The History of the United States, 2nd Edition

Allen C. Guelzo, Ph.D.
Gary W. Gallagher, Ph.D.
Patrick N. Allitt, Ph.D.

PUBLISHED BY:

THE GREAT COURSES
Corporate Headquarters
4840 Westfields Boulevard, Suite 500
Chantilly, Virginia 20151-2299
Phone: 1-800-832-2412
Fax: 703-378-3819
www.thegreatcourses.com

Copyright © The Teaching Company, 2003

Printed in the United States of America

This book is in copyright. All rights reserved.

Without limiting the rights under copyright reserved above,
no part of this publication may be reproduced, stored in
or introduced into a retrieval system, or transmitted,
in any form, or by any means
(electronic, mechanical, photocopying, recording, or otherwise),
without the prior written permission of
The Teaching Company.

Allen C. Guelzo, Ph.D.
Professor of American History
Eastern University

Dr. Allen C. Guelzo is the Dean of the Templeton Honors College at Eastern University, on Philadelphia's Main Line, where he is also the Grace Ferguson Kea Professor of American History. He holds an M.A. and a Ph.D. in history from the University of Pennsylvania, an M.Div. from Philadelphia Theological Seminary, and an honorary doctorate in history from Lincoln College in Illinois. Dr. Guelzo's special field of interest is American intellectual and cultural history in the period between 1750 and 1865. He has published several books on subjects in this period, including *Edwards on the Will: A Century of American Philosophical Debate* (1989); *For the Union of Evangelical Christendom: The Irony of the Reformed Episcopalians* (1994), which won the 1994 Outler Prize; *The Crisis of the American Republic: A New History of the Civil War and Reconstruction* (1995); and *Abraham Lincoln: Redeemer President* (1999), which won the Lincoln Prize. His essays and reviews have appeared in *American Historical Review*, *Journal of American History*, *William and Mary Quarterly*, *The Wilson Quarterly*, *Journal of the Abraham Lincoln Association*, *Civil War History*, *Journal of the Early Republic*, *Filson Club History Quarterly*, *Journal of the History of Ideas*, *Pennsylvania Magazine of History and Biography*, and *Anglican and Episcopal History*.

Dr. Guelzo has held fellowships from the American Council of Learned Societies, the Pew Evangelical Scholarship Initiative, the Charles Warren Center for American Studies at Harvard, and the James Madison Fellows Program at Princeton. He is a senior research associate of the McNeil Center for Early American Studies at the University of Pennsylvania. He serves as a member of the Board of Directors of the Abraham Lincoln Association, the Abraham Lincoln Institute of the Mid-Atlantic, the Lincoln Studies Center at Knox College (Illinois), and the Historical Society of the Episcopal Church and as a member of advisory panels for the President Lincoln and Soldiers Home Project, National Trust for Historic Preservation, the Abraham

Lincoln Presidential Papers, Library of Congress, and the Abraham Lincoln Bicentennial Commission. Dr. Guelzo has also contributed articles for *The Historical Times Illustrated Encyclopedia of the Civil War*, *Encyclopedia of African American Religions*, *Routledge Encyclopedia of Philosophy*, *The Biographical Dictionary of the Union*, *The Encyclopedia of the Enlightenment*, *The Encyclopedia of American Intellectual and Cultural History*, and *The American National Biography*, as well as journalism for *Civil War Times Illustrated*, *The Philadelphia Inquirer*, *The Wall Street Journal*, *Los Angeles Times*, *First Things*, and *The Washington Post*. ∎

Gary W. Gallagher, Ph.D.
Professor of History of the American Civil War
University of Virginia

Gary W. Gallagher is the John L. Nau Professor in the History of the American Civil War at the University of Virginia. Before coming to UVA, he was Professor of History at Pennsylvania State University—University Park flagship campus. He graduated from Adams State College of Colorado and earned both his master's degree and doctorate in history from the University of Texas at Austin. His research and teaching focus are on the era of the Civil War and Reconstruction.

Recognized as one of the top historians of the Civil War, Dr. Gallagher is a prolific author. His books include *The Confederate War*, *Lee and His Generals in War and Memory*, *Stephen Dodson Ramseur: Lee's Gallant General*, and *The Myth of the Lost Cause and Civil War History* (co-edited with Alan T. Nolan). He has also co-authored and edited numerous works on individual battles and campaigns, including Antietam, Fredericksburg, Chancellorsville, Gettysburg, Wilderness, Spotsylvania, and the 1864 Shenandoah Valley campaign and published more than eight dozen articles in scholarly journals and popular historical magazines. Virtually all his books have been History Book Club selections.

He has received numerous awards for his research and writing, including the Lincoln Prize (1998—shared with three other authors), the Fletcher Pratt Award for the best nonfiction book on the Civil War (1999), the Laney Prize for the best book on the Civil War (1998), and the William Woods Hassler Award for contributions to Civil War studies (1998). Additionally, Professor Gallagher serves as editor of two book series for the University of North Carolina Press ("Civil War America" and "Military Campaigns of the Civil War"). He has appeared regularly on the Arts and Entertainment Network's series *Civil War Journal* and has participated in other television projects. Active in historic preservation, Professor Gallagher was president of the Association for Preservation of Civil War Sites from 1987 through mid-1994, has served on the Board of Directors of the Civil War Trust, and on numerous occasions, has testified before Congress on battlefield preservation. ■

Patrick N. Allitt, Ph.D.

Professor of History, Emory University

Patrick Allitt is Professor of History at Emory University. He was born and raised in central England and attended schools near his home in Mickleover, Derbyshire. An undergraduate at Hertford College, Oxford, he graduated (1977) with honors in British and European history. After a year of travel, he studied for the history doctorate at the University of California, Berkeley. He was a postdoctoral fellow at Harvard in the mid-1980s and, since 1988, has been on the faculty of Emory University in Atlanta, Georgia. Professor Allitt is the author of three books, including *Catholic Converts: British and American Intellectuals Turn to Rome* (1997). He also writes frequent articles and reviews. In 1999, he won Emory's Excellence in Teaching Award and, in 2000, was appointed to the N.E.H./Arthur Blank Professorship of Teaching in the Humanities. Professor Allitt keeps in touch with his homeland by spending about two months every year on a working holiday in Britain, teaching the history of Victorian England with Emory's summer school, which is held at University College, Oxford. His wife, Toni, is American, a Michigan native, and they have a daughter, Frances, born in 1988. ■

Table of Contents

INTRODUCTION

Professor Biographies i
Scope for Lectures 1–36 1
Scope for Lectures 37–48 162
Scope for Lectures 49–84 239

LECTURE GUIDES, 1–36

LECTURE 1
Living Bravely 5

LECTURE 2
Spain, France, and the Netherlands 8

LECTURE 3
Gentlemen in the Wilderness 11

LECTURE 4
Radicals in the Wilderness 14

LECTURE 5
Traders in the Wilderness 17

LECTURE 6
An Economy of Slaves 19

LECTURE 7
Printers, Painters, and Preachers 22

LECTURE 8
The Great Awakening 24

LECTURE 9
The Great War for Empire 26

Table of Contents

LECTURE 10
The Rejection of Empire 28

LECTURE 11
The American Revolution—Politics and People 32

LECTURE 12
The American Revolution—Howe's War 34

LECTURE 13
The American Revolution—Washington's War 36

LECTURE 14
Creating the Constitution 38

LECTURE 15
Hamilton's Republic 41

LECTURE 16
Republicans and Federalists 44

LECTURE 17
Adams and Liberty 47

LECTURE 18
The Jeffersonian Reaction 49

LECTURE 19
Territory and Treason 51

LECTURE 20
The Agrarian Republic 53

LECTURE 21
The Disastrous War of 1812 56

LECTURE 22
The "American System" 60

Table of Contents

LECTURE 23
A Nation Announcing Itself..63

LECTURE 24
National Republican Follies...65

LECTURE 25
The Second Great Awakening...67

LECTURE 26
Dark Satanic Mills..69

LECTURE 27
The Military Chieftain..71

LECTURE 28
The Politics of Distrust..73

LECTURE 29
The Monster Bank...76

LECTURE 30
Whigs and Democrats..79

LECTURE 31
American Romanticism...82

LECTURE 32
The Age of Reform 86

LECTURE 33
Southern Society and the Defense of Slavery...................89

LECTURE 34
Whose Manifest Destiny?...93

LECTURE 35
The Mexican War 96

Table of Contents

LECTURE 36
The Great Compromise 100

SUPPLEMENTAL MATERIAL, 1–36

Maps 104
Timeline 116
Glossary 127
Biographical Notes 135
Bibliography 142

LECTURE GUIDES, 37–48

LECTURE 37
Sectional Tensions Escalate 164

LECTURE 38
Drifting Toward Disaster 168

LECTURE 39
The Coming of War 171

LECTURE 40
The First Year of Fighting 174

LECTURE 41
Shifting Tides of Battle 177

LECTURE 42
Diplomatic Clashes and Sustaining the War 181

LECTURE 43
Behind the Lines—Politics and Economies 185

LECTURE 44
African Americans in Wartime 189

Table of Contents

LECTURE 45
The Union Drive to Victory 194

LECTURE 46
Presidential Reconstruction 198

LECTURE 47
Congress Takes Command 201

LECTURE 48
Reconstruction Ends 204

SUPPLEMENTAL MATERIAL, 37–48

Maps 207
Timeline 209
Glossary 222
Biographical Notes 225
Bibliography 233

LECTURE GUIDES, 49–84

LECTURE 49
Industrialization 244

LECTURE 50
Transcontinental Railroads 248

LECTURE 51
The Last Indian Wars 251

LECTURE 52
Farming the Great Plains 254

LECTURE 53
African Americans after Reconstruction 258

Table of Contents

LECTURE 54
Men and Women 261

LECTURE 55
Religion in Victorian America 264

LECTURE 56
The Populists 268

LECTURE 57
The New Immigration 272

LECTURE 58
City Life 276

LECTURE 59
Labor and Capital 279

LECTURE 60
Theodore Roosevelt and Progressivism 282

LECTURE 61
Mass Production 285

LECTURE 62
World War I—The Road to Intervention 288

LECTURE 63
World War I—Versailles and Wilson's Gambit 291

LECTURE 64
The 1920s 295

LECTURE 65
The Wall Street Crash and the Great Depression 298

LECTURE 66
The New Deal 302

Table of Contents

LECTURE 67
World War II—The Road to Pearl Harbor 305

LECTURE 68
World War II—The European Theater 308

LECTURE 69
World War II—The Pacific Theater 311

LECTURE 70
The Cold War 314

LECTURE 71
The Korean War and McCarthyism 317

LECTURE 72
The Affluent Society..320

LECTURE 73
The Civil Rights Movement...323

LECTURE 74
The New Frontier and the Great Society 327

LECTURE 75
The Rise of Mass Media...331

LECTURE 76
The Vietnam War..335

LECTURE 77
The Women's Movement..339

LECTURE 78
Nixon and Watergate..343

LECTURE 79
Environmentalism...347

Table of Contents

LECTURE 80
Religion in Twentieth-Century America..350

LECTURE 81
Carter and the Reagan Revolution..353

LECTURE 82
The New World Order..357

LECTURE 83
Clinton's America and the Millennium..360

LECTURE 84
Reflections..364

SUPPLEMENTAL MATERIAL, 49–84

Timeline..367
Glossary...376
Biographical Notes 381
Bibliography..392

The History of the United States, 2nd Edition

Scope (Lectures 1–36):

This course chronicles the history of the United States from colonial origins to the beginning of the 21st century. The lectures focus on several key themes: (1) the exceptionalism of the American experiment, symbolized by the Puritan "city on the hill"; (2) the commitment to socioeconomic mobility and opportunity in the marketplace; (3) the expanding enfranchisement of citizens in the development of political democracy; and (4) the confirmation of the "melting pot" as a symbol of inclusion in the national body politic. The spread of literacy and mass information, the political and cultural importance of regionalism, and the central role of civilian government are also salient themes in the lectures that follow.

This portion of the The Great Courses' *History of the United States* survey course carries you from the beginnings of European settlement of what is now the United States to the end of the Mexican War and the Great Compromise of 1850. It covers, in other words, what historians like to call "Colonial America" and the "Early Republic." The 36 lectures in this first part are built around four important themes:

1. How did the experience of discovery and settlement change Europeans, American native peoples, African and Caribbean slaves, and all the other different and sometimes hostile populations that came (or were forced to come) to North America into an entirely different kind of people, the Americans? In what ways has that made America exceptional and unique among the other, older nations of the West and of the world?

2. How did the United States manage to assimilate so many different peoples from so many different places?

3. How did the geography, beliefs, and necessities of the settlements Europeans planted along the eastern coast of North America develop such unprecedented religious, political, and economic freedom?

4. How did the natural resources of North America, and the human resourcefulness of its people, generate such an abundance of wealth—and so many confrontations over the way to use it?

We will begin our expedition into the American past in Lectures One and Two with the first phases of European exploration and examine why it was that a continent Europeans at first thought was a disappointment quickly became an asset. From there, in Lectures Three through Five, we will look at how Europeans turned from organizing settlements whose chief purpose was simply extraction of resources for European use to the creation of settlements of occupation, or *colonies*. English colonization, in particular, had three very different patterns for settlement in New England, the Chesapeake, and the "middle colonies." The most significant development, however, will be the way in which these colonies matured, from being stages for Europeans to make fortunes to being homes for people who were no longer really Europeans (even when they tried to be). In passing, we will see in Lectures Seven and Eight how the colonials practiced and changed religious beliefs, created various levels of culture unique to their own worlds, and struggled to decide (in Lectures Nine and Ten) whether they were simply plantations on the periphery of someone else's empire or societies that had achieved identities of their own that their European sponsors needed to respect.

Much of the first 12 lectures will be about personalities—John Smith at Jamestown, John Winthrop and Cotton Mather in Boston, William Penn and Benjamin Franklin in Philadelphia, Jonathan Edwards in his pulpit, William Billings in his singing school, John Singleton Copley at his easel, and George Whitefield on his travels. This portion of the course will also be about war—at first, brushfire wars for the survival of individual settlements, then world wars in which the colonies were expected to serve as proxies for their empires. Of course, Lectures Eleven through Thirteen will be about the war that eventually separated 13 of these colonies from Great Britain and made them a new nation, the United States.

The American Revolution appeared to be a break with the past—it cut Americans loose politically from Britain, but even more fundamentally, it cut them off from the entire European political tradition. As we will see in Lecture Fourteen, the new American nation was a child of the

Enlightenment, and it was the first modern Western nation on any large scale to consciously abandon the age-old traditions of status and monarchy and experiment with an ideal form of enlightened government, a republic. But republics were a new and untested idea, and the newness of the idea was underscored by how quickly Americans developed radically different views about what a republic should look like. These views coalesce in Lectures Fifteen through Eighteen around two figures who are vitally important to these lectures: Thomas Jefferson and Alexander Hamilton. But they include a host of characters both great (George Washington) and small (William Maclay) as, of course, they should when our story is about the first great venture in popular government.

The Jefferson-Hamilton division begins a script that will be played out over Lectures Nineteen and Twenty, as Americans struggle to reconcile the impact of the Industrial Revolution with their allegiance to a republican system. Once again, it is the characters who come to the fore—Andrew Jackson, the bank-killer and apostle of agrarian democracy in Lectures Twenty-Seven through Twenty-Eight, and Henry Clay, the sophisticated statesman who, in Lecture Thirty, convinces us that the American experiment would never succeed until it built itself up as an industrial competitor of Europe. But Americans will work to find other ways of sorting out their new identity as distinct from the Old World, in literature and philosophy as much as politics. They will mark out a path of their own by giving religion an entirely new place in public life (Lecture Twenty-Five), by developing a collegiate moral philosophy that provides instruction for public virtue (Lectures Thirty-One and Thirty-Two), and by entertaining new assumptions about men and women, white and black, slave and free. And there will still be war, literal—the War of 1812 in Lecture Twenty-One; Indian war and the wars of expansion in Lectures Nineteen, Twenty-Two, and Thirty-Four; the Mexican War in Lecture Thirty-Five—and figurative—the Bank War in Lecture Twenty-Nine; the political warfare of Democrat and Whig in Lectures Twenty-Three and Twenty-Four and, again, in Lecture Thirty; the determination of abolitionists to rid America of slavery and of slaveowners to keep it in Lectures Thirty-Three and Thirty-Six.

This is the story of how to make a republic—make it in the midst of a hurricane of economic change in the late 18th and early 19th centuries, make it despite conflict and prejudice, make it so that it re-makes its own citizens into a people utterly different from anything the world has seen before—*and* how to keep it. Or, as we come to the close of Lecture Thirty-Six, how to very nearly lose it. ■

Living Bravely
Lecture 1

We're going to do it from soup to nuts, or, if you like, from Columbus to Clinton. This is a voyage that I can guarantee you is going to have more surprises than you might think. ... We're going to meet all sorts and conditions, and the kinds of change we'll see will positively make your head spin.

Christopher Columbus's voyage from Spain, across the Atlantic Ocean, marked the beginning of the most important encounter of places and peoples in human history. The New World that Columbus "discovered" was first inhabited anywhere from 40,000 to 12,000 years ago and was populated by successive waves of immigrants from eastern Asia.

The remains of Kennewick Man, uncovered in 1996 in Washington state, have contributed to the controversy regarding just who the first immigrants to the Americas were and where they came from. By 1500, Native Americans may have numbered as many as 15 million in North America and spoke some 300 different languages. Some native cultures, such as the Aztecs in Mexico and Incas in South America, were socially stratified and highly developed civilizations.

After the fall of the Roman Empire, Europe lapsed into a cultural and economic backwater. The continent was fragmented: controlled in the East by the Byzantine Empire and in the West by the remnants of Roman rule. It was politically disorganized. Its internal economy was reduced to the most primitive levels of barter and reciprocity. It demonstrates the difficulties ancient cultures had in reviving themselves, because the possibility of importing outside influences and new ideas was expensive and minimal.

The Crusades changed this picture. They opened the possibility for organized, state-supported exploration. They opened Europe to tremendous new possibilities of trade and culture with the Middle East and, beyond that, the

Orient. These possibilities encouraged Europeans and European governments to undertake new explorations for opening markets in the Middle East. Marco Polo demonstrated the opportunities of exploration by penetrating all the way to China but also the limitations on private expeditions. Mediterranean states and cities underwrote trading expeditions and colonies in the eastern Mediterranean and Black Sea. Not all these exposures were profitable—for example, the Black Death was imported into Europe over trade routes to the Black Sea.

> **Some of this was sheer, heartless slaughter and exploitation by the Spaniards, who enslaved conquered Indians and put them to work to support Spanish enrichment.**

Western European states, frustrated by lack of geographical proximity, the costs of transport, and eastern Mediterranean monopolies, began to underwrite their own expeditions. Prince Henry the Navigator made Portugal a major sponsor of explorations into the near Atlantic and down the coast of Africa. Vasco da Gama succeeded in rounding the Cape of Good Hope and establishing a trade route to India, which the Portuguese protected by means of colonies. The newly reunited Spanish came late to exploration and were willing to take the risk proposed by Columbus of gaining access to the Orient by sailing west across the Atlantic in 1492.

Surprisingly, Columbus's discovery was at first a great disappointment, because the American continents were an obstacle to reaching China. Subsequent expeditions attempted to find ways around the Americas. Magellan sailed around South America and into the Pacific, only to find it immensely more huge than anyone had thought the path to the East would be. Europeans found the physical appearance of North America alternately fascinating and frightening.

Balboa attempted to find a path across the narrowest part of the Americas in Panama. Other European adventurers looked for a Northwest Passage or a navigable water route through the continents. When no such path appeared to be open, the European states turned their attention elsewhere. This encouraged individual freebooters (Cortés, Pizarro) to launch their own expeditions, looking for treasure in the Americas rather than around it. With minimal state oversight, these freebooters found America to be a place where traditional European ideas of society and behavior no longer applied.

Colonial societies emerged that were open to social experimentation, to accumulations of unheard-of wealth by disenfranchised classes, to political or exploitative arrangements unthinkable to European society, and to the erosion of distinctions in status and religion. This frequently came at tremendous cost to the native ecology, native populations, and the slaves and servant classes who were used to extract the wealth and support the experimentations. ■

Suggested Reading

Cronon, *Changes in the Land*, chap. 2.

Morison, *The European Discovery of America: The Southern Voyages*, chaps. 1–7, 12.

Wright, *Stolen Continents*, chaps. 1–3.

Questions to Consider

1. What were the ecological consequences of European exploration?

2. What were the human consequences of European exploration?

Spain, France, and the Netherlands
Lecture 2

> Once the initial phase of Spanish conquest was over, the Spanish crown obtrusively shouldered its way in; retired or demoted the conquistadors, as Charles did with Cortés in 1535; and set about instituting formal governments that would be subservient to the Spanish crown.

Spaniards attempted to repeat the pattern of the first conquistadors and settlers in as many places in North and South America as they could. Spanish settlement of Mexico, the Pacific coast, and South America eventually required the institution of formal governments subservient to the Spanish crown. This called for organizing not only their own European societies but also those of the indigenous peoples they conquered. They moved through three stages: enslavement, dislocation, and confrontation (i.e, the Pueblo Revolt). The deadliest enemies of the indigenous populations were disease.

The Spanish New World settlements eventually matured from an extraction society to a permanent settler society. American wealth made Spain a world power in the 16th and 17th centuries. But Spain mismanaged its wealth, resulting in declining profitability of its settlements and diminishing interest in further expansion.

France emerged from civil war in the 16th century to European mastery in the 17th. France hoped to emulate the profitability of the Spanish New World expeditions by subsidizing its own. By the end of the 1500s, the first French expeditions had established French contact on the maritime coast of Canada and the upper Mississippi. Samuel de Champlain succeeded in building up the first significant French settlement along the St. Lawrence River at Quebec to exploit the fur trade. Robert La Salle explored the Gulf Coast, and the Company of the Indies began French settlements along the gulf and the mouth of the Mississippi. Champlain also helped set the pattern of European versus Indian military conflict with the Algonquian and Iroquian peoples of the northeastern woodlands.

The French did not, however, succeed in building a strong settler society. One of the principal activities of the French was religious proselytizing. The French government saw only minimal returns on its promotion of New World colonization, especially in Louisiana. The French forbade the emigration of religious dissidents. French adventurism in Europe drained the French population of potential settlers and the French treasury of funds whereby it could have further supported exploration under the French flag.

> **Unlike [in] many other places in Europe in the 1600s, Dutch women could own property in their own names even while married, could make their own contracts, [and] could conduct their own businesses.**

The 17th century saw the meteoric rise of the Dutch as a major world commercial power. Although newly independent from Spanish rule and with some of the most unproductive land in Europe, the Dutch succeeded in positioning themselves as the great financial and trading center of Western Europe. The Dutch East India Company organized an exploration of the Hudson River in 1609 and the creation of the New Netherland colony. Although the main settlement was established at New Amsterdam, the immediate goal was the exploitation of the fur trade in the woodland interior.

New Netherland, as a commercial subsidiary, became the most culturally and ethnically diverse settlement in North America. The colony attracted a wide variety of emigrants. The company's government practiced religious toleration. Women possessed more rights than they did in Europe. ■

Suggested Reading

Horgan, *Conquistadores in North American History*.

Morison, *The European Discovery of America*, chaps. 8–9, 11–14.

Taylor, *American Colonies*, chaps. 4–5.

Questions to Consider

1. Which of the three colonial empires—Spanish, French, or Dutch—was the best governed?

2. Which of the three colonial empires—Spanish, French, or Dutch—would have offered the most opportunity?

Gentlemen in the Wilderness
Lecture 3

All of this in-fighting exhausted and distracted England from undertaking any serious adventures in America, and it was not until Elizabeth had been securely on the throne for 20 years that English attention began to wander back over the western horizon.

England had been distracted by civil and religious instability through the early 1500s. Henry VIII had led his kingdom into ruinous wars and even more ruinous experiments with the Protestant Reformation. The English ventured into the Atlantic only as a means of preying on Spanish shipping. The earliest interest in settlements was shown by wealthy individuals (such as Sir Walter Raleigh) for the purpose of establishing bases along the North American coast for ambushing Spanish trade, most of which failed.

A joint-stock company, the Virginia Company, undertook to establish a settlement on the Chesapeake Bay at Jamestown. Even with corporate backing, the settlement nearly failed, and it never yielded any profit. Antagonism with the Powhatan tribes led to a near annihilation of the Virginia settlements in 1622.

The commercial failures of English colonization often stranded settlers in America. This gave several colonies, beginning with Virginia, freedom to experiment with establishing their own governments and assemblies, none of which were recognized by the crown but which the crown did nothing to suppress. The crown did not wish to assume financial liability for ruling these settlements, preferring to franchise out new settlements to those willing to take the risks, and let the colonies become dumping grounds for England's various uncooperative, unemployed, and unwanted inhabitants. Virginia organized a rough-and-ready government and the first American legislative assembly. The crown ignored its own ban on Roman Catholics and allowed English Roman Catholics to establish a settlement on the upper Chesapeake.

Political dissidents organized an experimental government in the Carolinas. An experiment in social benevolence was founded by aristocrats in Georgia. To the surprise of all beholders, by 1680, these settlements had achieved success. Principally, this success came through economic development. Virginia also developed the first great American commodity, tobacco.

> [The repression of Bacon's Rebellion] served as a useful reminder that Virginia was, after all the benign neglect, still a royal colony.

The Carolinas mimicked the pattern of the British West Indies and became a major source for rice and indigo. The Chesapeake solved the problem of creating a cheap labor force for these commodities by abandoning indentured servitude of whites and moving to a workforce of slaves, who were visibly marked by whites for service by being Africans.

All of this came at little cost to the royal government until the 1670s. The crown was able to practice a policy of benign neglect. Eventually, however, the royal government noticed that the settlements were beginning to compete with the economy of the home islands, which called forth the beginnings of economic regulation. Social unrest in 1676 (Bacon's Rebellion) also forced the crown to begin taking a more active interventionist role in colonial administration. ■

Suggested Reading

Greene, *Pursuits of Happiness*, chap. 4.

Kupperman, *Roanoke*.

Morgan, *American Slavery-American Freedom*, chaps. 4, 11, 15.

Questions to Consider

1. Was there another alternative to Virginia's turn to slave labor in the 17th century?

2. Did any of these colonies live up to the expectations of their founders?

Radicals in the Wilderness
Lecture 4

> The southern colonies were established mostly for the sake of profit or politics, but there were other English colonies to the far north that were founded mostly for the sake of ideas and religion. The difference has had a lasting impact on the nature of American culture.

The New England settlements were purposely founded as refuges for English radical Protestants—Puritans. The Puritans were refugees from the English government's demands for conformity to a single, mainstream, state-established church. They struggled to affirm their English identity, but in truth, they owed spiritual allegiance to a transnational ideological movement known as Calvinism.

Calvinism taught them theology, but it also taught them about social construction by making church membership a voluntary act to be tested by specific signs of sincerity and organized separately from the state. It imparted a short-term pessimism about human nature but a long-term optimism about the future of the Calvinist mission. It also made its members suspect in the eyes of the Stuart kings James I and Charles I. To leave England because of deliberate dissent was synonymous with treason.

The Puritans invented a subterfuge to cover their emigration in the form of another joint-stock company, the Massachusetts Bay Company. John Winthrop was appointed governor, and a corporate board was elected. Once in New England, Winthrop became de facto governor of a province, not a company, and the board became the legislative assembly. Under that authority, the Puritans were at last able to freely construct the kind of church and society that they believed conformed to the Calvinist vision—the "city on a hill."

However, under the seductions of profit and growth, the Puritan colonies were gradually pulled in the same direction as the southern colonies. Originally, the social picture of the New England colonies was starkly different from that of the southern colonies. New Englanders represented a different demographic cross-section. They attempted to organize themselves as communally as possible to maintain moral oversight.

Ideologically, the Puritans found it difficult to maintain a consensus. Evermore-radical Puritans attempted their own purifications and withdrawals, in the cases of Ann Hutchinson and Roger Williams. The enthusiasm for undergoing the tests of church membership diminished the eagerness of second- and third-generation New Englanders to join, forcing the churches to move back toward English patterns of church membership and state involvement.

> **The jeremiad, however, firmly set this notion of cultural revival into the cluster of basic American ideas that we all still live with.**

Socially, the Puritans found it difficult to maintain social cohesiveness. Communal organization broke down over the need for new land. New England grew into six separately organized settlements—Massachusetts Bay, New Hampshire, New Haven, Plymouth, Connecticut, and Rhode Island—which generated large-scale warfare with the Indian tribes, especially in King Philip's War. Commercial successes after 1700 made Boston a thriving town of merchants.

By the end of the 1600s, the original Puritan vision seemed to have faded. It was, however, rescued by the clergy and captured in the jeremiad. The jeremiad became the source for cultural revitalization in New England and, ultimately, in American thought thereafter. ■

Suggested Reading

Miller, *The New England Mind*, chaps. 4, 13.

Morgan, *The Puritan Dilemma*.

Morison, *Builders of the Bay Colony*, chap. 3.

Questions to Consider

1. What have been the long-term effects of the Puritans on American culture?

2. How does the stereotypical image of a Puritan contrast with the settlers of Massachusetts Bay in the 1600s?

Traders in the Wilderness
Lecture 5

A large part of the story of English exploration and settlement in North America is a story about geography, because so much of it revolves around the great ocean inlets of the North American coast: the Chesapeake Bay, the Hudson River, and Massachusetts Bay.

The coastal territory between the Chesapeake and Long Island was the last to be settled by the English. Unlike the south and New England, this territory had already been previously settled by Europeans. The Dutch in New Netherland controlled the Hudson River Valley from New Amsterdam to Fort Orange. The Swedes planted a small colony of New Sweden along the Delaware River from Cape May to Kingsessing.

Both colonies had been designed as extraction settlements and were comparatively feeble. The Dutch swallowed up the Swedes once Swedish military influence in Europe during the Thirty Years' War declined. The Dutch were almost destroyed by repeated conflicts with the Algonquian tribes and yielded easily to English conquest once Dutch maritime supremacy was eclipsed by the English. The Dutch settlements (renamed New York) developed into a major commercial center and, following the usual plan, created an upriver aristocracy based on the semi-slavery of tenant farming.

The Delaware settlements passed into the quixotic ownership of the influential Quaker William Penn. The Quakers were similar to the Puritans in their dissent and separatism. They were sharply persecuted by the English church and state, who sensed in them not merely dissent but social revolution for women and the economically marginalized.

Penn was an unusual convert to Quakerism, coming as he did from the aristocracy. His influence and wealth made him a major figure in English Quakerism and tempted him to try to achieve religious toleration through political action. When politics failed, he and the Quakers began looking to replicate the Puritan emigration. An initial colony was established in New Jersey.

Penn was offered a more desirable option by King Charles II on lands that were eventually named, to Penn's embarrassment, Pennsylvania. Like Winthrop, he hoped to create a consensual society around his model city, Philadelphia. But Penn's Pennsylvania passed even more quickly into the free-for-all phase.

By the 1750s, Pennsylvania had become an ethnically and religiously diverse society, rather than a consensual one, with a commercial aristocracy similar to that of Boston. Yet, like New England, Pennsylvania retained a core of Quaker idealism that rejected slavery and embraced radical notions of social equality. ■

> **[King Charles II declared] the new colony should be named in honor of Penn's father as "Pennsylvania." Penn was horrified at what his fellow Quakers would make of such a self-serving title.**

Suggested Reading

Kammen, *Colonial New York*, chaps. 2–3.

Kelley, *Pennsylvania: The Colonial Years*, chaps. 1–6.

Questions to Consider

1. In what ways was Penn's "holy experiment" in Pennsylvania similar to Winthrop's "city on a hill"?

2. Was there more or less ethnic diversity in 18th-century British North America than there is in the modern United States and Canada?

An Economy of Slaves
Lecture 6

There was no single pattern that governed how Europeans extended themselves to North America. Virtually all of it happened by fits and starts, without any coordination and, as we've already seen from some other results, without much in the way of forethought for how it was all going to unfold.

Each region of English settlement underwent a transition from radically different models toward convergence on a generally English model. This would not have been possible without a source of cheap labor. British America's great asset was an immensity of land, either legally claimed or waiting to be dispossessed of its native inhabitants. Its great deficit was a shortage of hands to develop the land. The English government showed little interest in sponsoring emigration. Those who did emigrate were often the least prepared or the most antisocial (for religious or other reasons), and when they did come, the availability of cheap land inclined them more to set up for themselves than as the employees of others.

As the 17th century progressed, Virginia's planters turned to slavery for labor.

The alternative to cheap labor was forced labor. Colonists already in America paid for the importation of convicts, beggars, prisoners-of-war, and indentured servants. The costs of such imports rose steeply through the 1600s. The colonists turned to an existing trade in forced labor in the form of slaves, carried by Spanish, Portuguese, and Dutch traders. The colonies developed their own domestic slave-trading industry, based on the three-way trade of the Middle Passage, and making Newport, Rhode Island, its center.

> Virginia's planters began turning increasingly to a form of forced labor that would never have the chance of turning into Nathaniel Bacon's rabble, and that form of forced labor was slavery.

To support their struggle to imitate the home culture, the English colonists fell back on a form of labor that resembled nothing in the home culture. Enslavement was an attractive option for labor-starved colonists. It was permanent and could be passed on generationally. The laws of slavery imposed "social death" on slaves from birth, thus eliminating a political life. Slavery was total—the slave had no identity apart from that conferred by the slaveowner.

Enslavement quickly became race-based, because racial coloring offered an easy basis for marking the enslaved apart from the English population and the surrounding Indian tribes. All told, 11 million Africans were torn from their homes as slaves. Most of them were shipped to the West Indies and South America, but a sizable proportion went to the North American colonies.

All the colonies participated in slavery, but the concentrations varied. The greatest concentrations of slave labor were in the Carolinas. Slave labor participated in almost every aspect of the colonial economy. Slave labor generated conflict and tension, resulting in slave revolts. ■

Suggested Reading

Kolchin, *American Slavery*.

Morris, *Southern Slavery and the Law*.

Thomas, *The Slave Trade*.

Questions to Consider

1. Why did American slavery become a racial institution rather than just an economic institution?

2. How widespread was the use of forced labor in the British North American colonies?

Printers, Painters, and Preachers
Lecture 7

> Culture, however, is a slippery, slippery term. In the most often used sense, it seems to me the artistic pastimes of the elite of any given society take the forms of literature, portraiture, and various forms of social or religious music. Culture exists in multiple forms, though, when you think about it.

Although Americans produced little in the way of their own music, art, or philosophy, they had great confidence that America would eventually outperform all other older civilizations. Culture in the 17th and 18th centuries can be understood in three ways: as vernacular (or folk) culture, in which production and consumption of symbols is for immediate use among a limited circle of persons; as urban culture, in which production can be for sale or exchange among wider areas; and as elite culture, in which production is by skilled professionals for display more than use.

New England was the most likely place to offer possibilities for urban and elite culture. Poetry was written by Michael Wigglesworth and Anne Bradstreet. Painting was produced by Joseph Badger, John Smibert, John Singleton Copley, and Benjamin West. Music was produced by William Billings, Francis Hopkinson, and James Lyon.

Americans were particularly productive at adapting and redeveloping European philosophy. Philosophy was closely tied to theology and was part of curricula aimed at training clergy. Harvard's curriculum was dominated by

Benjamin Franklin embraced New Philosophy.

Protestant Scholastics. However, even then, the authority of Aristotle had to compete with the subtle psychological twists introduced by William Ames and Peter Ramus.

The advent of the New Philosophy of Newton and Bacon in Europe induced gradual changes in the collegiate curricula in America. Harvard moved toward the new "logick" through William Brattle. Yale was organized as a conservative reaction to Harvard, but it, too, was influenced by the New Philosophy.

> **This New Philosophy became the foundation of what we call the Enlightenment ... especially in England.**

Americans developed three examples of how to cope with the New Philosophy: adaptation, as represented by the intellectual compromises of Cotton Mather; complete embrace, as represented by Benjamin Franklin; and creative dissent, as represented by Jonathan Edwards. ■

Suggested Reading

Edwards, *Works of Jonathan Edwards*, vol. 6, introduction.

Fiering, *Moral Philosophy at Seventeenth-Century Harvard*.

Flower and Murphey, *A History of Philosophy in America*, vol. 1, chaps. 2–3.

Questions to Consider

1. Has the distance between the various levels of culture grown greater or smaller since the 18th century?

2. On the whole, which was the wiser strategy for dealing with the New Philosophy, Mather's or Edwards's?

The Great Awakening
Lecture 8

> One of the great ironies of our history, and also one of the best things that happened to us, [is] that not a single one of the American colonies turned out quite as its promoters planned. Pennsylvania did not become a Quaker paradise. Virginia did not become a profitable corporate enterprise. New York did not become a Dutch wonderland.

America presented a frightening environment to Europeans. The American landscape was alien to European experience. It contained native inhabitants with no desire for assimilation, culturally or politically. Dramatic social inversions were the rule. The home government was distant and uninterested.

This stress triggered reactions that were aimed at regaining some sense of control, either over one's external circumstances or personal identity. One early example of this is the Salem witch trials of 1692. Other examples included rebellions and mob actions.

The most dramatic attempt to redirect American intentions was the Great Awakening. The Awakening was a revival of religious concern and interest. It followed a pattern of personal religious renewal already established in New England but made it collective. It was also linked to a larger pattern of evangelical Protestant renewal movements in Europe known as Pietism.

The first tremors of the Awakening occurred in the 1730s. Jonathan Edwards witnessed a strong revival of religious interest in western Massachusetts in 1734–1735. Another revival developed in New Jersey under Theodore Frelinghuysen.

The principal Awakening occurred in 1739–1742. It began with the preaching of the English itinerant George Whitefield in many of the coastal towns and cities. It was given a philosophical and psychological rationale by Jonathan Edwards. It had tremendous force in Pennsylvania under Gilbert Tennent. It was promoted in Virginia by migrants and missionaries from Pennsylvania.

The results of the Awakening were great and profound. Many of America's prestige educational institutions were founded as an outcome of the Awakening. Dartmouth was founded as a missionary college. Princeton was founded by Presbyterian awakeners who were sympathetic to Edwards.

> **[The Great Awakening] was the beginning of the most dramatic cultural upheaval and the most ambitious attempt to relocate a source of certainty in American history.**

The Awakening was the first authentically American cultural event. It established patterns of print communication that democratized public discourse. It empowered non-elites to set up standards of cultural value apart from their social superiors. It encouraged Americans, principally through missionary work, to see themselves as exporters of ideas to other cultures.

It revived New England's dormant notion of mission. The Puritan idea of mission was extended to all of America. A pattern of cultural renewal was established that has repeatedly given collective strength to Americans in times of crisis. ■

Suggested Reading

Edwards, *Works of Jonathan Edwards*, vol. 3, introduction.

Isaac, *The Transformation of Virginia*, chap. 8.

Winslow, *Jonathan Edwards*, chaps. 8–9.

Questions to Consider

1. What are some of the ways in which the Great Awakening had an impact on the American Revolution?

2. What are some of the similarities between the Salem witch trials and the Northampton revival of 1734–1735?

The Great War for Empire
Lecture 9

> For a century after Walter Raleigh's first attempts to plant an English settlement on the North American coast, the English government was happy to let those settlements and colonies run pretty much by themselves, under the policy [of] "benign neglect"—at least, the English government was happy to do that until the end of the 1600s.

Great Britain and France developed foreign empires around the world in the 17th and 18th centuries that dwarfed all other competitors. The British American colonies emerged from an era of benign neglect to become major economic players in the empire. British imperial planners sought to reintegrate the colonies into the British economy through regulation. The British government came to believe that it could survive only by conducting its empire defensively, on the basis of mercantilism. The British sought to recruit the colonies and colonists as resources in ongoing imperial skirmishes with France.

France was much less successful in mobilizing its colonial resources and preferred to concentrate on centralizing power at home and directing warfare in Europe. Restrictive immigration policies discouraged large-scale settlement. A badly flawed governmental structure in Canada generated constant internal conflict. Nevertheless, the French were successful in mobilizing Indian tribes to assist them in harassing the English frontier.

The Treaty of Paris finally ended the war in all the places where it had flared. All of New France was ceded to the British to become British Canada.

After a series of increasingly larger conflicts, a Great War for Empire (known as the Seven Years' War in Europe and the French and Indian War in America) resulted. The early conflicts in this war were uniformly disastrous for the British. An early reconnaissance by George Washington ended in surrender at Fort Necessity. A British force under General Edward Braddock was humiliated in the Battle of the Wilderness. Panicky colonists organized an ineffective Congress at Albany to deal with the situation.

Changes in British political leadership reversed the course of the war. New British generals—Amherst, Forbes, Wolfe—won major victories. Wolfe succeeded in capturing the French fortress of Quebec in 1759, effectively ending French resistance in Canada.

The Treaty of Paris ended France's empire in the New World. All of Canada was ceded to British control. The role the American colonists had played in the victory convinced them that they were finally equal players in the larger scheme of Britain's empire. ■

Suggested Reading

Gipson, *The British Empire before the Revolution*, vol. 6, chap. 4.

Kelley, *Pennsylvania: The Colonial Years*, chaps. 15–19.

Steele, *Warpaths*, chaps. 9–12.

Questions to Consider

1. Given the advantages they started with, why did it take so long for the British to win the French and Indian War?

2. Would the French have been better served to have concentrated more, or fewer, resources to the defense of Canada?

The Rejection of Empire
Lecture 10

> To finance a war that reached around the world, and especially to finance a war that had seen the sending of regular British troops to North America for the first time in any substantial numbers, the king's government had had to pile up a war debt of over £122 million.

Service alone on the English debt from the Great War for Empire would cost the government £4.5 million a year. The home islands were already the most heavily taxed in Europe. Costs of maintaining a military presence in the newly acquired regions would require £200,000 a year.

In addition to this economic hardship, the Great War for Empire left the British government in political disarray. The empire was riddled by a vast disagreement over the nature of governing power. The Stuart monarchy had attempted to establish a French-style absolute monarchy in the 1600s. This had triggered civil war on two occasions, first from the Puritans, then from Parliament.

At the beginning of the 18th century, the disagreement had resolved itself into two political ideologies, Whig and Tory. The Whig political literature was the strongest, with John Locke on political theory and such satirists as Trenchard and Gordon.

Parliament's solution was to compel the colonies to shoulder part of the burden of imperial debt. Parliament had never before levied *direct* taxes on the colonies. The colonies had raised their own money for government through their own assemblies, but with the empire providing defense, this taxation was small. Because the colonies were plantations (and, thus, their assemblies had no legal standing), Parliament insisted that it had the authority to levy direct taxes without seeking approval from the colonial assemblies. Moreover, the colonies should be compelled to support a permanent military garrison in America.

Implementation of the new taxation policies fell to George Grenville. Grenville imposed a series of direct levies, culminating in the Stamp Act. The colonial assemblies at once rose in protest. A Stamp Act Congress met in Albany to issue a Declaration of Rights and Grievances, denying that the colonies were plantations and insisting on taxation only through their assemblies. Crowd actions were organized by the Sons of Liberty. The Grenville government collapsed, succeeded by the Marquis of Rockingham, who sponsored the repeal of the Stamp Act.

A raid on Lexington and Concord ended in a pitched battle.

Americans found justification for resistance in Whig political writings. The American assemblies had always functioned in the manner described by Whig political theory as a "natural" form of government. Exposure to British troops in the Great War convinced Americans, like the Whigs, that England was awash in depravity. American elites resented the possibility that British officials would displace them and assume control of colonial affairs. American Protestants feared that, along with the Stamp Act, the Church of England would install a bishop in America to undermine non-Anglican churches.

Rockingham's government was superseded by a Whig government under William Pitt. Pitt was elderly and suffered a nervous breakdown, leaving running of the government to Charles Townsend. Parliament repudiated the Stamp Act but not the principle of direct taxation. Townsend imposed a series of new taxes, the Townsend Duties. This act touched off still more American protest. When the first elements of the British garrison arrived in Boston, they caused a confrontation that became known as the Boston Massacre (1770).

> This Boston Tea Party, as it became known, broke that last line of restraint. "We must master them," King George III remarked grimly, "or totally leave them to themselves."

A new government, headed by Lord Frederick North, suspended the Townsend Duties but would not concede the colonists the right to self-taxation. A new Tea Act (1773), designed to bail out the East India Company, imposed taxes on imported tea, which was already so cheap that it could undersell colonial merchants. The Sons of Liberty responded by dumping the tea into Boston harbor in the Boston Tea Party of December 16, 1773.

In retaliation, Parliament imposed the "Intolerable Acts." The port of Boston was closed, and the Massachusetts government was taken over by crown officials. Massachusetts responded with the Suffolk Resolves. A Continental Congress was called in Philadelphia (1774).

The British government resolved to suppress colonial dissent. Seizures of colonial military stores were arranged. A raid on Lexington and Concord in pursuit of John Hancock and Samuel Adams ended in a pitched battle between British troops and colonial militia (1775). ■

Suggested Reading

Bailyn, *The Ideological Origins of the American Revolution*, chaps. 2 and 5.

Fischer, *Paul Revere's Ride*.

Maier, *From Resistance to Revolution*, chap. 8.

Questions to Consider

1. Were Parliament's expectations that the colonies permit direct taxation reasonable?

2. What made the "Intolerable Acts" intolerable?

The American Revolution—Politics and People
Lecture 11

The incident at Lexington and Concord might have remained only that—an incident—and, in fact, only the most unpleasantly violent of several such face-offs between colonial militia and the British army in the winter of 1774–1775.

The British government's reaction to the outbreak of conflict at Lexington and Concord in 1775 played directly into the hands of the most radical Americans, who favored outright independence from Britain. The First Continental Congress was a triumph for radical politics, but second thoughts soon occurred. In the months following the First Continental Congress, loyalists began to be fearful that the radicals had other agendas. Challenges to the authority of Parliament could easily become challenges to the authority of colonial elites. Independence was what the loyalists feared most.

Parliament managed to subvert the best efforts of the loyalists to prevent a breakaway. Parliament approved the American Prohibitory Bill. In 1775, General Gage was forced to clear Bunker Hill of American militia to protect his hold on Boston, winning a victory but at frightening cost.

Radicals began seizing the initiative. The Massachusetts Provincial Convention petitioned the Second Continental Congress for recognition as the legitimate government of Massachusetts. The Congress gave the colonies sanction to reorganize their governments, and the new legislatures quickly filled with radicals. The legislatures, in turn, recalled loyalist delegates to the Congress and silenced loyalist opposition.

Congress moved to take up the identity of an independent nation. Richard Henry Lee moved that Congress declare independence, and a committee was set up to write a declaration explanatory of the motion. The committee delegated the writing of the declaration to Thomas Jefferson. Jefferson's Declaration of Independence (1776) was a memorable, compelling statement of both American independence and the political ideas underlying it.

A committee for drawing up a colonial constitution was organized. It would be impossible to expect economic and military aid if there was no government in the colonies for European nations to recognize.

Jonathan Dickinson became the chief architect of the Articles of Confederation, but the Articles were weakened by disagreements over representation, taxation, and control of the west. The colonies, once they became independent states, proceeded to behave as though they were also independent of each other.

> From the very first words, Jefferson cast his Declaration as an enlightenment and a Whig manifesto.

A committee for foreign alliances was established. Benjamin Franklin and John Adams were sent as America's chief representatives to France, Spain, and the Netherlands. The French were sympathetic but would not commit themselves until it was clear that the Americans could succeed militarily on their own. ■

Suggested Reading

Countryman, *The American Revolution*, chaps. 4–5.

Hyneman and Lutz, eds., *American Political Writings during the Founding Era*, vol. 1, documents 22–26.

Maier, *American Scripture*, chap. 3.

Questions to Consider

1. In what ways was the Declaration of Independence a philosophical, and not just a political, document?

2. By what means was the Continental Congress turned from a vehicle for loyal protest into an engine of independence?

The American Revolution—Howe's War
Lecture 12

> The conduct of the militia at Bunker Hill made the unhappy General Thomas Gage growl that "The Americans show a spirit and conduct against us they never showed against the French."

The Revolution was not a military success in its initial phases. The American attempt to contain the British army in Boston was only a partial success. The British held securely to Boston through the winter of 1775. Congress authorized George Washington to muster the militia into the service of Congress as the Continental Army.

Washington had only limited resources with which to form a regular army. Americans had never needed to formulate tactical or strategic doctrine on their own. Americans were undersupplied in weaponry and experienced officers. However, their morale compared favorably with that of the British line troops they were facing. The capture of siege guns and their transportation to Boston forced the British to evacuate Boston in the spring of 1776. General Gage was succeeded in command by General William Howe.

The British then staged a succession of well-planned strikes along the North American coast. The British landed at Long Island, routed Washington, and captured New York. The British occupied New Jersey but experienced a temporary setback through Washington's Christmas raid on Trenton. The British mounted a successful invasion of the Chesapeake, climaxing in the battles of Brandywine and Germantown and the capture of Philadelphia (1777). The Continental Congress was forced to find refuge in Lancaster. The Continental Army settled down to a miserable winter in Valley Forge. However, an attempted invasion from Canada under General Burgoyne was stopped and defeated at Saratoga.

The British failure to clinch complete victory opened diplomatic opportunities. Congress first appointed peace commissioners to treat with the British in 1776. General Howe disapproved of the war and was disinclined to press his military advantage. The subsequent conference was barren of

> **It was not until the victory at Saratoga that the French were persuaded that the British really could be defeated in North America.**

developments. The American victory at Saratoga forced Britain to make another offer, but it refused to go as far as independence.

Congress turned to France to negotiate an alliance. The French were still smarting from their defeat in the Seven Years' War. Saratoga persuaded the French that the British could be defeated in North America. The French put economic credits at the disposal of the United States and supplied troops and ships under French command. ■

Suggested Reading

Conway, *The War of American Independence*, chap. 4.

Ketchum, *Saratoga*.

Wright, *The Continental Army*, chaps. 3–4.

Questions to Consider

1. What incentives did France have for entering the war on the American side?

2. What factors caused the British to fail in what should have been an easy campaign to subdue the American rebels?

The American Revolution—Washington's War
Lecture 13

The French Alliance forced the British to completely rethink their strategic priorities in dealing with their rebellious colonies. Sir William Howe was replaced in command of the British armies in North America. He actually resigned in protest because of all the stinging criticism he had received for the surrender of Burgoyne.

The French intervention in the Revolution forced the British to completely rethink their strategic priorities. Howe's successor, Clinton, was ordered to abandon Philadelphia, withdraw to New York, and confine himself to naval operations. The Continental Army, coming out of Valley Forge, successfully harassed the retreating British at Monmouth (1778). British energies were redirected against the French in the West Indies, the New England coastline, and the western frontier.

In 1778, Clinton resolved to extend his coastal operations to the South. The British occupied Savannah and the Georgia hinterland. Clinton then organized an expedition that seized Charleston.

The ease of these conquests convinced Clinton that British control could be extended inland. Lord Cornwallis attempted to invade North Carolina but was stopped at King's Mountain (1780). Cornwallis's second attempt met with defeats at Cowpens and Guildford Courthouse (1781). Cornwallis attempted to set up a new base for operations at Yorktown, only to be hemmed in by French and American troops and forced to surrender, effectively eliminating the only sizable British land force left in America (1781).

The impact of the war was felt even before it had ended. The American economy was seriously disrupted. American shipping was hard hit and lost its former protection on the high seas from the British Navy. Slaves deserted southern plantations to join the British. The attempt to create an American currency was wrecked by disastrous inflation.

American politics on the local level were increasingly radicalized. The old colonial elite was either exiled or deposed. New state constitutions experimented with democratic politics.

The Treaty of Paris (1783) ended by recognizing American independence. The British conceded the legal existence of the colonies. British possessions west of the Appalachians were ceded to the United States. Franklin asked that Canada be ceded to America in return for a separate peace with Britain.

The army was demobilized peacefully, and Washington resigned, desiring only to return to Mount Vernon and the life of a gentleman planter.

Many of the officers had supported a military intervention to end mismanagement by Congress. Washington set an example by resigning from the army. This example of virtuous republicanism probably saved the Confederation. ■

Suggested Reading

Allen, ed., *George Washington: A Collection*, chap. 5.

Conway, *The War of American Independence*, chaps. 5–6.

Flexner, *George Washington in the American Revolution*.

Questions to Consider

1. Was it a blessing that the Continental Army had lost so many battles that it was not able to pose a political threat until the close of the war?

2. What roles did the interventions of France, the Netherlands, and Spain play in obtaining independence for the United States?

Creating the Constitution
Lecture 14

The American Revolution was ended by the Treaty of Paris, but it was not so clear that the Treaty of Paris ensured the survival of the nation the Revolution had created.

The Revolution gave independence to 13 new states, but both Congress and the states were hopelessly in debt by the end of the Revolution. Congress had taken to paying its bills in paper money, which was hemorrhaging value. Those who lent Congress money in return for Continental securities watched the value of these pledges dwindle away to nothing. In the summer of 1786, a rebellion led by Daniel Shays protested Massachusetts taxes. Virginia's westernmost settlements in Kentucky and Tennessee tried to organize their own state of Franklin.

By 1785, many members of the revolutionary leadership were being replaced by a new generation. They saw the nation, not the states, as the source of political authority. The best example among these new men was Alexander Hamilton. Under the new leadership, state constitutions began to revise the organization of power.

Two events finally triggered action. Virginia and Maryland called a convention to discuss river

James Madison (1751–1836): secretary of state, fourth president of the United States, and author of the Federalist Papers.

navigation rights and concluded by asking for a national convention to write a new constitution. The rebellion led by Shays threatened popular revolution, which the states feared they could not suppress themselves.

The Constitutional Convention met in Philadelphia in 1787. The most obvious issue was that of power. The national government was given the right to levy taxes on the states and on exterior commerce and to issue money. It was also given the power to maintain a national army and navy.

The second issue was who should control this government. The Virginia Plan called for a two-house legislature, an executive, and a judiciary. The New Jersey Plan called for a one-house legislature with each state having an equal vote.

Unhappily, Virginia, New York, North Carolina, and Rhode Island remained in the other column, and everyone knew that unless New York and Virginia embraced the Constitution, it had no hope of ever working.

The Great Compromise created two houses in the Congress, one elected according to population and the other composed of equal representation from each state.

The convention designed a surprisingly powerful presidency. The president was responsible for executing the laws, commanding the armed forces, and supervising foreign relations. This might have been a stumbling block had not the election process been amended so that the states elected the president through the electoral college and had it not been assumed that Washington would be the first president.

The new Constitution also had some striking omissions. No allowance was made for political parties. The principle of the supremacy of the national government over the states was implied but not stated. And no precise standard of citizenship was established.

The old radicals greeted the Constitution with a hail of abuse, but the "new men" were better organized in reply. The pro-Constitutionalists took the name Federalist, as though they were still sympathetic to the states. This left the old revolutionaries with no other choice but to bill themselves merely as the Anti-Federalists. Hamilton, Jay, and Madison undertook a propaganda campaign for the Constitution in the Federalist Papers. These initiatives paid off handsomely. By July 1788, the necessary number of states had ratified. Resistance was pacified by the promise of 10 amendments to the Constitution, which would act as a Bill of Rights. ■

Suggested Reading

Banning, *The Sacred Fire of Liberty*, chap. 9.

Hamilton, Jay, and Madison, *The Federalist* nos. 9–10, 15, 41–43, and 57, in Carey and McClellan, *The Federalist*.

Wood, *The Creation of the American Republic, 1776–1789*, chaps. 12–13.

Questions to Consider

1. Why did the Anti-Federalists object so strongly to the Preamble to the Constitution?

2. What has it taken to remedy the Constitution's omissions?

Hamilton's Republic
Lecture 15

Modern Americans take the Constitution of the United States so much for granted that it becomes difficult to appreciate the sense of suspicion and apprehension with which it was greeted when the government it created finally began to operate in the spring of 1789.

The United States had already gone through two ineffective governments. The Continental Congress was hardly more than an unofficial federation. The Articles of Confederation were weak and ramshackle.

Support for the Constitution had to be bought with promises to the states. It had to promise to do nothing to establish a state religion. It had to promise to do nothing to restrain freedom of speech. It would do nothing to meddle in a variety of state affairs.

Like most political compromises, these proved impractical from the first day. The Constitution made no provision for an executive staff, which meant that Washington had to create one. He authorized four departments—War, Treasury, State, and Attorney General. He appointed Alexander Hamilton, Thomas Jefferson,

John Adams (1735–1826) narrowly defeated Thomas Jefferson to become the second U.S. president.

The 1790s, the first decade of the new American Constitution, clearly belonged to Alexander Hamilton.

Henry Knox, and Edmund Randolph to head the newly created departments.

Because the new federal government had inherited war indebtedness, Hamilton had to design measures to restore the government to solvency. The Report on the Public Credit recommended the assumption of the debt. The Report on a National Bank recommended a public/private venture that would help pay off the debt. The Report on the Subject of Manufactures recommended government support for manufacturing.

Hamilton had to deal with the combined opposition of Jefferson and Randolph. In Congress, Hamilton relied on the support of members of Congress who were invested in government debt. Hamilton had the authority of Washington behind him, especially concerning the national bank. Jefferson resigned from the cabinet in frustration.

Hamilton stepped down as treasury secretary in 1795, but the decade was clearly Hamilton's. Hamilton's economic plans bore early fruit. Forty new corporations were chartered. State legislatures chartered new banks. Europeans began investing in America.

Nevertheless, Jefferson remained a serious opponent of the Hamiltonian vision. Washington's hand-picked successor for the presidency, John Adams, barely squeaked past Jefferson in the 1796 presidential election. Hamilton's friends in Congress turned out to be worse than his enemies. ∎

Suggested Reading

Elkins and McKitrick, *The Age of Federalism*.

Freeman, *Alexander Hamilton: Writings*.

McDonald, *Alexander Hamilton*.

Questions to Consider

1. In what ways does the modern American economy resemble the plan set out in Hamilton's three great reports?

2. Does Washington's role as president compare favorably or unfavorably with his achievements as a military commander in the Revolution?

Republicans and Federalists
Lecture 16

If there was one thing that Alexander Hamilton's argument for the Bank of the United States demonstrated, it was that the Constitution, while it was comprehensive, was not designed to anticipate every detail.

The formation of political parties was the most important detail unforeseen in the Constitution. In the 1790s, politics was dominated by faction, not party. Faction politics is temporary; parties are built around long-term, comprehensive goals. Faction politics is also local or oriented toward special interests; parties organize broad constituencies. Faction politics is small scale; parties are large scale. Faction politics is personal; parties survive the loss or defeat of leaders.

The idea of party was an offense to the republican ideology. Party politics cuts across the grain of the republican commitment to virtue. Party politics appeals to self-interest. Republicanism assumed that politics could point only in a single, nonpartisan direction, rather than sanctioning competing directions. Republics are fragile because they lack hierarchy, which makes them vulnerable to party corruption.

No one set out to create parties, but the split between Hamilton and Jefferson was so large that it made party formation inevitable. James Madison organized the Democratic-Republicans in Congress; John Beckley was their local organizer. Opposition to Hamilton in Congress was mobilized. Local campaigns

Alexander Hamilton (1757–1804), whose split with Thomas Jefferson was the seed of party formation.

employed publicity and get-out-the-vote organizing. By 1793, there were 11 Democratic-Republican societies.

The theorist of the Democratic-Republicans was John Taylor of Caroline. Taylor was an agrarian with no use for Hamilton's economics. Taylor blamed Hamilton for making parties necessary in *A Definition of Parties, or the Political Effect of the Paper System Considered* (1794). Hamilton began organizing himself under the name Federalist. He recruited Rufus King and Fisher Ames as congressional leaders. He established Federalist newspapers. Most Federalist support was in the urban seaports and depended on the national veneration of Washington.

By 1796, both Federalists and Republicans had taken on a political life of their own, and nominated their own choices for both president and vice president.

The Republicans were nearly wrecked at the outset by their association with the excesses of the French Revolution. Jefferson was tenacious in his faith in the French Republic, but the revolution embarrassed the Republicans more and more. Ministers preached against the revolution as anti-Christ. The French Republic's minister, Edmond Genet, outraged Washington.

Nevertheless, the Federalists managed to fumble away all these advantages. Hamilton could formulate policy but could not make it work. The Whiskey Rebellion made Hamilton and Washington appear heavy-handed. The Jay Treaty was so lopsidedly pro-British that the Federalist administration was embarrassed.

The 1796 election was won by Adams and the Federalists. However, under the Constitution's election procedures, Jefferson was elected vice president. Jefferson would use the vice presidency to frustrate Adams and the Federalists. ∎

Suggested Reading

Appleby, *Capitalism and a New Social Order*.

Banning, *The Jeffersonian Persuasion*.

Jefferson, "Notes on the State of Virginia," in Peterson, *The Portable Thomas Jefferson*.

Questions to Consider

1. Why did the Constitutional Convention miss so completely the likelihood that political parties would develop in the new republic?

2. Were there any points of shared values between Republicans and Federalists?

Adams and Liberty
Lecture 17

Few people in the American republic in the 1790s had a more distinguished record of public service than the second president of the United States, John Adams. Born and bred in Quincy, Massachusetts, Adams had spoken first for American liberty back in 1765 by denouncing the Stamp Act.

Despite his long career of public service, John Adams was not well liked. His personal temperament was unattractive. He was vain and uncooperative. His *Defence of the Constitutions of Government of the United States* (1787) appeared to favor quasi-monarchy. At the same time, Adams showed no enthusiasm for Hamilton's economic program.

Fortunately for Adams, his first challenge involved foreign policy. French ships at war with Britain were seizing American ships. Adams sent a three-man delegation—consisting of Pinckney, Marshall, and Gerry—to negotiate. They were met with demands for bribes. Adams released the news of the XYZ Affair to Congress and asked for military mobilization (1798). His particular triumph was the success of the American frigates.

But Adams proceeded to display the Federalist weakness for losing control. He created political martyrs out of the Republicans. In an effort to suppress French "sedition," Congress passed the Naturalization Act, the Act Concerning Aliens, the Act Concerning Alien Enemies, and the Sedition Act (collectively, the Alien and Sedition Acts; 1798). When the arrests centered on Republicans, public opinion swung against Adams. Jefferson and Madison drafted the Virginia and Kentucky resolutions, threatening nullification and secession.

The French Directory was overthrown by Napoleon, ending the immediate threat of war with France. Adams unwisely opened negotiations with France and demobilized the military. Hamilton was so outraged that he inaugurated a dump-Adams movement in 1800. Hamilton split the Federalists, enabling

Jefferson to capture the presidency and attempt the restoration of what he considered "true" republicanism. ■

Suggested Reading

Banning, *The Sacred Fire of Liberty*, chap. 7.

Ellis, *American Sphinx: The Character of Thomas Jefferson*.

McCullough, *John Adams*.

Questions to Consider

1. Could Adams have used the opportunity of war with France to solidify the Federalist grip on political power?

2. Were the Virginia and Kentucky Resolutions an appropriate response to the Alien and Sedition Acts?

The Jeffersonian Reaction
Lecture 18

There was no question in Thomas Jefferson's mind but that his election as the third president of the United States meant a completely new start for the practice of American republicanism.

The Federalists' opposition to the French Revolution was evidence of their common cause with Britain. Hamilton's reports were evidence of a determination to entangle America in British finance. Thus Jefferson was determined to do away with Federalist influence. His inauguration was the first to be held in Washington, free from corrupting influences in Philadelphia. He would dismantle the structure of federal government. He would contain the size of the military. There would be no favoritism in foreign policy.

However, Jefferson's administration turned out not to be as radical as it at first seemed. Jefferson made no effort

The French Directory was on the road to collapse, and collapse it finally did in November of 1799, when Bonaparte seized power in a massive *coup d'etat*.

to extend voting rights. In many states, voting rights were actually decreased. Jefferson's only solution was to increase property holding. Neither was he successful in promoting an agrarian agenda. He personally knew little about agriculture and had no objection against small-scale manufacturing. He was an ineffective administrator, failing to displace Hamilton's fiscal policies. He canceled military spending, only to be embarrassed by the Barbary pirates (1801–1804).

Jefferson attempted to solve the problem of British and French depredations on American commerce with a national embargo on exports. Renewal of war between France and Great Britain in 1803 made American ships sitting ducks. A British frigate, the *Leopard*, assaulted an American frigate, the *Chesapeake*, in 1807. Jefferson called for an embargo in 1808 to force the British and French to cave in. Instead, the embargo beggared the American economy.

Jefferson was hamstrung by the federal courts. John Marshall was one of Adams's last appointments, as chief justice of the U.S. Supreme Court. He successfully choked off the application of Jefferson's "revolution of 1800" through court decisions: *Marbury v. Madison* (1803) established the principle of judicial review. *Martin v. Hunter's Lessee* established the authority of the federal courts over the state courts. And *McCulloch v. Maryland* argued for the existence of "implied powers" in the federal government. ■

Suggested Reading

Hyneman and Lutz, eds., *American Political Writings during the Founding Era, 1760–1805*, vol. 2, documents 67–76.

Newmyer, *John Marshall and the Heroic Age of the Supreme Court*.

White, *The Marshall Court and Cultural Change*.

Questions to Consider

1. Do you believe the kind of court that Marshall created was what the Constitution originally envisioned in providing for a Supreme Court?

2. In what ways are the Marshall decisions still important today?

Territory and Treason
Lecture 19

Nothing terrified the thinking of the American Republic in the first 30 years of its existence more than the fear that somehow the United States would be ground to pieces between the conflicts of the great European powers and then re-colonized by one of them, or perhaps several of them.

Americans feared the European threat to their independence, and they feared military actions from the Europeans. Napoleon's armies toppled one European kingdom after another. The British responded by preemptive strikes against neutral powers. The British and French aggressively poached on American shipping in the West Indies.

Americans also feared betrayal to the European empires from within. Jefferson accused the Federalists of pro-British treason (for example, the Jay Treaty). Federalists were convinced that the Jeffersonians would plunge them into a pro-French proxy war against Great Britain.

Jefferson personally hoped to avoid any involvement with Europe by turning American attention westward, to ensure American self-sufficiency. By 1800, the American population in the trans-Appalachia had grown by 400 percent. Ohio was the first state to be organized from the Northwest Territory, in 1803.

The problem with westward expansion was that it oriented trade toward New Orleans, then in Spanish hands. Bonaparte intended to make New Orleans the center of a plan to revive France's colonial empire in North America. Bonaparte's plan failed because of the resistance of black San Domingue. Bonaparte then offered to sell Louisiana to the United States, and Jefferson accepted. Jefferson had already explored the Louisiana Territory by means of secret exploring parties under Lewis and Clark, Zebulon Pike, and commercial freelancers (such as John Jacob Astor).

Louisiana, however, also opened up opportunities for plotters. The most sinister of these plotters was Aaron Burr. Burr was the grandson of Jonathan Edwards and was Jefferson's former vice president. He goaded Alexander Hamilton into a fatal duel in 1804.

Burr plotted to set up an independent republic in Louisiana. He offered to make the territory a British dependency. He recruited General James Wilkinson to betray New Orleans. Wilkinson subsequently double-crossed Burr, and Burr was arrested.

> **On August 31, Marshall quashed the treason indictment of Burr on a technicality. Burr went off scot-free.**

Burr's treason trial was a fiasco for Jefferson. Burr had covered his tracks very effectively. Chief Justice Marshall was eager to even scores with Jefferson. Burr was acquitted, went into exile, and returned to the United States in 1812. ■

Suggested Reading

Ellis, *Founding Brothers*.

Kline, ed., *The Political Correspondence and Public Papers of Aaron Burr*, vol. 2.

McDonald, *The Presidency of Thomas Jefferson*.

Questions to Consider

1. What might have been the results for the United States had Burr's conspiracy to create an independent republic in the Southwest succeeded?

2. In what ways were Jefferson's actions as president inconsistent with the Republican Party attitudes?

The Agrarian Republic
Lecture 20

All through his life, the one fixed and unmoving star in Thomas Jefferson's political philosophy as a Republican was the importance of keeping the American Republic an overwhelmingly agrarian society.

Thomas Jefferson valorized farmers—those citizens who owned their own land and lived off their own subsistence. This meant an antidevelopment posture. Nevertheless, it reflected much of the reality of early America.

Jefferson was suspicious of the implications of market capitalism. Capitalism involved the exchange of goods at a profit and the conversion of those profits into more goods for exchange. It was perceived as a threat to the stability and ethical norms of many societies. No one did better in this than the English, who simplified the process through the conversion of economic exchange into cash. The English also set about overhauling their empire to balance supply and demand. The American colonies were kept deliberately agricultural. Jefferson inherited the system he loved from the people he hated.

Jefferson was also determined to keep America agrarian in culture. Agrarian culture was typified by independence. America had no aristocracy. They largely owned their land in fee simple. Wealth and power were diffused along a rough but recognizable equality.

Even more like the whites, the Indians had learned—even before the Revolution—how to find places in the white man's commercial networks.

Agrarian culture was typified by non-market agriculture. Because land titles were not jeopardized by taxes, the chief incentive for production was household consumption. Farm households produced as much as 75 percent of what they required. Cash was almost nonexistent in many places as a medium of exchange.

53

Agrarian culture was typified by patriarchy. The model for structuring the agrarian household was the rule of the adult male over women and children. Economic duties were divided along gender and age lines. Childhood scarcely existed as a separate category.

Agrarian culture was typified by the influence of community. The absence of cash exchange demanded a face-to-face relationship. Indebtedness was common, without interest, and often not repaid.

Tenskwatawa, a Shawnee leader defeated at the Battle of Tippecanoe.

The fatal flaw in this system was the increase in agricultural population. Reproduction of the subsistence household required the expansion of land to support it. This generated much of the westward expansion into the Northwest Territory. Such expansion spawned clashes with the Indian tribes of those regions.

Indian tribes were both numerous and well organized. Indian economies were fundamentally similar to Jefferson's. Instead of being a two-way relationship of colonists and British, the colonial economy was really three-way, including Indians.

As Americans poured into the Northwest Territory, Indians were confronted with two choices. They could accommodate themselves by signing over lands and accepting resettlement, by organizing themselves to mirror white society, or by undergoing revitalization. Or they could resist, a strategy adopted by Lalawethika, Tenskwatawa, and Tecumseh.

Resistance usually ended disastrously. Tecumseh's alliance was defeated at Tippecanoe in 1811. But it convinced Americans that the real enemy was the British. ■

Suggested Reading

Clark, *The Roots of Rural Capitalism: Western Massachusetts, 1780–1861.*

Sellers, *The Market Revolution*, chap. 1.

Wallace, *The Death and Rebirth of the Seneca.*

Questions to Consider

1. What would victory for the Tecumseh alliance have looked like if Tecumseh had been successful?

2. Does the agrarian ideal still have political force today?

The Disastrous War of 1812
Lecture 21

> The incidents at Macaw … reinforced the sense of helplessness that American ship owners and merchants felt at being caught on the high seas between the warring navies of Napoleon's France and Great Britain.

American commerce had frequently been caught in the crossfire of the Napoleonic Wars. The British reserved the right to board American ships looking for "deserters." This triggered such incidents as the *Caravan* and the *Diana*, and the *Diana* and the *Topaz*. Jefferson attempted to deal with this by imposing an embargo on American high-seas commerce.

The embargo failed to ease these confrontations. It wrecked the American economy. It wrecked the Republicans' hold on the government; they retained

British forces captured the city of Washington on August 24, 1814, and set government buildings ablaze.

the presidency by electing James Madison but lost other political ground to the Federalists.

The surviving Republicans in Congress were Jeffersonian radicals from the West who demanded retaliation against the British. Henry Clay of Kentucky vigorously attacked the British abroad and corporate privilege at home. He was joined by the War Hawks. They demanded the seizure of Canada as a hostage to British behavior toward American shipping on the oceans.

President Madison preferred diplomatic dealings, but the British undid all his efforts. British correspondence with New England Federalists revealed a plot to detach New England from the United States. In April 1812, Madison finally asked a willing Congress for a declaration of war against Britain.

The United States was woefully unprepared to wage war, much less against the British. Jefferson's administration had severely underfunded the American military. The federal budget was incapable of supporting a war The U.S. Army listed only 7,500 men. The U.S. Navy had only 16 ships in commission.

The military results of the war were humiliating for the United States. General William Hull surrendered Detroit. General Stephen Van Renssalaer invaded Canada but was forced to retreat. General W. H. Harrison's expedition to recover Detroit was massacred at the Raisin River. General James Wilkinson's army invaded upper Canada but went wild and burned the town of York.

Actual American victories were few and insubstantial. Oliver H. Perry defeated the British Navy's Lake Erie squadron and forced the evacuation of Detroit. General W. H. Harrison won a subsequent victory at the battle of Thames, where Tecumseh was killed. General Jacob Brown invaded Canada and defeated the British at Chippewa and Lundy's Lane but had to withdraw.

The British launched their own counterinvasions in 1814. Admiral George Cockburn raided the American coast and burnt Washington. Sir George

Prevost invaded New York but was stopped at Plattsburgh by Alexander Macomb and Thomas MacDonough.

The most substantial American successes were at sea and in the South. The American frigates failed to loosen a British blockade but scored several spectacular ship-to-ship battles. The *Constitution* fought and defeated the *Guerriere* and the *Java* (1812). The *United States* defeated the *Macedonian*. The *Essex* raided British shipping in the Pacific.

> **The War of 1812 was over, but its aftereffects would be felt for the next 40 years.**

The Red Stick Creeks were roused by Tecumseh to attack American settlements. The Tennessee militia under Andrew Jackson crushed the Red Sticks at Horseshoe Bend (1814). Jackson occupied Spanish West Florida, then repulsed a British attack on New Orleans.

By 1815, both Americans and British were ready for peace. The American war effort was exhausted. The treasury was depleted, and the war was being financed by borrowing. American commerce was suffering from the blockade.

The British were also exhausted. The defeat of Napoleon at Leipzig in 1813 allowed the British to hope for all-around peace. The British offered to begin direct negotiations at Ghent.

New England Federalists organized a break-away convention at Hartford. New England had suffered more than any other region. The Hartford Convention demanded new constitutional amendments to limit Madison's powers and threatened a second convention for the purpose of seceding from the Union. The signing of the Peace of Ghent ended these plans, but the effects of the War of 1812 would be felt for the next 40 years. ■

Suggested Reading

Banner, *To the Hartford Convention*.

Hickey, *The War of 1812*.

Remini, *The Battle of New Orleans*.

Questions to Consider

1. What would have been the consequences had Jackson failed to prevent a British seizure of New Orleans?

2. In what ways was the War of 1812 a direct result of Thomas Jefferson's policies?

The "American System"
Lecture 22

The War of 1812 started badly and, except for Andrew Jackson's lame-duck victory at New Orleans two weeks after the signing of the Treaty of Ghent, it ended badly, too.

The War of 1812 forced the Republican leadership into a series of initiatives that threatened a serious departure from Jeffersonian orthodoxy. President Madison called for reviving the American military. New fortifications, an enlarged army, and a naval construction program were proposed. To fund this, Madison asked for a continuance of wartime taxes and a doubling of the tariff rates.

Madison also called for a revival of the Bank of the United States. A second bank would be chartered along lines similar to Hamilton's. It would be capitalized at $35 million. Madison also proposed a national transportation initiative. He found his principal floor leaders in Congress in sadder-but-wiser War Hawks, such as Clay and Calhoun. These initiatives became known as National Republicanism. But these departures shocked Republican elders. Jefferson predicted that they would concentrate power and money in their own hands.

Therefore, Republicans sought an uncontroversial presidential candidate for 1816 and nominated James Monroe. In office, however, President Monroe disappointed the old-guard Republicans by continuing Madison's policies.

James Monroe (1758–1831), fifth president of the United States.

The Cumberland Road project was hesitatingly supported by Madison and Monroe and was followed by state turnpike projects. Steam-powered riverboats, beginning with Robert Fulton's *Clermont*, further cut shipping costs, especially on the Mississippi River. Canals provided artificial waterways to supplement the rivers, the most spectacularly successful being DeWitt Clinton's Erie Canal (1825). Railroads, introduced from Britain in 1828, cut shipping costs still further.

> **[Monroe] had such applause from both Federalists and his own party, the Republicans, that his admirers began to … dub Monroe's presidency as the Era of Good Feelings.**

The result was the undercutting of the agrarian economy and culture. Households stopped producing their own support and turned commercial. Face-to-face reciprocity yielded to formal contracts and distant market obligations. Following the Second Bank of the United States, new banks sprang into life with state charters, issuing a flood of paper bank notes.

Monroe's two terms as president became known as the Era of Good Feelings. Anxieties diminished as the social costs of market capitalism were outweighed by the prosperity that resulted. Nevertheless, Jefferson looked at the postwar policies as a betrayal of republicanism. ∎

Suggested Reading

Dawidoff, *The Education of John Randolph*.

Sheriff, *The Artificial River*.

Watson, *Liberty and Power*.

Questions to Consider

1. Why were Jeffersonians so suspicious of banks?

2. To what degree were slavery and Indian removal the byproducts of economic decisions?

A Nation Announcing Itself
Lecture 23

The year 1824 brought to a close the last term of James Monroe as president and set off plans for celebrations throughout 1825 of the 50th anniversary of the beginning of the American Revolution.

The 50th anniversary of American independence marked a turning point for the republic. The anniversary marked the passing of the revolutionary generation. The Marquis de Lafayette made a state visit in 1824–1825. The Bunker Hill Monument was dedicated in 1825. John Adams and Thomas Jefferson both died on July 4, 1826.

The anniversary also highlighted changes in American demography. Between 1790 and 1820, the American population more than doubled. Although domestic birth rates declined, the decline was more than offset by immigration from Europe. English-speaking emigrants amounted to 500,000 by 1840.

The anniversary pointed to immense geographical growth. The end of the War of 1812 led to tremendous sales of public lands. Most of this went to land speculators. Congress constantly lowered the restrictions to allow greater access to land purchases, but many simply "squatted" and claimed title preemption. The speculators were disliked but were crucial to land development.

The most unsettling development was the growth of American cities. Although predominantly agricultural, the United States saw a significant upswing in urban population. Between 1820 and 1850, the number of cities with more than 5,000 inhabitants rose from 12 to 150. Existing cities became denser. Many western pioneers went not to farm but to build cities in the interior.

Cities were the economic nerve centers of the republic. Home-based manufacturing yielded to the factory system. The imbalance of wealth distribution became acute. In theory, urban laborers had an "escape valve"

> **That new form of political organization is what we call "democracy," or, to be more accurate, it signaled the end of the republican ideology.**

available in western lands. That was not true for urban free blacks. White migrants discovered flimsiness and instability.

The ultimate casualty of these developments was republicanism. Republicanism feared a society built on self-interest rather than virtue. In the West and in the cities, self-interest reigned supreme. This signaled the conversion of republicanism into democracy. ■

Suggested Reading

Faragher, *Sugar Creek*.

Smith, *The "Lower Sort": Philadelphia's Laboring People*.

Tocqueville, *Democracy in America*.

Questions to Consider

1. Does the sale of federal lands constitute a governmental "intervention" in the economy?

2. How is democracy different from republicanism?

National Republican Follies
Lecture 24

Henry Clay was no one's fool, especially when it came to economic issues, and he had no illusions that pushing the United States into the networks of world markets was without risks. He declared, however, that he had closely studied the results of the wars in Europe and in America, and he had learned some lessons by it.

Aware of the risks of market involvement, the National Republicans believed it was essential to national greatness. But the rapid rate of American development came to a crashing halt in the economic panic of the year 1819.

The Panic of 1819 began with the state banks. State banks could not issue coin, but they could issue paper bank notes. The collapse of British cotton prices set off a run on the state banks. The state banks and the Second Bank of the United States, in turn, called in loans.

The panic generated massive popular unrest. Debtor relief laws were passed by state legislatures. Every Western legislature adopted measures to postpone foreclosure sales, restrict liquidation sales, close state courts to creditors, and force creditors to accept bank notes. These measures were risky because they were unconstitutional.

Banks were closed or outlawed by legislatures. Some states permitted the establishment only of a state-controlled bank. Even nonbank corporations became the targets of legislative control.

Voter reform admitted thousands of new voters to the franchise by eliminating property qualifications. Republicanism was suspicious of concentrations of power, even when that power was in the hands of the people. The economic crisis led to an explosion in demands to widen voting rights to the victims of the panic. Voter participation now surged from 27 percent in 1824 to 80 percent in 1840. Presidential nominations began moving out of party caucuses and into national conventions.

The principal restraint on this popular backlash was the Supreme Court. Law shifted from concentrating on the regulation of behavior to the protection of property and contract. Law did this because of its kinship to the capitalist ethic. Lawyers became the shock troops of capitalism. The principal example of this was John Marshall. The Marshall Court heard appeals in a series of critical cases that restrained popular attacks on corporations and contract: *Dartmouth College v. Woodward* prevented the state of New Hampshire from interfering in the corporate charter of Dartmouth College. *Sturgis v. Crowninshield* struck down New York state bankruptcy laws. *Gibbons v. Ogden* invoked the Commerce Clause to prevent states from interfering in the competitive operations of the market. The success of the Marshall Court outraged Jeffersonians, who looked for a candidate to turn the tide against the market and found him in Andrew Jackson. ■

> **As commercial capitalism came to be the dominant economic engine of prosperity and growth in the British Empire, though, British and American law stopped being a monitor of behavior and became an arbitrator of contracts.**

Suggested Reading

Freehling, *The Road to Disunion*, vol. 1: *Secessionists at Bay*.

White, *The Marshall Court and Cultural Change, 1815–1835*, chaps. 8–9.

Questions to Consider

1. How did the roles of lawyers change from the colonial era to the early republic?

2. Why did the application of Missouri for admission as a slave state trigger a controversy in 1819, but not the applications of Ohio, Mississippi, Indiana, or Alabama?

The Second Great Awakening
Lecture 25

It was more than just the impact of reading the skeptical writers of the Enlightenment that dislocated American religion in the first decades of the American Republic, however. It was, in fact, the ideology of republicanism itself, which, as the offspring of the Enlightenment, had little need or little room for public Christianity.

The Enlightenment had little use for religion as sanctioning or confirming its ideas, and as an Enlightenment ideology, republicanism too had little need for religious sanction. Republicanism based itself entirely on human longings, human morals, and human nature. Jefferson was openly critical of Christianity.

Christianity had rarely enjoyed a stable footing in American life even before the Revolution. Most colonial religious groups were antiauthoritarian come-outers. The English state church had been indifferent to colonial religious life. The Great Awakening revived antiauthoritarian instincts.

The Revolution cost American religious groups dearly in public influence. Loyalist Anglicans fled the country and reduced the Church of England to a tiny group. Wartime disruptions interfered with stable religious life. State governments disestablished churches. The federal Constitution forbade federal support for religious denominations.

As formal Christianity declined, unusual substitutes sprang up. Deists were usually belligerent, skeptical, and anti-Calvinist. Unitarianism offered an alternative to New Englanders who could not stomach revivalism. Freemasonry offered secular ritualism as an alternative to religion.

But instead of fading into the background, Christian churches staged a remarkable comeback. The organization of congregations went on the upswing. Congregationalists went from about 750 to 2,200 congregations. Methodists went from nothing to 20,000 congregations by 1860. Roman Catholics went from 50 congregations to 2,500 by 1860.

This upswing grew from three factors. Based on the example of the Great Awakening, revivals proved to be a vigorous way of renewing Christian conversion. The virtue republicanism saw as vital to a republican order was claimed by the churches as religion's special province. Churches co-opted republican optimism about the future with religious optimism in the form of millennialism.

> "There is no country in the whole world in which the Christian religion retains a greater influence over the souls of men than in America."
> —Alexis de Tocqueville

By 1835, Christianity had recovered much of its lost ground. Religious leaders identified Christianity as the best friend of republicanism. However, it would have to cope with the challenge posed by the materialism of the market. ∎

Suggested Reading

Butler, *Awash in a Sea of Faith*, chap. 9.

Cross, *The Burned-Over District*.

Johnson, *A Shopkeeper's Millennium*.

Questions to Consider

1. What role did the Founders intend for religion to play in the new republic?

2. How did churches adapt themselves and recover influence once they had been stripped of public support?

Dark Satanic Mills
Lecture 26

Our images of the Industrial Revolution are surprisingly contradictory ones. The glittering, humming efficiency of brass and iron machines is set in the midst of gloomy, smoke-begrimed factories. The incredible volume of cheaply produced goods stands beside the incredible volume of resentment and violence by the factory workers.

Republicanism was built on the pillars of liberty, virtue, and commerce, but democracy and revivalism challenged the first two, and the Industrial Revolution challenged the third. The Industrial Revolution was built around four important developments: the substitution of machines for production of commodities; the application of artificial power for human, wind, or animal power; the organization of labor into the factory system; and the funding of enterprise through commercial capitalism.

It took 50 years after the Industrial Revolution in Great Britain for these developments to mature in the United States. British colonial policy had obstructed American industrial development. Not until 1789 did a British emigrant, Samuel Slater, build a cotton-spinning mill in Rhode Island from his memories of English models. New England merchants built up fortunes in trade, allowing the formation of sufficient capital to fund the building of factories.

America's first major experiments in factory organization took place in in New England. Francis Cabot Lowell organized a textile mill at Waltham and Chelmsford, Massachusetts with a workforce of single women recruited from the countryside.

The McCormick reaper, one of the first successful reaping machines.

Mills experienced tremendous growth and profitability. Eli Whitney introduced assembly-line manufacturing. Alfred Jenks opened a steam-powered mill. Cyrus McCormick mechanized agriculture with the mechanical reaper. But the success of the factory system also generated problems and opposition. The multiplication of mills created greater supply. As supply increased, demand fell, and so did prices and wages. Industrial workers began to organize and form unions and stage strikes, which were treated by the courts as breaches of contract.

> **In Boston, working men actually forced the adoption of a new city charter and threatened to step in "with our leathern aprons on and choose a man of our own sentiments for the city's government and the city's mayor."**

Working men then turned to political solutions. Working men's parties were organized. These parties found their champion in Andrew Jackson. ■

Suggested Reading

Anthony, *Wallace, Rockdale*.

Cochran, *Frontiers of Change: Early Industrialism in America*.

Wilentz, *Chants Democratic*.

Questions to Consider

1. Would the Industrial Revolution have been possible if the federal government was understood in the minimal terms it was in the 1800s?

2. What were the components of an early textile factory?

The Military Chieftain
Lecture 27

Ever since 1800, Thomas Jefferson's Republicans had held a locked grip on the presidency. In fact, after the Federalists had committed political suicide in convening the Hartford Convention in the midst of the War of 1812, the Republicans had been virtually the only functioning political party with anybody to elect.

The election of 1824 represented a break in the normal presidential nominating process. As the reigning political organization, the Republicans chose their candidates by caucus. The president usually sent in the name of his secretary of state as his successor. Under this plan, in 1824, James Monroe would nominate John Quincy Adams.

The expansion of voting rights forced a change in this process in 1824. The caucus system seemed like an insider process. Divisions had grown up within the Republicans, with the National Republicans and the Democratic-Republicans sponsoring differing agendas.

The likelihood of Adams's succession to the nomination became clouded. Although he had substantial experience as a diplomat, he still resembled a Federalist. His father was the Federalists' last president. He espoused the National Republican agenda.

Adams had a challenger in Henry Clay. Clay represented the interests of the West. He was the Speaker of the House of Representatives and was in a position to obstruct an Adams nomination. He was also becoming the exponent of the "American System."

Republican Party regulars used the caucus to nominate William Crawford. Clay arranged for a rival nomination by the Kentucky legislature. Adams arranged for a counter-nomination by New England and New York. The split made it likely that the election would be thrown into the House of Representatives, where Clay was confident of victory.

Clay had reckoned without the popular emergence of Andrew Jackson. Andrew Jackson had become the favorite of Western Republicans and an enemy of the National Republican agenda. He was a self-made lawyer who rose to prominence and wealth in Tennessee. He was possessed of a volcanic temper and given to dueling. He established a reputation as a ruthless Indian fighter. He won the War of 1812's greatest victory at New Orleans. He nearly triggered war with Great Britain again in 1818 by hanging two British subjects and occupying Florida.

The Panic of 1819 pushed Jackson back into politics. He was an enemy of the banks. He was more of a Democrat than a classical Republican. Jackson became the favorite candidate of Republicans who liked neither Clay nor Adams. The Tennessee legislature nominated Jackson. In 1824, Jackson swept the popular vote but failed to garner sufficient electoral votes to beat Clay, Adams, and Crawford. ■

> **[Andrew Jackson] returned to Tennessee to find his state wracked with the agonies of the Panic of 1819, and himself pushed to the brink of financial ruin.**

Suggested Reading

Remini, *Henry Clay*, chaps. 14–15.

——, *John Quincy Adams*.

Rogin, *Fathers and Children: Andrew Jackson and the Subjugation of the American Indian*.

Questions to Consider

1. Did Clay have good reason to believe he could defeat Adams?

2. What made Jackson so much more attractive politically to American voters than Clay or Adams, with their wide experience in national government?

The Politics of Distrust
Lecture 28

Clay was fairly certain that he would probably not win a majority of electoral votes the first time around. He was certain, however, that once the election was thrown into the House of Representatives, where he was, of course, the Speaker of the House, well, that was about as good as throwing it into his own lap.

The stalled election of 1824 was thrown into the House of Representatives. Although Clay finished fourth in electoral votes, he used his position as Speaker of the House to recruit votes. Clay was rumored to have struck a corrupt bargain with Adams to permit an Adams election, after which Clay would become secretary of state. Adams was elected on the first ballot.

The corrupt bargain besmirched the reputations of both Adams and Clay. Adams tried to prove his innocence by including Jackson's supporters in his administration, only to have them sabotage it. Adams got no support for implementing the National Republican economic agenda.

Jackson gathered his forces for the election of 1828. Jackson won an overwhelming victory, especially among new voters. He was supported by an alliance of antitax, anti-bank, and anticorporate farmers and workers. Ironically, Jackson himself was a slaveholder and a wealthy man. But Jackson appeared as the enemy of great concentrations of power and the friend of territorial expansion.

Henry Clay (1777–1852), Speaker of the House and Kentucky's candidate for president in 1824.

73

The election of 1828 marked a shift from republican politics to democratic politics. Democracy was the answer to distrust. In contrast to the private swearing-in ceremonies of previous presidents, thousands flooded unbidden into Washington. Jackson's inaugural reception resembled a democratic bacchanal.

Jackson instituted an internal administrative revolution. Nearly 1,000 officers, from the cabinet down to postmasters, were turned out. They were replaced by Jackson's personal friends: Martin Van Buren, Samuel Ingham, John H. Eaton. Jackson insisted on conducting the appointment process by the spoils system.

While Jackson worked to promote agricultural interests, he fought government support for manufacturing and commerce, although he allowed neither to threaten the permanence of the federal union. Jackson used his veto to strike down a number of congressionally funded projects. He vetoed the Maysville Road project. He signed a tariff bill in 1832, but only with the understanding that it would be used to permanently eliminate the national debt.

When Jackson signed the tariff, Calhoun had no other honorable option but to resign as vice president and return to South Carolina.

Southern interests were aghast at Jackson's approval of the tariff. John Calhoun wrote two major protests advocating state nullification of the tariff. Calhoun delegated defense of nullification in the Senate to Robert Hayne, who was out-argued by Daniel Webster. Calhoun failed to enlist Jackson's endorsement of nullification at the 1830 Jefferson's birthday dinner. Calhoun prompted South Carolina to challenge the tariff by nullifying it within state boundaries, only to be forced by Jackson to back down. ∎

Suggested Reading

Belz, ed., *The Webster-Hayne Debate on the Nature of the Union*, p. 3–134.

Freehling, *Prelude to Civil War: The Nullification Controversy in South Carolina*.

Remini, *Andrew Jackson and the Course of American Freedom*.

Questions to Consider

1. Was Calhoun or Jackson more attuned to the ideas of Thomas Jefferson?

2. How did Jackson align his promotion of southern interests with his hostility to South Carolina and nullification?

The Monster Bank
Lecture 29

> In times of prosperity, the demand for specie could keep banks from overextending themselves through excessive loans and excessive issues of paper currency. In harder economic times, the Bank of the United States could ease the strain by relaxing its demands for specie from the local banks.

The Second Bank of the United States (BUS) had been the prime symbol of National Republicanism ever since its original chartering in 1816. It served to regulate the national money supply. All federal customs duties and taxes were payable to the BUS. It could demand repayment for bank notes from the original issuers in specie. This power restrained banks from overextending themselves by overprinting bank notes.

The BUS provided resources for national investment. As a mixed public/private corporation, it could put government economic clout behind private enterprises. The constant inflow of government revenues gave it constant liquidity and vast financial reserves. The BUS could step in to fund development projects that Congress could not.

The power of the BUS outraged Democratic-Republicans. The BUS did nothing to allay these suspicions. Its first president, William Jones, helped trigger the Panic of 1819.

Nicholas Biddle (1786–1844), second president of the Second Bank of the United States

Its second president, Nicholas Biddle, used the BUS's resources to protect the BUS politically.

Jackson would have moved more dramatically against the bank in his first term but didn't. He was restrained by other political problems, and the BUS had a 20-year charter.

Biddle's blind spot was power, and to increase the power of the bank, he was willing to use the bank's privileges to buy political security.

Biddle actually provoked a confrontation by appealing to Congress in 1832 for an early rechartering. Henry Clay advised in favor of rechartering. It would pass Congress without difficulty. If Jackson vetoed it, the veto would be overridden by Congress and alarm the electorate. If Jackson signed it, it would destroy his reputation with his own party.

A rechartering petition was submitted by Clay in 1832. Jackson vetoed it. Accompanying the veto was a veto message that identified the BUS's supporters as foreigners, financiers, and usurpers. The veto message was instantly popular. Clay called for an override of the veto. He warned of dire financial consequences if the BUS was shut down. Jackson's logic in the veto was identical with nullification. However, the veto was not overridden. When Clay attempted to make the BUS an issue in the 1832 election, he was soundly defeated by Jackson.

The veto inaugurated a bank war. The BUS still had four more years to run on its charter. Jackson went on the offensive and removed government deposits from the BUS. Two successive treasury secretaries refused to obey Jackson's order. Finally, Jackson recruited Roger Taney to remove the deposits.

Government funds were now deposited in seven "pet" state banks. The redeposit led Clay to ask Congress for a motion of censure against Jackson. Biddle retaliated by calling in loans. The result was a major financial panic in 1837. Jackson eventually increased the number of pet banks to more than 300. He used the pet banks to pay off the national debt. He parceled out government revenue surpluses to the states. He issued a Specie Circular, which required that payment for federal lands be made only in specie, thus nudging the country away from the use of bank notes.

The bank war left Jackson with an even more secure grip on power. The BUS was reduced to seeking a state charter from Pennsylvania to keep operating. Jackson rewarded Taney by making him chief justice after the death of John Marshall. ■

Suggested Reading

Schlesinger, *The Age of Jackson*.

Sellers, *The Market Revolution*, chap. 11.

Silbey, *The Partisan Imperative*.

Questions to Consider

1. What aspects of the economy were most likely to be hit by Jackson's veto of the BUS charter?

2. Why was destroying the "monster bank" essential to Jackson's political vision?

Whigs and Democrats
Lecture 30

The bank war destroyed all illusion that a single Republican Party, the party of Jefferson, and the party of the revolution of 1800 still existed. For years, ever since the election of John Quincy Adams in 1824, that pretense had been evaporating. With the bank war, it was gone entirely.

The National Republicans had organized themselves around the need for a national banking system. The attack on the BUS exposed the central line of division in the Republican house. In 1832, the National Republicans organized their own national nominating convention.

In 1834, Clay nicknamed the National Republicans "Whigs." This was originally the name of the British party dedicated to resistance against monarchical tyranny. It was applied by Clay to stigmatize Andrew Jackson as a would-be king.

The Whigs came to stand for a cluster of ideas that sharply differentiated them from the Jacksonians: The Whigs encouraged economic dynamism. They became associated with small-scale urban business and finance. Whig farmers tended to be commercial farmers. Whigs did not tie themselves to local or state identities. This attracted them to Clay's American System. It also opened them to the charge of being the "party of the rich."

Martin Van Buren (1782–1862), eighth president of the United States.

The Whigs looked to create a place for social morality in a secular republic. The Whigs established a close alliance with moderate Protestants. These moderate Protestants sought to rebuild religious influence in society. Whig Protestants sought to rationalize and sanction the market system. They often ignored the costs of private opportunism but were incensed by departures from public morality.

> **Even though Harrison was a military chieftain himself and a man of no ordinary wealth, the Whigs billed Harrison as a man of the people who would out-Democrat the Democrats.**

The Whigs thought of themselves as the protectors of national union. The key to establishing a national economy and national morality was the preservation of the Union in the face of democratic individualism. Whigs tended to attack extremists from both South and North. Whig politicians liked to think of themselves as disinterested statesmen who concentrated on formulating compromises to save the Union rather than tearing it apart to satisfy regional agendas.

The Whig mentality contained some important connections to European liberalism. It was based on reason, especially the rationalism of the marketplace. It glorified the Union but applauded individual self-help. It revered the past but believed confidently in progress. It was suspicious of democracy and believed that only an enlightened elite was fit to govern.

By contrast, Jackson's Democrats liked to think of themselves as the "party of the people." Democrats called for laissez faire to reign in private but not public spheres. Political virtue became synonymous with the public will. Democrats resisted the intrusion of religion into public affairs.

Democrats increasingly came to see liberty as negative rather than positive. Whigs wanted economic diversity and cultural uniformity. Democrats favored economic uniformity and cultural diversity.

Democrats had more to fear than they expected from the Whigs. Jackson confidently anointed his vice president, Martin Van Buren, as the Democratic candidate in 1836, who easily defeated a divided Whig Party. Van Buren turned out to have little talent for the presidency. Without the BUS, the American economy slid into a panic in 1837. Van Buren attempted to shore up the collapse by half-restoring the BUS in the form of the Independent Treasury. But the Independent Treasury only provided a safe haven for federal funds and did nothing to revive the overall economy. Van Buren also cultivated an offensively ostentatious lifestyle.

Clay hoped that Van Buren's unpopularity would finally give him the chance to win the presidency. Whigs decided not to risk Clay and nominated William Henry Harrison for president in 1840. The Harrison campaign artfully reinvented Harrison as a "man of the people." Harrison easily won the election, thus ending three decades of nearly continuous rule by Jefferson and his heirs. ■

Suggested Reading

Howe, ed., *The American Whigs: An Anthology*.

———, *The Political Culture of the American Whigs*.

Meyers, *The Jacksonian Persuasion*.

Questions to Consider

1. What were the chief problems faced by the Whigs in gaining voter allegiance?

2. How did the various parts of the Whig political agenda fit together?

American Romanticism
Lecture 31

> Emerson was addressing a sort of intellectual desert in America, with American thinkers gnawing out a bare subsistence from the cactus of European philosophy. Emerson was a bit too pessimistic of how vital and bouncy and ingenious American intellectual life really was, though.

The American Republic was shaped, intellectually as well as politically, by the Enlightenment. A broad variety of American thinkers embraced the universality of natural law, as did Jefferson in his Declaration of Independence and Madison and Hamilton in the Federalist Papers.

Scottish "common sense" philosophy had provided a realist underpinning for natural-law thinking. The most popular tool for inquiry across many disciplines was the Baconian method—in theology, as demonstrated by Charles Hodge; in medicine, as demonstrated by Benjamin Rush.

American law was codified to create a system, based on English common law, that avoided both religion and utilitarianism. The first law schools and legal theorists tried to create a system as regular and scientific as nature itself. The process of codifying American law is amazingly fast, from almost nothing in 1790 to the great commentaries of Joseph Story and James Kent by 1850.

There were, however, many other forces at work in the United States in the early 19th century that cut against the grain of the Enlightenment heritage to create a "Romantic rebellion," including evangelical Protestantism. Many Protestants saw the Enlightenment as synonymous with religious unbelief. The Princeton theology was a major attempt to reconcile the demands of reason and experience.

The historic appeal of personal experience to radical Protestants manifested itself in public revivals of religion, modeled after the Great Awakening, with steadily more exotic aspects. Charles Grandison Finney became the most significant popularizer of the triumph of religious emotion.

American art moved out of its infancy as chiefly portraiture for the mercantile classes (as practiced by artists such as Ralph Earl) into glorification of the American landscape. American architecture abandoned the Georgian classical for Gothic. American Romantic art reached its highest point in the Hudson River School.

Resentment of the rule of lawyers broke out into criticism of law as a profession; ordinary justice based on honesty was championed, along with equity over legal theory. The classic case for antilegalism was made by the popularity of Davy Crockett.

The most important expression of a Romantic rebellion was in philosophy. The Romantic rebellion was originally a European movement and featured the following characterizations: A sense of admiration for, and harmony with, nature (Rousseau); A revolt against reason as senseless formality and cold logic; the glorification of emotion, or "the sublime"; a new understanding of language; and the cult of the artist.

> **Davy Crockett's legal thinking could be reduced to this one single and favorite legal maxim of his: "Be sure you're right, and then go ahead."**

Romanticism's first appearance in America was in the work of James Marsh. Marsh produced an edition of Samuel Taylor Coleridge's *Aids to Reflection* and introduced American readers to Kant. Marsh became the founder of Vermont Transcendentalism.

American Romantic philosophy was matched by a new Romantic theology. Horace Bushnell was a Connecticut Congregationalist and Yale graduate. He called for a revision of the Calvinist understanding of human nature and of the nature of religious language. Bushnell's comments on language were echoed by other New England Calvinists, most importantly, Edwards Amasa Park.

John Williamson Nevin was a product of the Princeton theology but abandoned it under German philosophical influences. Nevin became a theology teacher at the small German Reformed Seminary at Mercersburg, Pennsylvania, and developed a theology based on organic tradition and the use of liturgy for religious experience.

Anglo-Catholicism was a Romantic religious movement founded in England by John Henry Newman. It captured the Episcopal Church in America and converted it from a Protestant identity to a Romantic "Catholic" one.

In turn, American Romanticism came to its fullest flower in literature. The earliest representatives of Romantic literature were Charles Brockden Brown and James Fenimore Cooper. Brown's horror novels (such as *Wieland*) show the weakness of reason and the power of the passions. Cooper's *Leatherstocking Tales* (1823–1841) praise the untutored natural wisdom of Natty Bumppo and his Indian friends over against organized society.

The center of American Romanticism shifted rapidly to Boston and its environs. Ralph Waldo Emerson gave American Romanticism its classic expression in his essays. Emerson was the chief of a literary circle of Transcendentalists that included Margaret Fuller, Elizabeth Palmer Peabody, Henry David Thoreau, and George Ripley. Transcendentalism's greatest literary talents, however, also became its harshest critics, especially in the case of Nathaniel Hawthorne. ■

Suggested Reading

Conkin, *The Uneasy Center: Reformed Christianity in Antebellum America.*

Murphey and Flower, *History of Philosophy in America*, vol. 1, chaps. 4–7.

Richardson, *Emerson*, chaps. 23–25, 40, 43.

Questions to Consider

1. What point was Emerson trying to make by complaining about the need for a new kind of American scholar?

2. What made Scottish "common-sense" philosophy so attractive to American thinkers?

The Age of Reform
Lecture 32

> If you had gotten [Americans] to talk on any other subject [than politics], however, they suddenly turned into the greatest optimists the world had ever seen, which suggests that the American habit of prophesying doom if the next unfashionable candidate gets elected might itself have been a political pose.

Americans adopted an optimistic view of what their new republic was capable of achieving. They believed that the American experiment was unheralded in human history and that having once begun, the path to further improvement lay open. Andrew Jackson's political philosophy glorified American progress. American iconography spoke for confidence in American possibilities.

Americans also feared that this experiment could be compromised. They continued to resent humiliations visited on them by Great Britain. The European monarchies remained a threat. Americans dreaded the influence of material success on public virtue. Immigrants, with different languages, folkways, and versions of Christianity, provoked fear that immigrant minorities could be easily seduced and turned into instruments of political corruption.

This pushing for more reform was combined with a pulling away to guarantee the survival of reform in the midst of a threatening and unstable society. Many Americans were convinced that the threat to their republican purity was so great that it was necessary for them to withdraw from society. Examples of this were offered by America's own colonial past and by emigrant colonies organized by Gustavus Unonius and Morris Birkbeck.

Some of these reform efforts were religious. Movements for social improvement were inaugurated by many churches as a way of recapturing their lost position as the moral arbiters of American society. Churches attempted to promote the idea that Christianity was part of the common law. Churches sought to gain special exemptions and sought to veto objectionable legislation.

On the other hand, many religious movements withdrew from contact with society to set up separatist colonies, either because they were convinced their purity was at stake or because they espoused beliefs unpopular in the larger society. The Shakers practiced absolute celibacy and subordination to the teachings of Mother Ann Lee. The Millerites literally believed they would be taken up out of the world by the Second Coming of Jesus Christ in 1843. The Mormons organized their own colony at Nauvoo, Illinois, then withdrew still further to the West because of persecution for their practice of polygamy.

> **The shrewdest observer of American culture, though—the Frenchman Alexis de Tocqueville—saw the excesses of reform as part of the overall health of American democracy.**

Secular reform movements called for a rethinking of American participation in the world of market capitalism, education, diet, and women's rights. Many secular reform movements were attempts to reorganize society. Economic protest took the form of the creation of working-men's parties. Education reform was championed by Horace Mann. Dietary reform was promoted by Sylvester Graham and W. K. Kellogg. Temperance was promoted by a full spectrum of organizations and leaders.

Other reform movements, however, copied religious come-outers by attempting to create secular philosophical reform colonies. Brook Farm was a Transcendentalist experiment in communal living. The Northampton Association tried to organize an industrial, noncapitalist economic cooperative. Oberlin, Ohio, was organized as both a colony and a college, with the college based on a philosophy of self-sufficient manual labor.

The obsession with reform movements drew severe criticism from Americans and foreign observers, who equated the reform frenzy with the influence of democracy. American critics feared that the reformers were making democracy ridiculous. Orestes Brownson thought that reform enthusiasm was the logical fruit of Protestant individualism. Nathaniel Hawthorne believed that most reform movements were based on a flawed overestimate of human nature.

Foreign critics retailed stories of American reform movements that seemed to underscore all the frailties of democracy. George Featherstonhaugh, Frederika Bremer, and Michel Chevalier ridiculed American excesses. However, the shrewdest foreign observer, Alexis de Tocqueville, saw the excesses of reform as part of the overall health of American democracy. ■

Suggested Reading

Brooke, *The Refiner's Fire*.

Howe, *Making the American Self*.

Smith, *Revivalism and Social Reform*.

Questions to Consider

1. In what ways did the come-outer reform movements resemble earlier religious movements?

2. What in the nature of American government made the resort to private voluntary agencies necessary?

Southern Society and the Defense of Slavery
Lecture 33

"Emancipation," wrote Ralph Waldo Emerson, "is an American idea." If it was, though, it was an idea that had to live locked in a grotesque embrace with the pervasive reality of slavery, which was legal, prominent, and flourishing in American life.

Slavery was considered a contradiction of the spirit of liberty. To hold some people in bondage while theorizing about liberty seemed ridiculous. Numerous states and some prominent individuals began emancipation movements. Most of these emancipations were not immediate. Most emancipation programs favored colonization to Liberia or elsewhere. Many of them were made possible by competition from immigrant labor.

Slavery became an offense to religious conviction. It was opposed by increasing numbers of New England Calvinists, beginning with Samuel Hopkins. It was denounced by marginal religious groups, beginning with the Quakers.

In the South, where slavery was the most heavily concentrated, many southerners were inclined to agree with the criticism. Slavery was ceasing to be profitable. The principal cash crops for which slavery was vital began to decline. British interference with the Atlantic slave trade diminished the prospect of sustaining slave imports.

Southerners allowed the federal Constitution to begin whittling away at slavery. The slave trade was to be abolished in 1808. All mention of slavery was avoided. Southern representation in Congress could be based on counting only two-fifths of the slave population, rather than all of it. The Northwest Territory was organized without slavery.

Southern opposition to slavery began to weaken by the 1830s. Slavery in the South returned to profitability. Southerners turned to a new staple crop, cotton—the "white gold" of the Industrial Revolution. Cotton became the principal export commodity of the United States. The invention of the cotton gin by Eli Whitney made the aggressive use of slave labor economically dominant.

The possibility of slave revolts made southerners fearful of ending slavery. There were early revolt plots in Charleston and Richmond, as well as slave-ship uprisings, such as that of the Amistad in 1839. The most successful revolt was the most unplanned, that of Nat Turner in southside Virginia in 1831. Turner raised the specter of mass racial murder and convinced hesitant whites that slavery was the only means of protecting themselves from the bloody consequences of emancipation.

> Even religious denominations—like Baptists, Methodists, and Presbyterians—were split by southerners who could not rest with anything less than complete and total approval of the slave system.

Southerners created a proslavery ideology to suit their economic needs and racial fears. One part of this ideology was based on racial difference theory. European Romanticism glorified racial and national identities of blood (Gobineau, H. S. Chamberlain). Hierarchies of races were created that subordinated Africans. The characteristics of Africans were supposed to make them fit only for enslavement (Josiah Nott). It was never explained how this made blacks equally capable of revolt.

Another part of the proslavery ideology was based on paternalism. Some sections of the South liked to defend slavery as a household institution. Paternalism, however, was usually contradicted in practice.

Others defended slavery on simple economic grounds. It was in the interest and power of southerners to exploit others, and those others might as well be of another race (James Henry Hammond). They argued that Southern slavery was actually more socially responsible than the wage-slavery of northern factory workers (George Fitzhugh).

Nevertheless, many southern slaveholders were plagued with doubt about slavery. They feared the resentment of nonslaveholding whites and tried to deal with that by promoting white-man's democracy. They were conscious of the exploitation they were guilty of, and religious conviction doomed them to constant self-torment. They feared that slavery was dying out in the upper South and would cost the slave South the loyalty of its most settled regions.

Southerners were outraged when, after 1831, a northern abolition movement appeared. Unlike earlier antislavery movements, the new abolitionism was immediatist. William Lloyd Garrison demanded an immediate end to slavery and popularized his views in The Liberator. The new abolitionism was also opposed to colonization.

Abolitionism displayed many of the internal problems of other reform movements. Garrison favored withdrawal from the political process and criticized religious influences. He split the American Anti-Slavery Society over women's issues. Evangelical abolitionists resented Garrison's criticism of religion. They attracted more hatred than recruits from other northerners. Many of the abolitionists were themselves racists who were more concerned about the ill effects of slavery on whites than on blacks.

Nevertheless, southerners feared the abolitionists and tried to suppress them. They purged abolitionist literature from the federal mail. They organized elaborate systems of supervision and repression. They split several religious denominations. They installed a "gag rule" on abolitionist petitions in Congress.

Was the defense of slavery irrational? Not on the basis of economic profitability. Not on the basis of the reproduction of the slave population. Not on the basis of slavery's capacity for expansion. Not on the basis of slavery's adaptability from agricultural to industrial labor. Not on the basis of the resources available to the South and West in the form of land that could easily be seized from weaker nations and converted to slave agriculture. ■

Suggested Reading

Genovese, *Roll, Jordan, Roll.*

Mayer, *All on Fire.*

Oakes, *The Ruling Race.*

Questions to Consider

1. Was slavery an outmoded throwback to feudalism or a modern aspect of market economies?

2. Was Garrison's absolutism helpful or harmful in the crusade against slavery?

Whose Manifest Destiny?
Lecture 34

One other aspect of that potent optimism that helped to fuel the era of reform in American life in the 19th century was the belief Americans had that the westward sway of empire would carry republicanism, civilization, and Christianity into the uninhabited western regions of the United States.

Ever since the 18th century, Americans believed that the westward sway of empire would carry republicanism and Christianity into the uninhabited western regions of the United States. These regions, however, were "uninhabited" only in the sense that they contained few English-speaking white people. French-speaking and Spanish-speaking settlements covered the Mississippi valley, and until 1821, Spain still ruled an empire that covered the modern Southwest.

The woodland Indian tribes had to be legally dispossessed. Several of these tribes possessed cultural organization rivaling and sometimes mimicking that of American whites. Dispossession triggered armed conflict in the case of the Black Hawk War in Illinois. Dispossession triggered civil litigation and forced transfer in the case of the Cherokees and other tribes. "Indian removal" caused the loss of thousands of Indian lives. Once dispossession had removed the woodland tribes, Americans encountered a new cultural phenomenon in the form of the nomadic Plains Indians.

Certain regions, especially the lower Mississippi valley and the prairies of the Northwest Territory, turned out to contain some of the finest agricultural land in the world. The agricultural possibilities of both Mississippi and Illinois astounded foreign observers. Title to these lands was easy, dependable, and cheap to obtain. Although technically supervised by Congress, occupation of these lands often proceeded by simple squatting and preemption.

American expansion and settlement into the trans-Mississippi proceeded far faster than anyone, including Thomas Jefferson, had predicted. The structure of territorial government allowed settlements to organize themselves politically at a very fast rate. By 1818–1819, Illinois, Indiana, Alabama, and Mississippi passed through the territorial phase and were admitted as states.

The relentless expansion of American settlement generated two major conflicts that overshadowed all the others. Missouri was the first territory carved out of the Louisiana Purchase to apply for admission to the Union as a state, in 1819. As part of the Louisiana Purchase and not the Northwest Territory, Missouri had been settled by slaveholders. The territorial legislature asked for admission as a slave state. This generated protests from northern members of Congress, who saw the recognition of slavery in the Purchase as a symbolic attempt by slaveholders to identify slavery with expansion. A year of angry debate ensued to be resolved only by Henry Clay's proposal of the Missouri Compromise (1820), which drew a line through the Purchase, dividing the portions that could be admitted as slave states and the portions that could be admitted as free states.

American expansion across the West created friction with Great Britain over what the actual boundaries with Canada in the West were to be.

Slavery also became an issue in another incident of expansion in Texas. Texas was the most northeastern province of the Spanish viceroyalty of Mexico. When Mexicans overthrew Spanish rule in 1821 and proclaimed a republic, Texas passed under Mexican control. Texas remained sparsely settled.

When a revolution brought a military dictator, Antonio de Santa Anna, to power in Mexico, Santa Anna proposed to develop Texas by inviting American settlers on generous terms, provided they embraced Roman Catholicism and renounced slavery. Americans, under the impresario Stephen Austin, took up Santa Anna's offer but refused to subscribe to its conditions. As the number of American settlers increased, Santa Anna attempted to cut off immigration and disarm the Texans. The Texans revolted in 1835 and defeated Santa Anna. Congress balked at annexing another slave state, and for 11 years, Texas remained an independent republic.

Western expansion fed the notion that the United States had a manifest (that is, "plainly obvious") destiny to rule the North American continent. Western expansion began to acquire the status of romantic legend. This legend was fed by American artists depicting the Plains Indians as noble savages and the mystique of the mountain men. The legend was also fed by tales of missionary martyrs. It was given literary status by the histories of Francis Parkman.

Expansionism began to have real political consequences. It created friction with Great Britain over boundaries with Canada. It encouraged filibustering. It destroyed Henry Clay's last chance for election to the presidency in 1844, and it paved the way for the election of an outright expansionist and protégé of Andrew Jackson, James Knox Polk. ■

Suggested Reading

Benson, *The Concept of Jacksonian Democracy*.

Lord, *A Time to Stand*.

Schoelwer, *Alamo Images: Changing Perceptions of a Texas Experience*.

Questions to Consider

1. Why should Americans have regarded expansion to the Pacific coast as a "manifest destiny"?

2. What role did Romantic visions of the West play in promoting western expansion?

The Mexican War
Lecture 35

> "Personally, I could have no objection to the annexation of Texas, but I certainly would be unwilling to see the existing Union dissolved or seriously jeopardized for the sake of acquiring Texas."—Henry Clay

Clay's statement immediately horrified northern Whigs, who saw the annexation of Texas as nothing more than a stalking horse for Democratic expansion for southern agricultural interests and, of course, southern slave interests.

James Knox Polk's election was the signal for confrontation for the sake of expansion. The Polk administration made demands on the British government. Polk demanded recognition of the 54°40′ line as the northern border of the Oregon Territory. Eventually, this demand was settled by negotiation. Many critics of Polk believed that he backed down because expansion to the north would not have created new opportunities for slavery.

After Polk's election, the disheartened resistance to the annexation of Texas withered. Texas was annexed in 1845 as a state by a simple resolution of Congress. The Mexican government refused to recognize the annexation and refused to recognize the Rio Grande River as a legitimate boundary.

Polk invited a clash with Mexico as a means of seizing still more territory. Polk shared a general contempt for Mexico. The instability of the Mexican government and the bloody example of the Alamo during the Texan War of Independence appalled and embarrassed the American confidence in republicanism. White Americans stigmatized Mexicans on racial grounds, despite the fact that Mexican culture was as thoroughly Europeanized as their own.

In January 1846, Polk ordered American troops to occupy and patrol the Rio Grande River region. Troops under Zachary Taylor were ambushed by Mexican cavalry on April 23, 1846. Polk asked Congress for a declaration of war on May 11, 1846.

The first phase of the Mexican War began with an invasion of northern Mexico under Zachary Taylor and the conquest of New Mexico and California. Although outnumbered, American troops won repeated victories along the Rio Grande and in the Mexican province of Nuevo León. Taylor won two small-scale victories above the Rio Grande at Palo Alto and Resaca de la Palma in May 1846, then crossed the Rio Grande and occupied Monterey in September. Taylor won a major victory over Santa Anna at Buena Vista on February 22–23, 1847.

Stephen W. Kearney's "Army of the West" crossed the New Mexico desert. Kearney occupied New Mexico, capturing Santa Fe. Kearney then conquered California, aided by ships of the U.S. Navy and a domestic uprising of American immigrants who briefly organized themselves as the "Bear Flag Republic."

The second phase of the Mexican War began with an ambitious invasion of Mexico from the Gulf of Mexico under Winfield Scott. Scott's expedition was one of the most ambitious and well-coordinated military operations

The bloody example of the Alamo shocked and appalled Americans.

carried out since the Napoleonic Wars. Scott landed and seized Vera Cruz in March 1847. He then marched inland and won victories over Santa Anna at Cerro Gordo, Contreras, Churubusco, Molino del Rey, and Chapultepec Castle and occupied Mexico City.

With the fall of Mexico City, the war was effectively over. The war involved only 115,000 American soldiers, with only 1,721 battle deaths. However, the army was plagued by desertion, disease, and conflict between soldiers and officers of the regular army and state volunteers. The war provided a practical training ground for many officers who would later rise to command in the Civil War.

The war was officially concluded with the Treaty of Guadelupe-Hidalgo in February of 1848. Mexico was forced to submit to American demands for territory and reparations. Mexico ceded two-fifths of its territory, including California and New Mexico, and recognized the Rio Grande as the boundary of Texas. Mexico agreed to pay $15 million to settle all Mexican claims and debts to the United States. The treaty was followed in 1853 by an additional purchase of land along the Gila River (known as the Gadsden Purchase).

> **The war ended officially with the Treaty of Guadelupe-Hidalgo in February of 1848, a treaty whose terms sowed seeds of bitterness that still taint Mexican/American relations.**

The acquisition of this territory aroused rejoicing and criticism. Gold was discovered at Sutter's Mill in California in 1848, setting off the world's greatest gold rush, just in time for the benefits to flow entirely to the United States. Opposition to expansion and fear that the Mexican Cession would be used to open up room for the expansion of slavery provoked opposition from figures as varied as Henry David Thoreau and Abraham Lincoln. ■

Suggested Reading

Eisenhower, *So Far from God*.

Holt, *Rise and Fall of the American Whig Party*.

Questions to Consider

1. Was the Mexican War a justifiable response to aggression?

2. How did the performance of the American army in the Mexican War contrast with its performance in the War of 1812?

The Great Compromise
Lecture 36

> The great Louisiana Purchase of 1803 had bought for the United States title to half of the American West, and since most of that purchase looked like it was going to fall into the hands of free state settlers ... southerners were happy to get the compromise they did get in the Missouri Compromise of 1820.

Even before the Mexican War was over, controversy stirred in Congress over whether slavery should be admitted to any territory acquired from Mexico as a result of the war. Four alternatives emerged between 1846 and 1850 for dealing with the future of the Mexican Cession. David Wilmot proposed a rider to an appropriations bill, known as the Wilmot Proviso, which banned slavery completely from the Mexican Cession.

President Polk proposed to extend the division line of the Missouri Compromise through the Cession, which would have thrown almost all of it open to slavery. John Calhoun demanded that the Cession be recognized as "common property" among all U.S. citizens to enable slaveowners to take slaves with them anywhere into the Cession. Lewis Cass outlined a plan, known as popular sovereignty, which allowed settlers in the Cession to make their own decisions for or against slavery as they organized the Cession into territories and states.

Disagreements between northern and southern Democrats over these alternatives split the Democratic Party, which nominated Lewis Cass for president. The split allowed the Whigs to nominate Zachary Taylor for president in 1848. Taylor was a southern slaveholder but had no known stand on the Cession question. Once elected, Taylor had his own plan for the Cession, which involved admitting California and New Mexico as free states. Southerners were so angered by Taylor's proposal that a convention was called to discuss withdrawing from the Union.

The situation was rescued by the elderly Henry Clay, who stepped forward to produce one more Union-saving compromise. In January 1850, Clay laid eight resolutions before Congress. Clay proposed admitting California as a free state. New Mexico and Utah would be allowed to organize themselves according to popular sovereignty. A new Fugitive Slave Law would be adopted, and Congress would be barred from interfering with the interstate slave trade.

Clay made the tactical error of insisting that all the resolutions be voted on together as an omnibus bill. Partisans of slavery opposed it because it seemed to give everything away. Critics of slavery disliked the possibility that popular sovereignty might open New Mexico and Utah to slavery. In an effort to save Clay's compromise and the Union, Daniel Webster took the floor of the Senate to endorse the compromise, earning himself the denunciations of New England antislavery advocates. President Taylor, who saw Clay as a rival for leadership of the Whigs, gave no aid to Clay's compromise. The compromise was defeated in the Senate in July 1850.

The compromise was revived, however, by Illinois Senator Stephen A. Douglas. Douglas was born in Vermont but emigrated to Illinois. He was short, stout, and energetic, with a powerful and persuasive speaking manner. He rose quickly from the Illinois state legislature to the judiciary, then to the Senate, becoming one of the up-and-coming personalities of the Democratic Party.

Douglas was aided by the deaths of Calhoun and President Taylor in 1850. Taylor was succeeded by Vice President Millard Fillmore, who backed the compromise. When Clay withdrew from the Senate, Douglas assumed management of the compromise. Douglas reorganized the compromise into a more palatable format. He broke the eight resolutions into five separate bills and built separate coalitions around each bill. Fillmore rallied Whigs to support the reshaped compromise in Congress. By mid-September, Douglas had managed each of the bills through Congress, and the compromise was a fact.

The passage of the Compromise of 1850 was a great achievement of practical politics, but what did the compromise actually accomplish? It staved off civil war for another decade. The movement for southern secession quietly receded for the time being. Southerners interested in expanding the domain of slavery increasingly turned to the idea of annexing Cuba.

It allowed the immediate admission of California as a free state. As a result of the gold rush, California's population soared. Statehood allowed the federal government to stabilize law and order in California.

By endorsing popular sovereignty, the compromise asserted the right of Congress to legislate for the territories on the slavery issue. One of Calhoun's contentions was that because the territories were common property, Congress had no authority to legislate against the ownership of the property of some citizens. On the other hand, the great weakness of popular sovereignty was its assumption that settlers in the territories would be willing to arrive at peaceful conclusions to the slavery question.

The Compromise of 1850 allowed the old Missouri Compromise to stand as law in the old Louisiana Purchase territories, but it established the new principle of popular sovereignty as the rule for organizing the Mexican Cession.

The compromise also created a new fugitive slave law to succeed the original Fugitive Slave Law of 1793. Originally, this was the most unnoticed part of the compromise. However, it was a time bomb waiting to explode, because its terms threatened to make every northerner complicit in slave pursuit and rendition.

The compromise made Douglas a nationally famous figure. Douglas was reelected to the Senate in 1852. He now began to be spoken of as a possible presidential candidate. ■

Suggested Reading

Bartlett, *Daniel Webster*.

Hamilton, *Prologue to Conflict*.

Lence, *Union and Liberty: The Political Philosophy of John C. Calhoun*, "Speech on the Admission of California."

Questions to Consider

1. Why was the popular sovereignty solution so popular?

2. What enabled Douglas to succeed with the Compromise where Clay had failed?

Maps (Lectures 1–36)

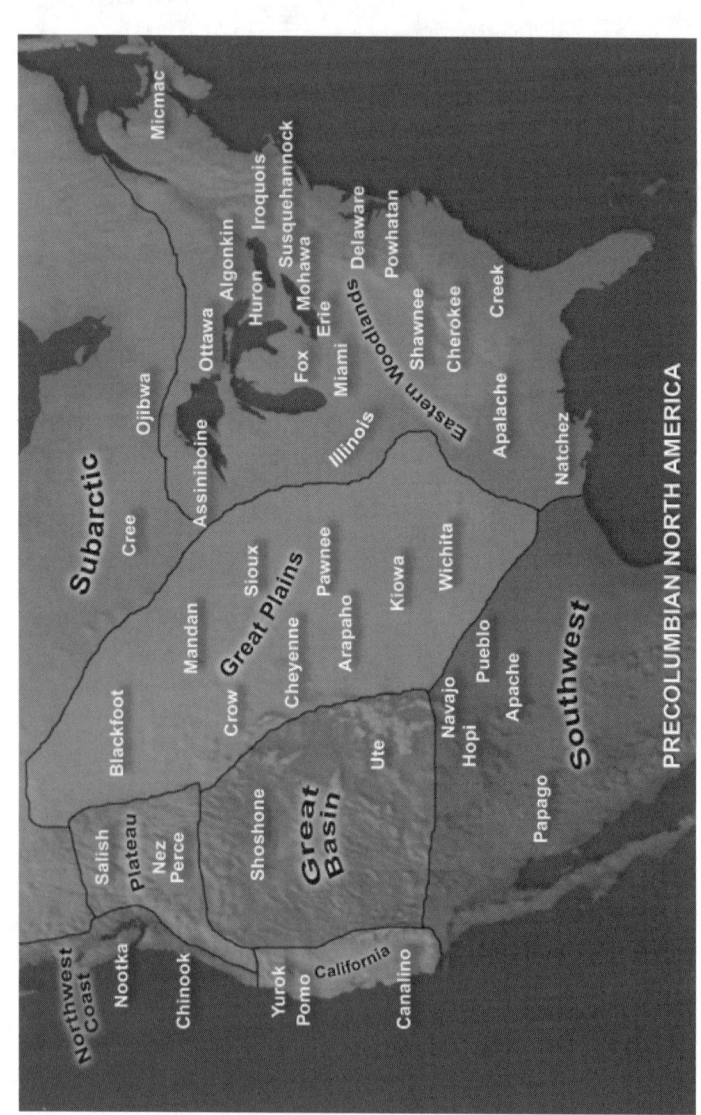

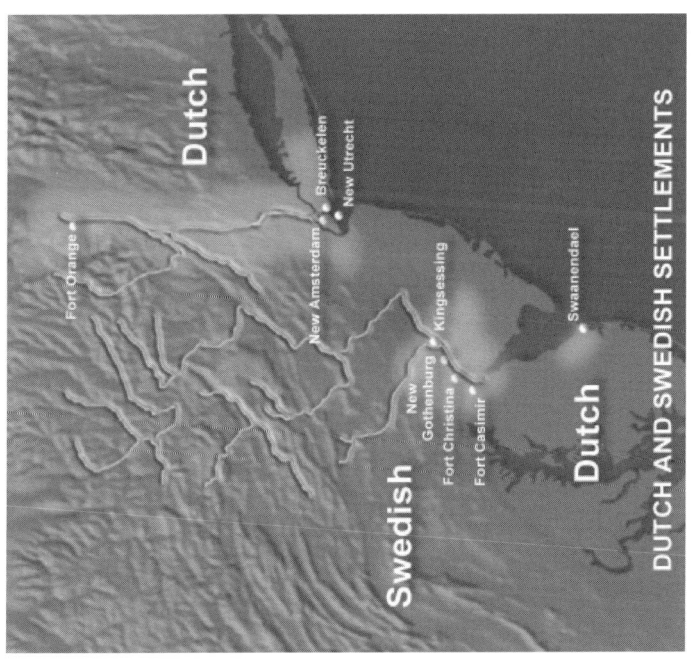

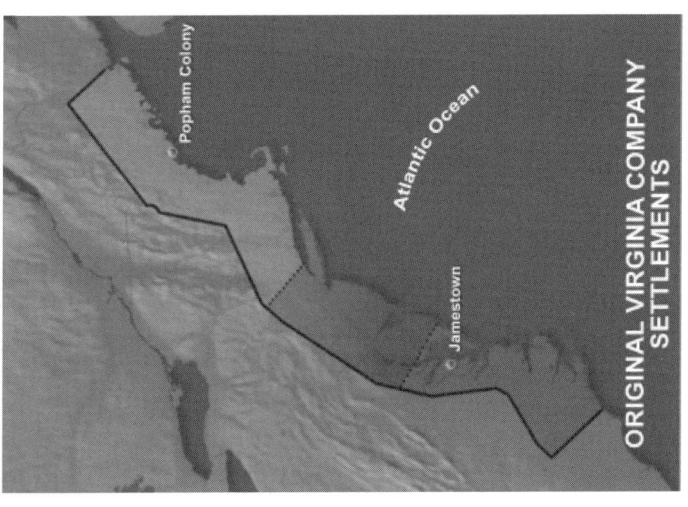

Maps (Lectures 1–36)

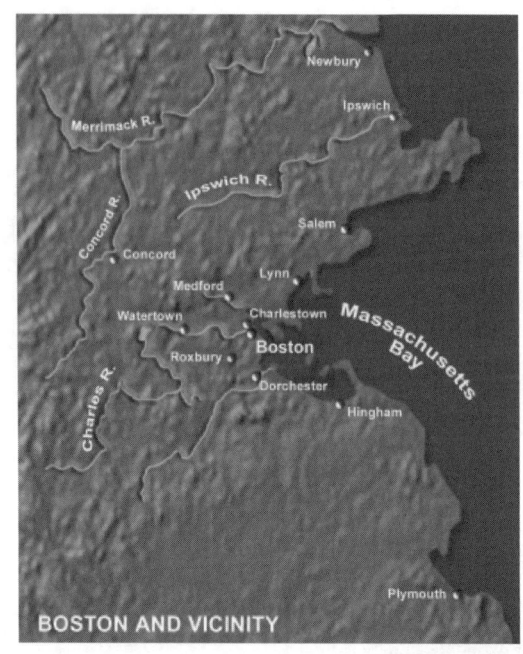

BOSTON AND VICINITY

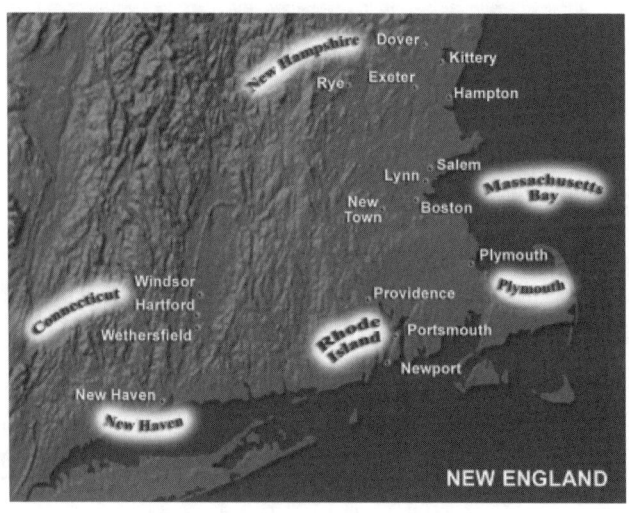

NEW ENGLAND

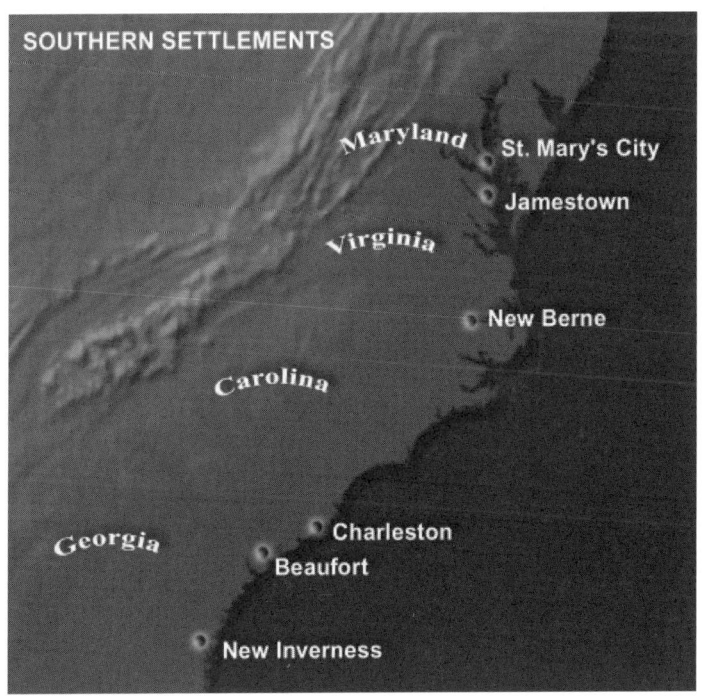

Maps (Lectures 1–36)

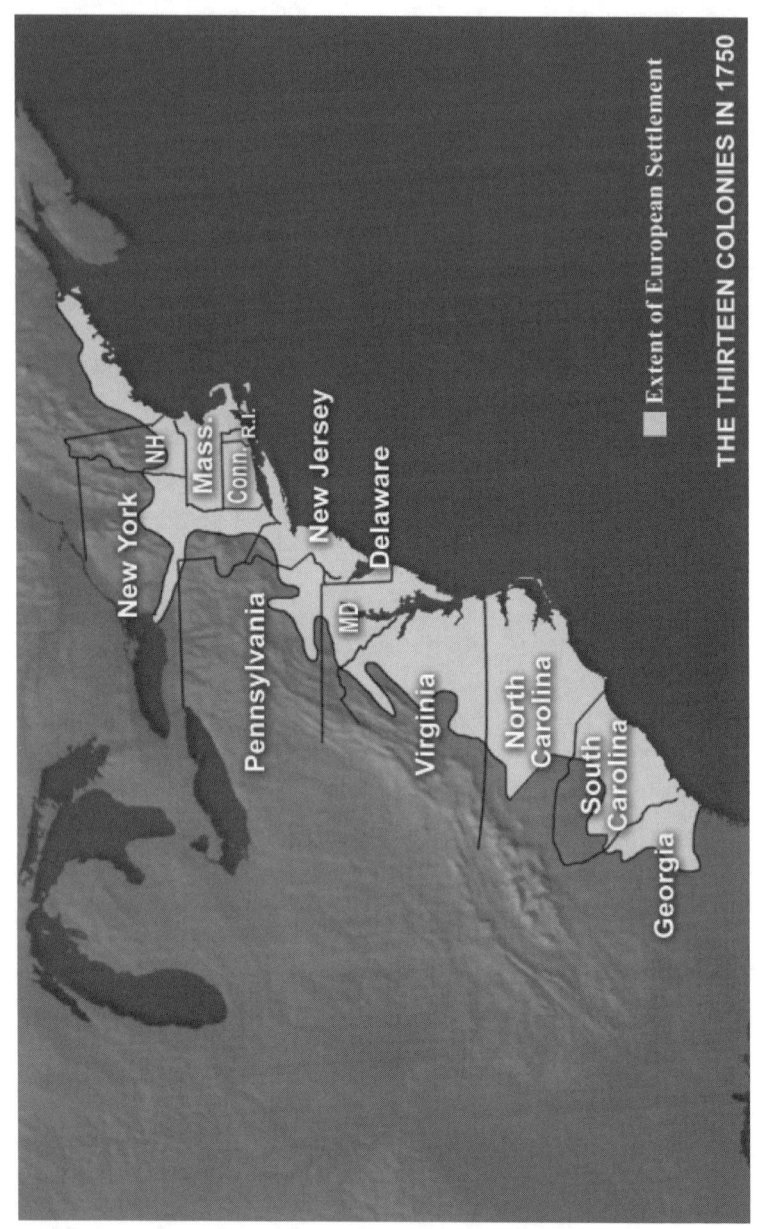

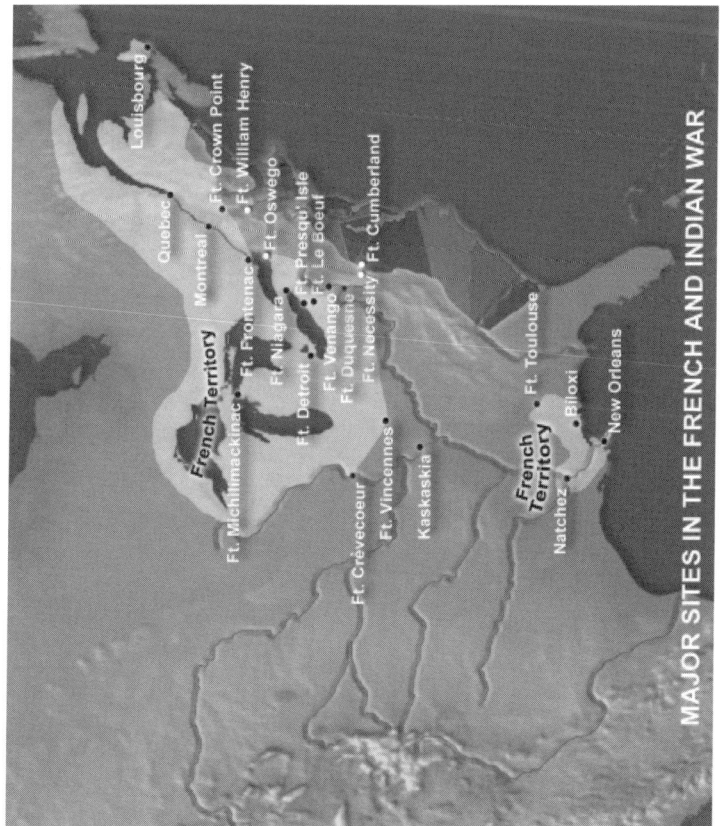

Maps (Lectures 1–36)

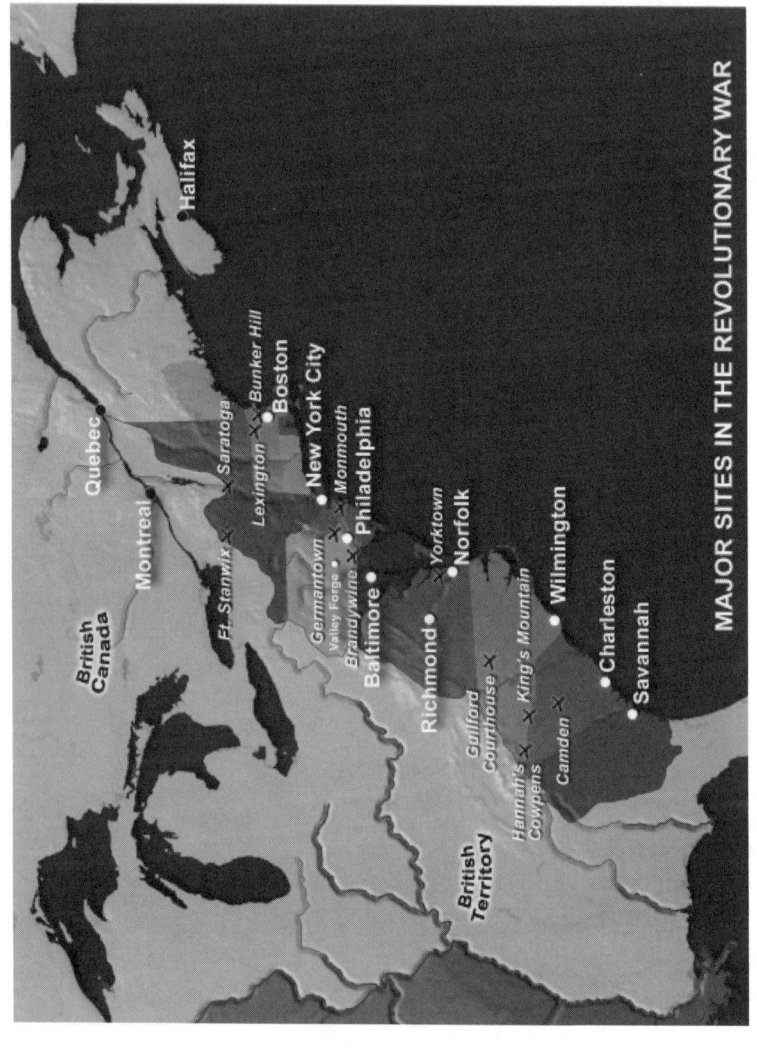

MAJOR SITES IN THE REVOLUTIONARY WAR

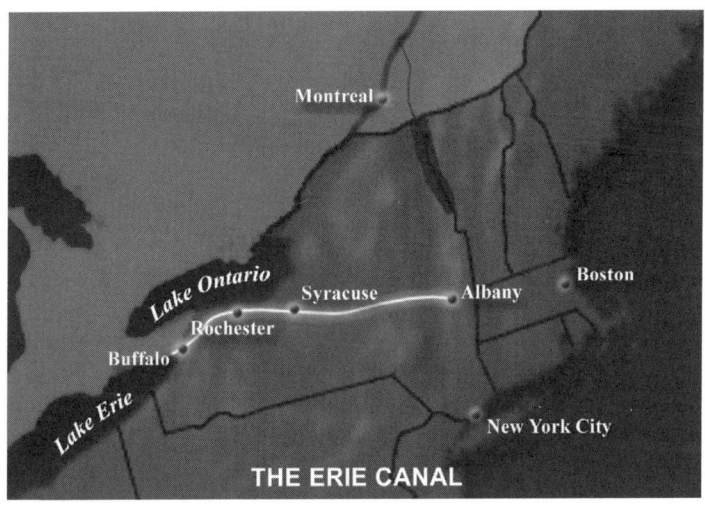

Maps (Lectures 1-36)

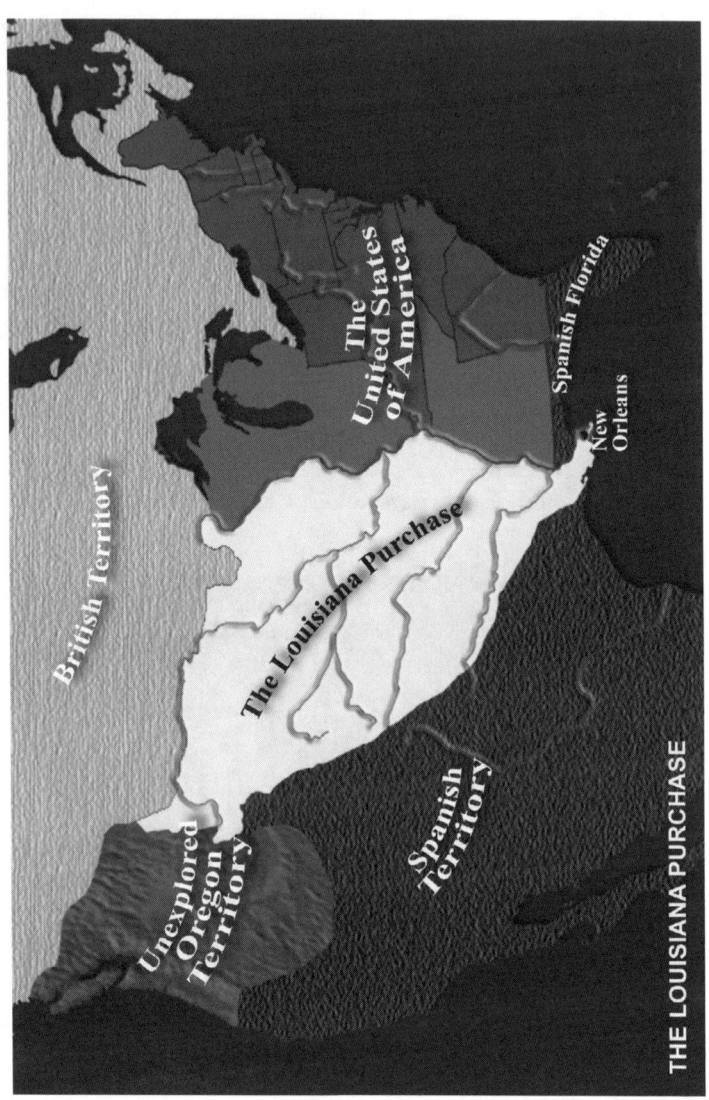

THE LOUISIANA PURCHASE

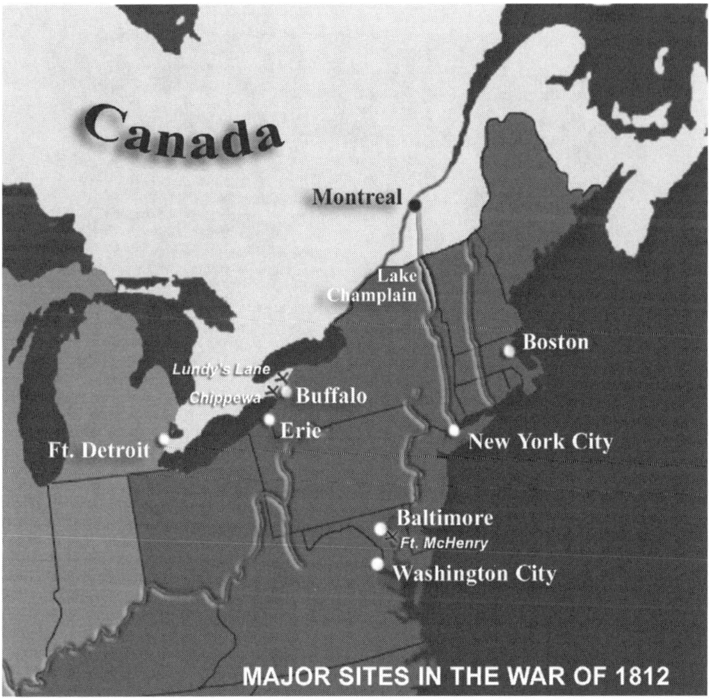

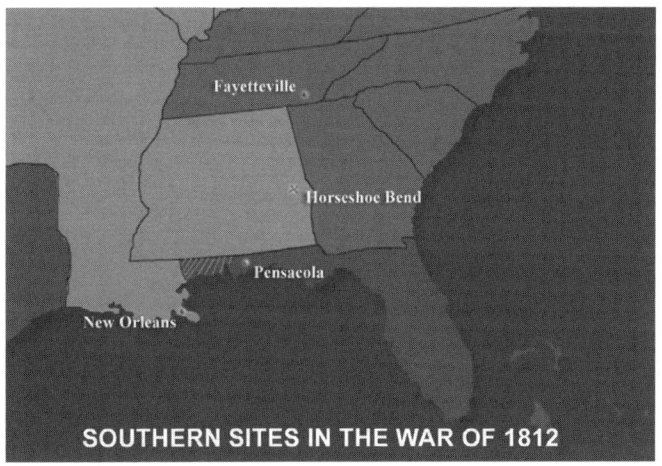

THE REPUBLIC OF TEXAS

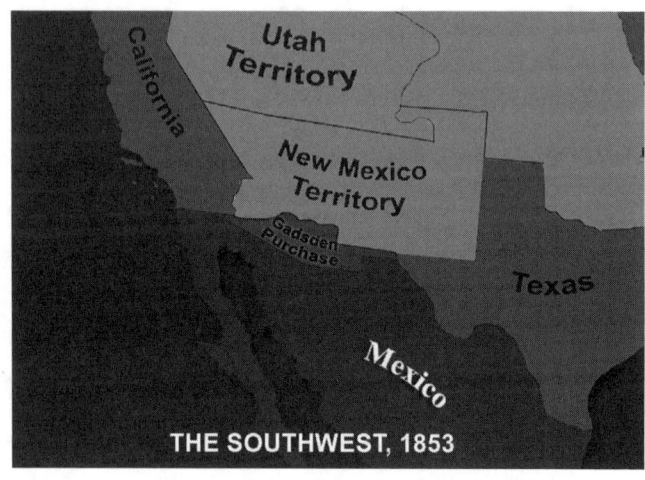

THE SOUTHWEST, 1853

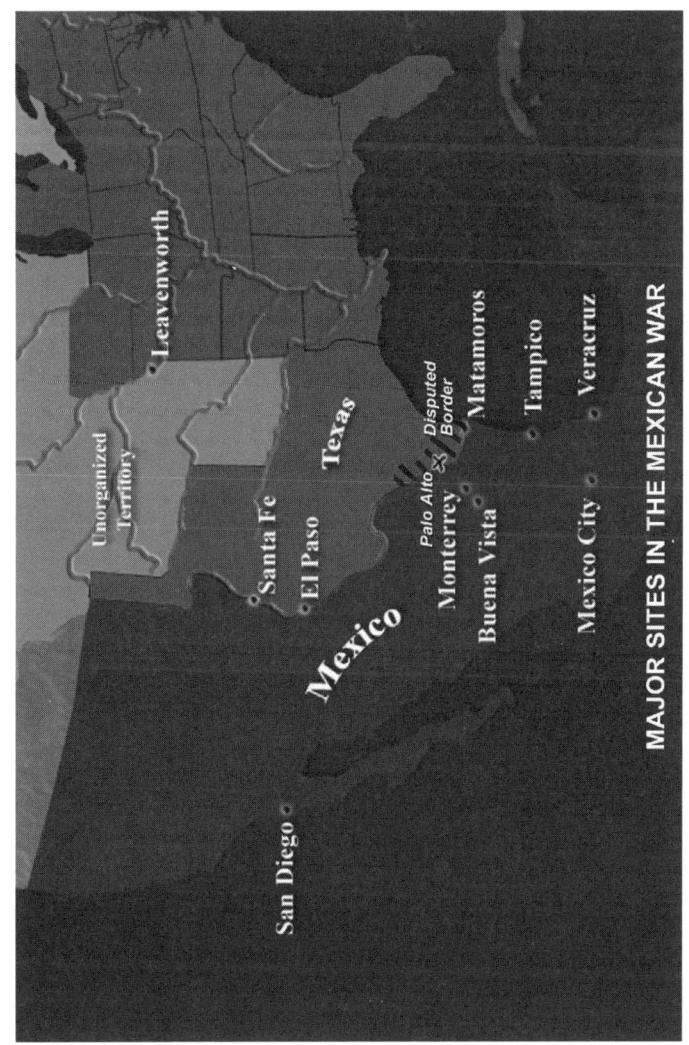

Timeline (Lectures 1–36)

Oct. 12, 1492	Christopher Columbus makes the first modern transatlantic crossing from Europe.
Feb. 19, 1519	Hernando Cortez sets sail from Cuba to begin the conquest of Mexico.
1585–1587	Sir Walter Raleigh twice is unsuccessful in planting English colonies on the Outer Banks.
May 24, 1607	The Virginia Company establishes an English colony on the James River at Jamestown.
Summer 1608	Quebec established by Samuel de Champlain.
Sept. 12, 1609	Henry Hudson begins exploration of the Hudson River for the Dutch West Indies Company.
May–June 1626	Dutch purchase ground to establish a colony, New Amsterdam, on Manhattan Island.
June 17, 1630	Massachusetts Bay Company arrives to begin settlement at Boston.
Oct. 28, 1636	Harvard College founded in Cambridge, Massachusetts.

Aug. 27, 1664 .... Peter Stuyvesant surrenders New Amsterdam to the British, who rename it New York.

1675–1676 .... King Philip's War ravages New England.

1679–1682 .... La Salle explores the Mississippi River and claims Louisiana for France.

Aug. 10, 1680 .... Pueblo Revolt begins, destroying Spanish churches and settlements in New Mexico.

Oct. 27, 1682 .... William Penn takes possession of Pennsylvania at New Castle.

Dec. 11, 1688 .... Glorious Revolution topples King James II and replaces him with William and Mary as monarchs.

Feb. 8, 1693 .... Charter granted to found the College of William and Mary.

Nov. 8, 1739 .... George Whitefield arrives in Philadelphia as part of his first evangelical preaching tour.

July 2, 1741 .... Jonathan Edwards delivers his sermon "Sinners in the Hands of an Angry God" at Enfield, Massachusetts (now Connecticut).

May 28, 1754 .... George Washington surrenders Virginia militia at Fort Necessity, beginning the French and Indian War.

July 9, 1755	British troops under General Edward Braddock defeated by French and Indians near Fort Duquesne.
Sept. 18, 1759	British capture Quebec, and effective military resistance by the French in Canada ends.
Oct. 25, 1760	George III becomes king of England.
1761–1766	Controversy in the colonies over writs of assistance.
Feb. 10, 1763	Treaty of Paris signed, making Great Britain dominant in North America.
May 7–Nov. 28, 1763	Pontiac lays siege to Fort Detroit as part of Pontiac's Rebellion.
March 22, 1765	Parliament imposes the Stamp Act, then rescinds it after violent colonial protests.
July 2, 1767	Townsend Duties enacted.
March 5, 1770	The Boston Massacre leaves five dead in front of the Boston Customs House.
May 10, 1773	Tea Act becomes law.
Dec. 16, 1773	Boston Tea Party.
Sept. 5–Oct. 26, 1774	Meeting of the First Continental Congress in Philadelphia.
April 18–19, 1775	Battles of Lexington and Concord.

May 10, 1775	Second Continental Congress meets.
June 17, 1775	Battle of Bunker Hill.
Jan. 10, 1776	Thomas Paine publishes Common Sense.
July 4, 1776	Declaration of American Independence.
Dec. 18–June 9, 1777–1778	Continental Army's winter encampment at Valley Forge, Pennsylvania.
March 1, 1780	Pennsylvania Act for Emancipation, first provision for gradual abolition of slavery in America.
March 1, 1781	Articles of Confederation ratified.
Oct. 19, 1781	Lord Cornwallis surrenders British forces at Yorktown.
1782	Hector St. John Crèvecoeur publishes Letters from an American Farmer.
Sept. 3, 1783	Treaty of Paris confirms independence of the United States from Great Britain.
May 20, 1785	Confederation Congress passes Land Ordinance on the organization of the western lands.
Jan. 25, 1787	Shay's Rebellion climaxes in an assault on the federal arsenal at Springfield, Massachusetts.

May 25–Sept. 17, 1787	Constitutional Convention meets in Philadelphia and draws up a new federal Constitution.
July 13, 1787	Confederation Congress adopts the Northwest Ordinance.
Oct.–Aug. 1787–88	James Madison, Alexander Hamilton, and John Jay publish The Federalist.
April 30, 1789	George Washington sworn in as the first president of the United States.
Jan. 14, 1790	The first of Hamilton's three "reports"—the Report on the Public Credit—is read to Congress.
Aug. 7–Nov. 19, 1791	Whiskey Rebellion in western Pennsylvania.
Dec. 15, 1791	Bill of Rights ratified.
March 14, 1794	Eli Whitney files a patent on the cotton gin, which he had designed and built the previous year while working as a family tutor on a Georgia plantation.
Oct. 8–Nov. 8, 1797–98	XYZ Affair outlined in dispatches from John Marshall, Timothy Pickering, and Elbridge Gerry.
Summer 1798	June 18, 25/July 6, 14: Alien and Sedition Acts passed by Congress.

Fall/winter 1798	Nov. 13, Dec. 24: The legislatures of Kentucky and Virginia adopt the Virginia and Kentucky Resolutions as drafted by Madison and Jefferson.
Feb. 17, 1801	Thomas Jefferson elected in the House of Representatives as third U.S. president.
March 5, 1801	John Marshall becomes chief justice of the U.S. Supreme Court.
Feb. 24, 1803	Chief Justice Marshall writes opinion for unanimous Supreme Court in *Marbury v. Madison*.
April 30, 1803	U.S. negotiators approve Louisiana Purchase; *Marbury v. Madison* establishes principle of judicial review.
May 14, 1804	Meriwether Lewis and William Clark lead "Corps of Discovery" up the Missouri River in exploration of the purchase.
July 11, 1804	Alexander Hamilton is shot by Aaron Burr in a duel.
Feb. 19, 1807	Aaron Burr arrested for his part in a conspiracy in the Southwest Territory.
Dec. 22, 1807	Congress passes the Embargo Act, cutting off American commerce with France and Great Britain.

Oct. 11, 1811	The New Orleans, the first steamboat on the western rivers, leaves Pittsburgh on a voyage down the Ohio and Mississippi to New Orleans.
Nov. 7, 1811	Battle of Tippecanoe.
June 1, 1812	President Madison asks for declaration of war against Great Britain, beginning the War of 1812.
Oct. 5, 1813	William Henry Harrison wins a victory for the United States at the Battle of the Thames.
Dec. 24, 1814	Treaty of Ghent ends the War of 1812.
Jan. 9, 1815	Andrew Jackson victorious at the battle of New Orleans.
March 14, 1816	Second Bank of the United States chartered by Congress.
March 20, 1816	Justice Joseph Story hands down Supreme Court decision in *Martin v. Hunter's Lessee*.
July 4, 1817	Work begins on the Erie Canal.
Feb. 2, 1819	*Dartmouth College v. Woodward* upholds the sanctity of contract.
Feb. 17, 1819	Chief Justice Marshall writes opinion for unanimous Supreme Court in *Sturgis v. Crowninshield*.

March 6, 1819	*McCulloch v. Maryland* establishes supremacy of federal jurisdiction over state.
Spring 1819	Panic of 1819 begins with fall in British commodity prices.
Feb. 16, 1820	Missouri Compromise adopted.
July 1822	Slave conspiracy under Denmark Vesey prompts panic and retribution in Charleston.
Dec. 2, 1823	President James Monroe's annual message to Congress articulates the Monroe Doctrine; James Fenimore Cooper begins his "Leatherstocking Tales" with the publication of The Pioneers.
Jan. 14, 1824	Henry Clay begins exposition of the "American System" before Congress.
March 2, 1824	Chief Justice Marshall hands down opinion for a unanimous Supreme Court in Gibbons v. Ogden.
Feb. 9, 1825	Election of John Quincy Adams as president in the House of Representatives, after the "corrupt bargain."
March 1, 1826	East Chelmsford, Massachusetts, incorporated as Lowell as it becomes the most important center of textile manufacturing in the United States.

July 18–25, 1827	New Lebanon Conference on revivalism.
July 4, 1828	Construction begins on Baltimore & Ohio Railroad.
Jan. 19–27, 1830	Webster-Hayne debates.
Jan. 1, 1831	William Lloyd Garrison begins publishing The Liberator.
Aug. 22, 1831	Nat Turner leads a bloody slave insurrection in southeastern Virginia.
July 10, 1832	President Jackson vetoes re-charter of the Second Bank of the United States.
Nov. 24, 1832	South Carolina state convention nullifies federal tariffs of 1828 and 1832.
Dec. 4, 1833	Founding of the American Anti-Slavery Society.
April 14, 1834	Henry Clay applies the term Whig to the anti-Jackson opposition.
March 6, 1836	Fall of the Alamo.
April 10, 1836	Charles Grandison Finney opens the Broadway Tabernacle in New York City.
Feb. 12, 1837	Chief Justice Roger Taney writes opinion for a narrow majority in Charles River Bridge v. Warren Bridge.

Aug. 31, 1837	Ralph Waldo Emerson delivers "The American Scholar" to the Harvard Phi Beta Kappa society.
Aug.–Dec. 1838	Forcible removal of 15,000 Cherokee Indians (the "Trail of Tears") begins.
Sept. 3, 1838	Frederick Douglass flees slavery to Philadelphia.
July 1840	Margaret Fuller begins publication of The Dial.
March 9, 1841	Justice Joseph Story, in *U.S. v. The Amistad*, frees slaves who rose in mutiny aboard slave ship Amistad in 1837.
April 4, 1841	President William Henry Harrison, the first Whig president, becomes the first president to die in office.
May 11–12, 1846	Congress approves President Polk's request for a declaration of war, beginning the Mexican War.
June 19, 1846	First game of baseball played on rules designed by Alexander Cartwright.
Feb. 22–23, 1847	Battle of Buena Vista.
Sept. 14, 1847	Winfield Scott captures Mexico City.
Feb. 2, 1848	Treaty of Guadalupe Hidalgo ends the Mexican War and provides for cession of 500,000 square miles to the United States.

July 19–20, 1848 .... Seneca Falls Convention on women's rights.

Jan. 19, 1850 .... Henry Clay introduces the bills that will make up the Compromise of 1850.

Glossary (Lectures 1–36)

abolitionism: A movement that gathered public visibility beginning in the 1830s; dedicated to the immediate and complete abolition of slavery in the United States.

agrarian: A term describing a cluster of ideas that located political economic virtue in agricultural employment, including independent land ownership and self-provision from the land, minimal land taxation, decentralized patterns of living, and patriarchy (in both gender and racial terms).

American System: Popularized by Henry Clay, this became the Whig economic platform and included federal government sponsorship for infrastructure ("internal improvements"), federal subsidies for manufacturing, and a fiscal system that helped fund entrepreneurship and contain the costs of risk.

Anglican: Term applied to describe the Church of England and its doctrines or to individual members of that Church; not actually used before the 19th century.

antislavery: The larger segment of opinion that opposed slavery, but not necessarily through immediate abolition.

assimilation: The process by which immigrants are brought into conformity with the dominant culture around them and in which they embrace the dominant values and reject those associated with their culture or country of origin.

business cycle: The pattern of alternating economic expansions and contractions that characterizes production and consumption in the various forms of unregulated market economies.

Calvinism: A system of religious doctrine developed by John Calvin that taught the unlimited sovereignty and power of God in ordering all human affairs and, thereby, undercut the demands for loyalty required by many governments and state-sponsored churches; its specific teachings are sometimes defined by the acronym TULIP (total depravity, unconditional election, limited atonement, irresistible grace, perseverance of the saints).

capitalism: An economic system in which (a) goods and services are sold at prices higher than their actual cost of production, with the difference between the two saved or reinvested in the production of still more goods and services; (b) resources for exchange and for initial investments in production are made available in the form of credit from financial institutions, such as banks; (c) minimal state regulation allows free movement of credit, resources, and commercial strategies; and (d) a spirit of entrepreneurship, rational abstraction, and disciplined work habits prevails.

class: A system of hierarchical social organization, based on acquired or inherited property holding and wealth and attaching various cultural attributes to each class.

colonization: In the 19th century, this term described a variety of plans proposed for repatriating freed slaves back to Africa rather than integrating them into civil and social life.

common sense philosophy: Term used to describe a system of presentational realism that asserted that the mind could directly know the objects of its ideas and, as such, could have direct and accurate intuitions of both objective reality and the moral content of objects and of internal mental processes, from which a rational and orderly system of understanding can be constructed on inductive (or Baconian) principles.

culture: The production and organization of symbols, attitudes, ideas, processes, and entertainment that express the common assumptions of a society or of groups in that society; can exist as folk, vernacular, or elite culture.

deism: General term describing a religion based on rational deduction from the evidences of nature of the existence and attributes of a supreme deity, rather than from an authoritative supernatural revelation.

democrat: Term for the political party begun as the Democratic-Republicans under Jefferson and Madison; sometimes shortened to "Republicans." In the 1820s, when a splinter group of National Republicans developed and split off to become the Whigs, the party became known simply as "Democrats" and became the vehicle for expressing the political attitudes and culture symbolized by Andrew Jackson.

electoral college: A provision in the Constitution designed to de-politicize the presidential election process by having electors in each state cast votes, based on the winner of the most votes in their states, for the president and vice president, with each state having as many votes as its combined number of senators and representatives in Congress.

Enlightenment: An intellectual movement born out of the scientific revolution of the 17th century that flourished on both sides of the Atlantic in the 18th century. The movement was characterized by confidence in reason as the means of solving practical, religious, and philosophical problems; an effort to approximate the order of nature; and a commitment to criticism as a means of discovery.

Evangelicalism: A form of Protestant Christian religious expression growing out of the Great Awakenings of the 18th century; marked by dramatic religious transformation, the location of religious authority in the Bible rather than in reason or in religious authorities, and a disposition to extend moral reform generally across society.

factory: A system in which workers trained in the production of a specific commodity or similar commodities labor for wages, produce individual parts of such commodities for assembly by other workers (rather than each worker producing the entire commodity), and use a common source of artificial power for the production process.

free labor: An economic system in which an individual, protected by natural and civil rights, is free to seek terms of employment, look for pay in the form of cash wages, and may accumulate sufficient capital through work and savings to acquire property and hire others.

frigate: A warship of the last era of wooden fighting ships, of medium size and armament (carrying anywhere from 44 to 56 cannon of varying weight), between a sloop and a ship-of-the-line.

Half-Way Covenant: A redefinition of the exacting standards of church membership originally laid down by New England Puritans, so that those children of church members who had not experienced religious conversion for themselves could nevertheless be admitted to one of the sacraments, baptism, and brought under church discipline.

indentured servant: An individual who sells rights to a term of service (usually seven years) in exchange for the costs of passage to America.

Jeffersonian: Refers to a system of ideas articulated by Thomas Jefferson, John Randolph of Roanoke, and John Taylor of Caroline that promoted agrarianism and states' rights and discouraged concentrations of fiscal and commercial power in governments, cities, institutions, and industries.

joint-stock companies: An early form of corporate organization, designed to limit risk and maximize resources by allowing individuals to contribute to a capital fund through the purchase of shares; this system limited losses to the value of shares bought and permitted sharing of profits through the payment of dividends based on the number of shares.

judicial review: The power of the federal courts to determine the legal standing and/or constitutionality of state or federal legislative actions.

jurisprudence: The theory of law; for example, a jurisprudence of "judicial restraint" would favor minimizing the intervention of judges in legislative matters.

laissez-faire: From the French, "let it be as they wish"; an economic attitude springing from Adam Smith that held that governments should exercise as small an active role as possible in a nation's economic activities and decisions.

liberalism: From the Latin *liber*, for "free"; a political and economic attitude developed at the end of the 17th century and growing to full stature in the late 18th and early 19th centuries. This view based organization of human societies on (a) the possession of natural rights rather than inherited status; (b) the notion of a "state of nature" in which the unrestrained competition for scarce resources induced people to create civil societies as a "social contract" for the purpose of acquiring and protecting property; and (c) the notion that the legitimacy of civil societies depended entirely on the securing of natural and civil rights and could be changed if it failed to do so.

Manifest Destiny: Phrase coined by Jacksonian journalist John O'Sullivan in 1845 that expressed the belief that the United States was clearly, or "manifestly," destined by divine providence, cultural superiority, or racial paternalism to extend U.S. sovereignty over the entire North American continent.

market: Originally a literal physical location but, in the 19th century, increasingly an abstract "place" in which sellers of goods and services compete with other sellers for the attention and business of consumers.

mercantilism: The view that national economies constitute resources that the state must manage in order to maximize, through regulation and subsidization, the survival of the state; especially applicable to the preservation of domestic resources and reserves of gold or silver.

militia: The civilian military forces of each state, who trained for military purposes on indifferent and occasional schedules and were available for active duty on the call of the state's governor or, in time of war or insurrection, by the president of the United States.

mobility: The concept that class, tradition, ethnicity, or religion are no barriers to economic or geographical movement.

moral philosophy: The study of practical applications of religious or philosophical teaching that formed the core of 18th- and 19th-century college curricula.

nativism: Fear of, or prejudice against, those not native born in the United States or those retaining loyalty to foreign languages, ethnic identities, or religions.

nullification: The doctrine, articulated first in the Virginia and Kentucky Resolutions, then by John Calhoun in the Nullification Crisis, that held that state governments have the power to veto, or nullify, the operation of federal laws within their bounds.

plantations: Term used to describe Britain's North American colonies from the view of the royal government. The implication was that the North American colonies were merely settlements with no forms of self-government that the crown was obligated to consult.

public lands: The vast holdings owned by the federal government in the areas ceded to the United States by the Treaty of Paris or acquired by the Louisiana Purchase or the Mexican Cession and whose sales were a major source of revenue for the federal government.

Puritanism: A religious protest movement in English Protestantism that identified itself doctrinally with Calvinism, set extremely high moral standards for admission to church membership, and insisted on disentangling the church from state control, even to the point of authorizing individual congregations to manage their own affairs (Congregationalism).

racism: A belief that certain physical marks categorize people into races and that these can be ranked hierarchically in moral, intellectual, or physical terms that permit members of a "superior" race to stigmatize, oppress, or exploit members of an "inferior" race.

Republicanism: Any form of political organization or ideology that (a) repudiates monarchy, oligarchy, or tyranny; (b) replaces government by self-interest and patronage with public spirit and considerations of merit; (c) lodges political authority in the community as a whole while restricting legislative, judicial, or executive responsibilities in the state to those enjoying popular endorsement; and (d) may be more or less democratic in the identification of those who are accorded civil rights, especially the vote.

Sometimes distinguished into "classical" republicanism, which stresses public spirit and community, and "liberal" republicanism, which legitimates the pursuit of economic and political self-interest as leading to the greatest good.

Romanticism: A reaction to the rationalism of the Enlightenment that valued community with nature; the power of emotion, passion, or sentiment over reason; a belief that "organic" and nonrational factors governed human behavior; and an individual subjectivity.

sedition: Treason, as in the Alien and Sedition Acts.

specie: Hard coin, in gold or silver, as opposed to paper money, stock certificates, or credit.

states' rights: A political doctrine rooted in the view that the states of the Union are its primary political units and have surrendered only limited aspects of sovereignty to the federal government.

suffrage: The civil right to vote.

tariffs: A tax laid on imported goods to be paid by the importer, often levied as a way of adding to the costs of foreign-produced goods in order to give competitive advantage to domestically produced goods.

temperance: A reform movement beginning in the 1820s that sought to restrict the consumption of hard alcoholic spirits through moral exhortation; eventually, the movement became interchangeable with the idea of total abstinence from all fermented liquors and political movements to ban alcohol production and distribution.

transcendentalism: Describes the beliefs of a group of New England Romantic philosophers who sought to "transcend" the Realist epistemology of the dominant "common sense" philosophy by discovering ideas of moral truth and beauty apart from sensation. The transcendentalists espoused reform movements based on communities that identified norms for behavior through mystical delight in nature and the discovery of "authenticity."

Unitarianism: A religious movement in 18th- and 19th-century New England Congregationalism that rejected the traditional tenets of Calvinism, in particular, the notion that God existed as three persons in a Trinity (composed of God the Father, Jesus Christ the Son, and the Holy Spirit), in favor of a "rational" reading of the Bible that found only one "person" in God and, therefore, redefined Jesus Christ as a being of a separate and lower order.

Utopianism: From Thomas More's *Utopia* (as derived from the Greek, *eutopia*, or "good place"), the quest for a perfectly ordered society in which inequality, crime, poverty, and suffering have been abolished by a readjustment of social relations, either through rational management or strict adherence to religious revelation.

veto: From the Latin for "I prevent," the term is used in article 1, section 9, of the Constitution to describe the power of the president to prevent Congressional legislation from passing into law.

voluntary societies: Describes self-organized associations of citizens for specific goals, usually religious, moral, or philanthropic, that the federal government was restricted by the Constitution from publicly pursuing or was given no mandate to pursue.

Whig: Originally, in English political history, the "country" party, opposed to the "court" party and absolute monarchy, this became the name of a party described in 1834 by Henry Clay as the new opposition to "King" Andrew Jackson and the Democrats.

Biographical Notes (Lectures 1–36)

John Adams (1735–1826). American lawyer, member of the Continental Congress, and second president of the United States. Moving force for American independence in the Revolution and major figure in the Federalist Party.

John Quincy Adams (1767–1848). American lawyer and sixth president of the United States. Elected president by the House of Representatives in the contested election of 1824 but tainted by suspicion of a "corrupt bargain" struck with Henry Clay.

Nicholas Biddle (1786–1844). American financier. President of the Second Bank of the United States, who triggered the "Bank War" of 1832 by applying for re-chartering of the bank in the face of Andrew Jackson's opposition.

John Burgoyne (1722–1792). British playwright, politician, and general. Commanded British invasion force from Canada in 1777, only to be defeated and forced to surrender his army at Saratoga, New York.

Aaron Burr (1756–1836). American lawyer and vice president of the United States. Allied himself with Thomas Jefferson and served as Jefferson's first vice president but alienated many Jeffersonians and was dropped from the ticket in 1804. Notorious for having killed Alexander Hamilton in a duel in 1804. Indicted for treason in 1807 after a plot to set up a separate republic in the southwest.

Horace Bushnell (1802–1876). American Congregational theologian. Proposed new ways of understanding traditional Calvinist religious language.

John Caldwell Calhoun (1782–1850). American politician and vice president of the United States. Attempted to shield the South from nationalist economic schemes; Calhoun proposed "nullification" of federal tariffs as a state's right and later demanded the opening of the Mexican Cession to slavery.

Henry Clay (1777–1852). American politician and secretary of state. Originally one of the "hawks" who agitated for the War of 1812, he became the author of the "American System" and founder of the Whig Party.

DeWitt Clinton (1769–1828). American politician and governor of New York. Proposed construction of the Erie Canal in 1816.

James Fenimore Cooper (1789–1851). American novelist. Introduced Romanticism to American literature through his series of "Leatherstocking Tales" (1823–1841), including *The Last of the Mohicans* (1826).

Charles Cornwallis (First Marquis and second Earl Cornwallis, 1738–1805). British general. Served in the Seven Years' War and the Revolution, in which he commanded the major British field force in the American South. Forced to surrender at Yorktown, Virginia, in 1781.

John Dickinson (1732–1808). American lawyer and politician. Served in the Continental Congress and was largely responsible for drafting the Articles of Confederation. Chaired the Annapolis Convention in 1786 and wrote on behalf of the new federal Constitution.

Jonathan Edwards (1703–1758). American Congregational theologian. Pastor of Northampton, Massachusetts, during the Great Awakening and author of important treatises defending the awakening and traditional Puritan Calvinism.

Ralph Waldo Emerson (1803–1882). American essayist and philosopher. Originally a Unitarian minister, he became the leading light of transcendentalism and popularized Romanticism in American philosophy.

Charles Grandison Finney (1792–1875). American Presbyterian theologian and educator. The most famous preacher of the Second Great Awakening, he helped found Oberlin College and served as pastor of Oberlin's First Church.

Benjamin Franklin (1706–1790). American printer, publisher, politician, scientist, and diplomat. Served in the Second Continental Congress and helped negotiate the Treaty of Paris. Signed both the Declaration of Independence and the Constitution.

Robert Fulton (1765–1815). American inventor. Designed and built the first commercially successful steamboat, the *Clermont*.

Thomas Gage (1720–1787). British general. Commanded British forced in North America from 1763 to 1775. Organized the raid that became the battles of Lexington and Concord.

William Lloyd Garrison (1805–1879). American newspaper editor and abolitionist. Founded the abolitionist newspaper *The Liberator* in 1831 and founded the American Anti-Slavery Society.

Alexander Hamilton (1757–1804). American lawyer, soldier, and first secretary of the treasury. His three Reports to Congress as treasury secretary helped shape the economic development of the American Republic.

William Henry Harrison (1773–1841). American soldier, politician, and eighth president of the United States. Cleared the Northwest Territory of Indian resistance at the battle of Tippecanoe in 1811 and defeated the British at the battle of the Thames in 1813 during the War of 1812. The first Whig president and the first president to die in office.

Nathaniel Hawthorne (1804–1864). American novelist. Originally influenced by transcendentalism, he turned to crafting an outstanding series of historical novels, especially *The Scarlet Letter* (1850) and *The House of Seven Gables* (1851).

Charles Hodge (1797–1878). American Presbyterian theologian. As seminary professor at Princeton Theological Seminary, he was the principal figure in the creation of the Princeton Theology.

Sir William Howe (1729–1814). British general. Commanded British forces in North America from 1775 to 1778, winning a series of victories over the Continental Army at Long Island, Brandywine, and Germantown, but he was unsuccessful in completely snuffing out the Revolution.

Henry Hudson (d. 1611). British navigator and explorer. Sponsored by the Dutch West Indies Company, he discovered the Hudson River in 1609 but died in a futile attempt to discover a northwest passage to China.

Andrew Jackson (1767–1845). American soldier and seventh president of the United States. Lionized for his victory over the British at New Orleans in 1815, Jackson was denied the presidency through the "corrupt bargain" of 1824 but was elected in 1828 and 1832 and pursued aggressive policies against the Second Bank of the United States, the Cherokee Indians, and southern threats of nullification of federal legislation.

Thomas Jefferson (1743–1826). American lawyer, author, first secretary of state, and third president of the United States. Author of the Declaration of Independence and enemy of the Federalists, he was the architect of the Democratic-Republican Party's agrarian ideology.

Marie Joseph Paul Yves Roch Gilbert du Motier, Marquis de Lafayette (1757–1834). French nobleman who volunteered his services as an aide to George Washington during the Revolution.

Robert Cavelier, Sieur de La Salle (1643–1687). French explorer. Explored the Great Lakes and Mississippi River valley for France and died trying to establish a settlement at the mouth of the Mississippi in 1687.

Ann Lee (1736–1784). English religious mystic. Founder of the communitarian sect known as the "Shakers" in 1774.

Meriwether Lewis (1774–1809). American soldier and explorer. Together with William Clark, he was commissioned by Thomas Jefferson to survey the Louisiana Purchase and carried out Jefferson's directive with a Corps of Discovery from 1804 to 1806, having reached the Pacific Ocean and returned with the loss of only one member of the expedition.

Francis Cabot Lowell (1775–1817). American industrialist. Founded the Boston Manufacturing Company and created the first large-scale textile mills in America at Waltham, Massachusetts.

James Madison (1751–1836). American lawyer, secretary of state, and fourth president of the United States. Joined with Hamilton and John Jay to argue for ratification of the Constitution by writing *The Federalist Papers* but supported Jefferson in the political conflict with federalism. Presided over American involvement in the War of 1812.

Horace Mann (1796–1859). American lawyer and educator. Designed a comprehensive renovation of the Massachusetts public education system and created the outline of the modern public school system.

John Marshall (1755–1835). American lawyer and chief justice of the U.S. Supreme Court. A Federalist appointed by John Adams to the Supreme Court, his long tenure as chief justice allowed Marshall to establish important principles of judicial review, the supremacy of federal over state authority, and the protection of the manufacturing economy.

Cotton Mather (1663–1728). American Congregational clergyman. Tireless promoter of schemes for public welfare and the reconciliation of Calvinism with the New Philosophy.

James Monroe (1758–1831). American diplomat and fifth president of the United States.

William Paterson (1745–1806). American lawyer and politician, born in Ireland. Architect of the "New Jersey Plan" at the Constitutional Convention in 1787.

Charles Cotesworth Pinckney (1746–1825). American lawyer, judge, diplomat, and politician. One of three American diplomats sent by President Adams to negotiate with the French Directory, only to be confronted by demands for bribes in the XYZ Affair.

Pontiac (1720–1769). Ottawa chieftain. Organized an intertribal offensive against the British at the close of the French and Indian War.

Paul Revere (1735–1818). Boston artisan. Carried warning of British raid to Lexington on the night of April 18–19, 1775.

Winfield Scott (1786–1866). American soldier. Commanded the principal American field force in the Mexican War, winning successive victories in 1847 that culminated in the capture of Mexico City.

Elizabeth Cady Stanton (1815–1902). American feminist. A pioneer of awarding civil equality to women, she organized the first women's rights convention at Seneca Falls, New York, in 1848.

Friedrich Wilhelm Ludolf Gerhard Augustin von Steuben (1730–1794). Prussian mercenary. Hired in 1777 to train the Continental Army at its winter encampment in Valley Forge, Pennsylvania.

Tecumseh (1768–1813). Shawnee chieftain. Organized a coalition of Indian tribes to resist white expansion in the Northwest Territory. After his forces were defeated at Tippecanoe by William Henry Harrison, he fled to Canada and fought with the British in the War of 1812. He was killed at the battle of the Thames.

George Washington (1732–1799). first president of the United States. Commanded the Continental Army in the Revolution, presided over the Constitutional Convention, and became a leading figure of the Federalists.

Daniel Webster (1782–1852). American lawyer and politician. Involved in the major cases of the Marshall Court, including *Gibbons v. Ogden*, *McCulloch vs. Maryland*, and *Dartmouth College vs. Woodward*. The greatest orator in the Senate, he attacked nullification and disunion in his great Second Reply to Hayne (1830).

Eli Whitney (1765–1825). American inventor. Inventor of the cotton gin, which made the commercial growth of cotton feasible, and the manufacturing system of interchangeable parts.

John Winthrop (1588–1649). English lawyer and Puritan, first governor of Massachusetts Bay. Led the Puritan exodus to New England in 1630 and founded the town of Boston.

John Witherspoon (1723–1794). American Presbyterian clergyman and president of Princeton College, born in Scotland. Became president of Princeton in 1768 and served in the Continental Congress. Advocate of Scottish "common sense" philosophy and the necessity of public religion to ensure virtue in a republic.

Bibliography (Lectures 1–36)

Essential Reading

Bailyn, Bernard. *The Ideological Origins of the American Revolution*. Cambridge, MA: Harvard University Press, 1967. A path-breaking work that reoriented our understanding of the political ideas of the American revolutionaries and their roots in five major sources of Whig thinking.

Boorstin, Daniel. *The Lost World of Thomas Jefferson*. New York: Henry Holt, 1948. An "intellectual biography" of the mind and ideas of Thomas Jefferson.

Butler, Jon. *Awash in a Sea of Faith: Christianizing the American People*. Cambridge, MA: Harvard University Press, 1990. Argues that religion established a comparatively feeble presence in early America, despite the presence of radical religious groups, such as the Puritans and Quakers, but eventually, through its own energies, succeeded in rising to cultural prominence in the early republic.

Carey, George W., and James McClellan. *The Federalist*. Indianapolis, IN: Liberty Fund, 2001. The best collection of the famous articles by Hamilton, Jay, and Madison advocating ratification of the federal Constitution, with the text of the Constitution keyed to all relevant sections of *The Federalist*.

Clark, Christopher. *The Roots of Rural Capitalism: Western Massachusetts, 1780–1861*. Ithaca, NY: Cornell University Press, 1990. A thorough and eye-opening investigation of the opening of rural western Massachusetts to commercial market agriculture, with its attendant social dislocations.

Elkins, Stanley, and Eric McKitrick. *The Age of Federalism: The Early American Republic, 1788–1800*. New York: Oxford University Press, 1993. The finest single-volume political history of the federal era.

Fogel, Robert William. *Without Consent or Contract: The Rise and Fall of American Slavery*. New York: W.W. Norton, 1989. The best survey of the economic nature of slavery, which Fogel argues developed into a dangerously profitable labor system before the Civil War.

Gipson, Lawrence Henry. *The British Empire before the American Revolution*. New York: Knopf, 1958–1968. A massive survey of Britain's North American colonies and their place in the larger scheme of the British Empire, from 1748–1776, in 14 volumes.

Holt, Michael F. *The Rise and Fall of the American Whig Party: Jacksonian Politics and the Onset of the Civil War*. New York: Oxford University Press, 1999. An enormous, highly detailed history of the fortunes of the Whig Party, with particular attention to its organization for elections and its successes and failures on the state and local levels.

Howe, Daniel Walker. *The Political Culture of the American Whigs*. Chicago: University of Chicago Press, 1979. Classic explanation of the values and attitudes that stood behind the public policies of the Whigs, with separate chapters on the major Whig leaders.

Kolchin, Peter. *American Slavery, 1619–1877*. New York: Hill and Wang, 1993. A thorough survey of the social, economic, and racial aspects of southern slavery.

McCusker, John J., and Russell R. Menard. *The Economy of British America, 1607–1789*. Chapel Hill, NC: University of North Carolina Press, 1985. The standard work on the nature of the various colonial economies of British North America.

Miller, Perry. *The New England Mind: The 17th Century*. Cambridge, MA: Harvard University Press, 1939. One of the greatest pieces of American historical writing, this volume (the first of three) is an "intellectual history" of the Puritanism carried to New England in the 1600s, written around the issues of reason, scholasticism, rhetoric, and covenant theology.

Morgan, Edmund S. *American Slavery-American Freedom: The Ordeal of Colonial Virginia*. New York: W.W. Norton, 1975. A meticulous history of the settlement of Virginia, from Jamestown through Bacon's Rebellion, showing how the demand for labor shaped the movement toward slavery and how slavery, in turn, shaped the notions of freedom brought to the Revolution by the Virginia elite.

Morison, Samuel Eliot. *The European Discovery of America: The Northern Voyages, A.D. 500–1600.* New York: Oxford University Press, 1971. A narrative history of the voyages of discovery to the North American continent before the beginning of permanent English settlements.

———. *The European Discovery of America: The Southern Voyages, A.D. 1492–1616.* New York: Oxford University Press, 1974. A sequel to the previous volume, tracing the voyages, beginning with that of Columbus, that explored the Caribbean, Gulf of Mexico, and Pacific coast.

Sellers, Charles G. *The Market Revolution: Jacksonian America, 1815–1846.* New York: Oxford University Press, 1991. A highly influential survey of the era, arguing forthrightly for the importance of the penetration of capitalist markets into American life as the chief issue in American politics and culture.

Smith, Billy G. *The "Lower Sort": Philadelphia's Laboring People, 1750–1800.* Ithaca, NY: Cornell University Press, 1990. A classic social history of the working class of Philadelphia in the early republic, analyzing the city's economy, wealth-holding patterns, and the family and working lives of the poor, but without illusions about a pre-industrial "golden age."

Tocqueville, Alexis de. *Democracy in America.* Harvey C. Mansfield and Delba Winthrop, eds. Chicago: University of Chicago Press, 2000. The authoritative translation of Tocqueville's massive commentary on the nature of American democracy.

Wood, Gordon S. *The Creation of the American Republic, 1776–1789.* Chapel Hill, NC: University of North Carolina Press, 1967. Depicts the creation of an independent American Republic as the product of a violent and complex crosscurrent of conflicting ideas of liberty in the colonies and new states, rather than a single, straightforward notion of liberty.

———. *The Radicalism of the American Revolution*. New York: Knopf, 1992. Argues that American republicanism was founded on aristocratic values that the Revolution undermined, leading to the swift development of a democratic, rather than a republican, political consciousness.

Supplementary Reading

Note: Some of the following books may be out of print. Internet sites such as www.abebooks.com and www.amazon.com may be helpful in locating copies.

Alden, John Richard. *George Washington: A Biography*. Baton Rouge, LA: Louisiana State University Press, 1984. An excellent one-volume survey of Washington's life.

Appleby, Joyce. *Capitalism and a New Social Order: The Republican Vision of the 1790s*. New York: New York University Press, 1984. Appleby argues that the republican ideology always had a strong bias toward liberal capitalism rather than toward non-market forms of "classical" republicanism.

———. *Inheriting the Revolution: The First Generation of Americans*. Cambridge, MA: Harvard University Press, 2000. A group biography of a cross-section of Americans between 1776 and 1826.

Ashworth, John. *Slavery, Capitalism, and Politics in the Antebellum Republic*. Cambridge: Cambridge University Press, 1996. A lengthy examination of the economic presuppositions of Whig and Democratic political thought.

Baker, Jean H. *Affairs of Party: The Political Culture of Northern Democrats in the Mid-nineteenth Century*. Ithaca, NY: Cornell University Press, 1983. An outstanding survey of the attitudes that formed Democratic "political culture" and underlay explicit Democratic policies.

Banner, James M. *To the Hartford Convention: The Federalists and the Origins of Party Politics in the Early Republic, 1789–1815*. New York: Knopf, 1967. Analyzes the rise and decline of New England federalism up to the party's collapse after the Hartford Convention.

Banning, Lance. *The Jeffersonian Persuasion: Evolution of a Party Ideology.* Ithaca, NY: Cornell University Press, 1978. Explains the components and details of Jeffersonian politics and policies.

———. *The Sacred Fire of Liberty: James Madison and the Founding of the Federal Republic.* Ithaca, NY: Cornell University Press, 1995. An in-depth analysis of James Madison that sees Madison as a consistent Jeffersonian throughout his career.

Bartlett, Irving H. *Daniel Webster.* New York: W.W. Norton, 1973. A biography of Webster emphasizing the contradictions within the man and his image.

Benson, Lee. *The Concept of Jacksonian Democracy: New York as Test Case.* Princeton: Princeton University Press, 1961. A classic work asserting that Jacksonian politics was organized less around ideas and policies and more by ethnic and religious group identities.

Brooke, John L. *The Refiner's Fire: The Making of Mormon Cosmology, 1644–1844.* New York: Cambridge University Press, 1994. Fascinating tour through the world of early American mystical and cultic beliefs that eventually formed the core of Mormonism.

Brown, Thomas. *Politics and Statesmanship: Essays on the American Whig Party.* New York: Columbia University Press, 1985. Essays on Whig Party attitudes and Whig leaders.

Bushman, Richard L. *The Refinement of America: Persons, Houses, Cities.* New York: Vintage, 1992. Studies the emergence of rules and handbooks on fashion, decoration, appearances, and self-presentation in the early republic.

Carwardine, Richard J. *Evangelicals and Politics in Antebellum America.* New Haven: Yale University Press, 1993. Strongly detailed picture of the issues that bound Protestant evangelicals to the Whigs and, later, to the Republicans.

Cochran, Thomas Childs. *Frontiers of Change: Early Industrialism in America*. New York: Oxford University Press, 1981. The standard introduction and survey of the beginnings of American industrialization.

Conkin, Paul K. *The Uneasy Center: Reformed Christianity in Antebellum America*. Chapel Hill, NC: University of North Carolina Press, 1995. Discusses the major ideas and thinkers among American Calvinists in the early republic, including Nathaniel William Taylor, Charles Hodge, and John Williamson Nevin.

Conway, Thomas. *The War of American Independence, 1775–1783*. London: Edward Arnold, 1995. The American Revolution from a delightfully literate English historian's perspective, measuring the worldwide scope and impact of the Revolution.

Countryman, Edward. *The American Revolution*. New York: Hill and Wang, 1985. A social history of the American Revolution.

Cronon, William. *Changes in the Land: Indians, Colonists, and the Ecology of New England*. New York: Hill and Wang, 1983. An innovative history of the impact of European settlement on the ecology and native societies of New England, full of many surprises about both the agents and recipients of those changes.

Cross, Whitney R. *The Burned-over District: The Social and Intellectual History of Enthusiastic Religion in Western New York, 1800–1850*. Ithaca, NY: Cornell University Press, 1950. A social history of western New York and the causes and impact of the revivals and religious cults that swept through it.

Dawidoff, Robert. *The Education of John Randolph*. New York: W.W. Norton, 1979. A raffish but sympathetic biography of the savagely articulate Jeffersonian.

Demos, John Putnam. *Entertaining Satan: Witchcraft and the Culture of Early New England*. New York: Oxford University Press, 1982. A history of witchcraft in the larger context of 17th-century American culture, along with a detailed analysis of the 1692 panic in Salem, Massachusetts; the individuals who fostered it; and those who were its victims.

Douglas, Ann. *The Feminization of American Culture*. New York: Knopf, 1977. A pioneering cultural history of pre-Civil War America, with emphasis on how religion and literature came to be "feminized," or seen as primarily the sphere of women.

Dwight, Timothy. *Travels in New England and New York*. Barbara Miller Solomon, ed. Cambridge, MA: Harvard University Press, 1969. Dwight, the grandson of Jonathan Edwards, embarked on a tour of New England in 1821–1822 to capture oral histories and impressions of the region as the last colonial generation was fading from the scene.

Eisenhower, John S. D. *So Far from God: The U.S. War with Mexico, 1846–1848*. New York: Random House, 1989. The best and most thorough modern narrative of the Mexican War.

Ellis, Joseph J. *American Sphinx: The Character of Thomas Jefferson*. New York: Knopf, 1997. An analysis of the character of Jefferson, who is portrayed as a collection of ideas whose parts did not all communicate with each other.

———. *Founding Brothers: The Revolutionary Generation*. New York: Knopf, 2000.

Faragher, John Mack. *Sugar Creek: Life on the Illinois Prairie*. New Haven: Yale University Press, 1986. Focuses on the transformation of a village in central Illinois from its prairie condition to the arrival of white agricultural pioneers and, eventually, the coming of the transportation revolution and commercial agriculture.

Fiering, Norman. *Moral Philosophy at 17th-Century Harvard*. Chapel Hill: University of North Carolina Press, 1981. An important description of how the curriculum of Harvard College witnessed the replacement of Christian scholasticism with a naturalistic moral philosophy, with particular attention to the principal textbooks and the development of a distinctive psychology.

Finney, Charles Grandison. *The Memoirs of Charles G. Finney: The Complete Restored Text*. Garth M. Rosell and Richard A. G. Dupuis, eds. Grand Rapids, MI: Academie Books, 1989. A superb edition of Finney's autobiography, with a reconstructed text and elaborate notes and identifications.

Fischer, David Hackett. *Paul Revere's Ride*. New York: Oxford University Press, 1994. Story of the first conflict of the Revolution, with the twin figures of Thomas Gage and Paul Revere at the forefront.

Flexner, James Thomas. *George Washington and the New Nation, 1783–1793*. Boston: Little, Brown, 1970. This is the third volume in the best multivolume survey of Washington's life.

———. *George Washington: Anguish and Farewell, 1793–1799*. Boston: Little, Brown, 1972.

———. *George Washington in the American Revolution, 1775–1783*. Boston: Little, Brown, 1968.

———. *George Washington: The Forge of Experience, 1732–1775*. Boston: Little, Brown, 1965.

Flower, Elizabeth, and Murray G. Murphey. *A History of Philosophy in America*. New York: G.P. Putnam's Sons, 1977. The first volume of this two-volume survey of American philosophy offers an invaluable overview of the main currents of American philosophical thought from the Puritans through transcendentalism.

Frederickson, George M. *The Black Image in the White Mind: The Debate on Afro-American Character and Destiny, 1817–1914.* New York: Harper & Row, 1971. Investigates the emergence of racism and racist justifications for the social marginalization and alienation of blacks, both free and slave.

Freehling, William W. *Prelude to Civil War: The Nullification Controversy in South Carolina*. New York: Harper & Row, 1966. Standard account of the controversy between Calhoun and South Carolina, and President Andrew Jackson, over the attempted nullification of the federal tariff.

———. *The Road to Disunion*, vol. 1: *Secessionists at Bay*. New York: Oxford University Press, 1990. A large-scale study of the slave South and its internal differences over slavery.

Genovese, Eugene D. *The Political Economy of Slavery: Studies in the Economy and Society of the Slave South*. New York: Pantheon, 1965. Analyzes the connections between slaveholding and pro-slavery ideology and market capitalism.

———. *Roll, Jordan, Roll: The World the Slaves Made*. New York: Pantheon, 1972. An intriguing interpretation of southern slavery as a pre-modern, pre-capitalist society in which slaves seized control of much of the dynamic of authority in their lives and compelled slaveowners to treat with them as workers rather than chattels.

Green, James A. *William Henry Harrison: His Life and Times*. Richmond, VA: Garrett and Massie, 1941. The principal modern biography of the first Whig president and the first president to die in office.

Greene, Jack P. *Pursuits of Happiness: The Social Development of Early Modern British Colonies and the Formation of American Culture*. Chapel Hill, NC: University of North Carolina Press, 1988. Focuses on the Chesapeake, rather than New England, as the settlement that most determined the development of American culture and offers a three-part formula of simplification, elaboration, and replication as an alternative to the New England preoccupation with "declension" as a way of understanding cultural change.

Gutman, Herbert. *The Black Family in Slavery and Freedom, 1750–1925*. New York: Pantheon, 1976. Pioneering study arguing that enslaved blacks successfully maintained family structures under the pressure of slavery and that the modern disintegration of the black family was a recent political phenomenon.

Hall, David D. *Worlds of Wonder, Days of Judgment: Popular Religious Belief in Early New England*. New York: Knopf, 1989. An innovative look into the practical beliefs and non-beliefs of New England Puritans, as opposed to an intellectual history of the clergy, concluding that the gap between the two was not nearly as wide as might be supposed.

Hambrick-Stowe, Charles E. *The Practice of Piety: Puritan Devotional Disciplines in Seventeenth-Century New England.* Chapel Hill, NC: University of North Carolina Press, 1982. A sympathetic and in-depth examination of Puritan spiritual disciplines and devotional reading.

Hamilton, Holman. *Prologue to Conflict: The Crisis and Compromise of 1850.* New York: W.W. Norton, 1964. The standard account of the political conflict over the extension of slavery into the Mexican Cession and its resolution in the Great Compromise.

Hatch, Nathan O. *The Democratization of American Christianity.* New Haven: Yale University Press, 1989. Argues that evangelical Protestants were influenced by democratization in church structure, leadership, and theology but also contributed tremendously to it, as well.

Hickey, Donald. *The War of 1812: A Forgotten Conflict.* Urbana, IL: University of Illinois Press, 1989. A dependable narrative of the Anglo-American conflict of 1812–1815.

Hodges, Graham Russell. *Slavery and Freedom in the Rural North: African-Americans in Monmouth County, New Jersey, 1665–1865.* Madison, WI: Madison House, 1997. Studies the lives of slave and free African Americans in a central New Jersey county.

Horgan, Paul. *Conquistadors in North American History.* New York: Farrar, Straus, 1963. A delightfully written and short survey of the Spanish colonial empire in northern Mexico.

Howe, Daniel Walker. *Making the American Self: From Jonathan Edwards to Abraham Lincoln.* Cambridge, MA: Harvard University Press, 1997. Examines the creation of an American model personality, based on notions of self-control and self-transformation, which played large roles in the formation of the Whig and evangelical Protestant minds.

———. *The Unitarian Conscience: Harvard Moral Philosophy, 1805–1861*. Cambridge, MA: Harvard University Press, 1970. An engaging examination of Unitarianism's capture of Harvard and its major personalities and ethical teachings.

Isaac, Rhys. *The Transformation of Virginia, 1740–1790*. Chapel Hill, NC: University of North Carolina Press, 1982. Explores the way in which radical evangelicalism in Virginia undermined the authority of traditional Virginia elites in the 18th century and prepared Virginians for participation in the Revolution.

Jennings, Francis. *The Invasion of America: Indians, Colonialism, and the Cant of Conquest*. New York: W.W. Norton, 1975. A radical view of American colonial history that treats the process of settlement as destructive, murderous, and ruthless.

Johnson, Paul E. *A Shopkeeper's Millennium: Society and Revival in Rochester, New York, 1815–1837*. New York: Hill & Wang, 1978. Argues for a causal relationship between economic changes brought by the transportation revolution to western New York and the release from social anxiety brought by the Second Great Awakening.

Kammen, Michael. *Colonial New York: A History*. New York: Scribner, 1975. A thorough survey of New York history from the Dutch founding to the first state constitution in 1777.

Kelley, Joseph J. *Pennsylvania: The Colonial Years, 1681–1776*. A lengthy but well-written narrative of colonial Pennsylvania from William Penn to Washington's crossing of the Delaware.

Ketchum, Richard M. *Saratoga: Turning Point of America's Revolutionary War*. New York: Henry Holt, 1997. Popular account of the Revolution's most important battle.

Kramnick, Isaac. *Republicanism and Bourgeois Radicalism: Political Ideology in Late Eighteenth-Century England and America*. Ithaca, NY: Cornell

University Press, 1990. The development and radicalization of middle-class Whig Republicans in the 18th-century on both sides of the Atlantic.

———, and R. Laurence Moore. *The Godless Constitution: The Case against Religious Correctness*. New York, NY : W.W. Norton & Company, 1996. A controversial and spirited argument against the notion that Christianity was ever intended by the Founders to have a public role in American political life.

Kupperman, Karen Ordahl. *Roanoke: The Abandoned Colony*. Savage, MD: Rowman and Littlefield, 1984. An intriguing and thorough history of the ill-fated Roanoke colonies.

Lambert, Frank. *Inventing the "Great Awakening."* Princeton, NJ: Princeton University Press, 1999. A cultural analysis of the way the religious revivals of the 1740s were depicted, interpreted, and reproduced.

Lebsock, Suzanne. *The Free Women of Petersburg: Status and Culture in a Southern Town, 1784–1860*. New York: W.W. Norton, 1984. Uses Petersburg, Virginia, women as models for understanding the economic and social lives of women and the numerous ways in which they carved out pockets of independence while still suffering legal disabilities.

Lepore, Jill. *The Name of War: King Philip's War and the Origins of American Identity*. New York: Knopf, 1998. A cultural history of the devastating Indian war of 1675–1676 in New England.

Lockridge, Kenneth. *A New England Town: The First Hundred Years*. New York: W.W. Norton, 1970. A social history of Dedham, Massachusetts, from its founding in 1635 as a "closed, corporate Christian community" to its social fracturing under the stresses of demography and economics.

Lord, Walter. *The Dawn's Early Light*. New York: W.W. Norton, 1972. A popular history of the British attack on Fort McHenry in Baltimore Harbor, which not only failed to seize the fort and city, but helped produce the national anthem.

———. *A Time To Stand*. New York: Harper, 1961. A fast-paced, popular history of the fall of the Alamo, but with careful attention to a full reading of original sources.

Maier, Pauline. *American Scripture: Making the Declaration of Independence*. New York: Knopf, 1997. A vivid analysis of the sources Jefferson used in constructing the Declaration of Independence and the Declaration's subsequent standing in American history.

———. *From Resistance to Revolution: Colonial Radicals and the Development of American Opposition to Britain, 1765–1776*. New York: Vintage Books, 1972. Surveys the movement of American opposition from the Stamp Act to independence.

May, Henry F. *The Enlightenment in America*. New York: Oxford University Press, 1976. An enormously literate and clear-headed analysis of the "four" Enlightenments that emerged in colonial and revolutionary America.

Mayer, Henry. *All on Fire: William Lloyd Garrison and the Abolition of Slavery*. New York: St. Martins, 1998. An admiring, almost partisan, but thorough biography of the premier abolitionist.

McCoy, Drew R. *The Last of the Fathers: James Madison and the Republican Legacy*. New York: Cambridge University Press, 1989. Studies the later years and influence of James Madison in the creation of the politics of the early republic.

McCullough, David G. *John Adams*. New York: Simon & Schuster, 2001. A notable and highly sympathetic biography of the second president.

———. *The Presidency of George Washington*. Lawrence, KS: University Press of Kansas, 1974. A careful analysis of the politics of Washington's two administrations.

McDonald, Forrest. *Alexander Hamilton: A Biography*. New York: W.W. Norton, 1979. A detailed and sympathetic treatment of Hamilton, which is especially illuminating in explaining Hamilton's economic policies as secretary of the treasury.

———. *The Presidency of Thomas Jefferson*. Lawrence, KS: University Press of Kansas, 1976. Part of the University of Kansas *Presidency* series, McDonald surveys Jefferson's two terms in office.

Meyers, Marvin. *The Jacksonian Persuasion: Politics and Belief*. Stanford, CA: Stanford University Press, 1957. Classic study of the political ideas and ideals of Jackson and his followers.

Morgan, Edmund S. *The Puritan Dilemma: The Story of John Winthrop*. Boston: Little, Brown, 1958. One of the great American biographies, it sympathetically portrays Winthrop as a Puritan determined to find a middle ground between moral indifference and moral absolutism in managing public affairs.

Morison, Samuel Eliot. *Builders of the Bay Colony*. Boston: Houghton, Mifflin, 1930. Twelve masterful portraits of the political, religious, economic, and intellectual leaders of the first generation of Massachusetts Bay Puritans, told with the verve of a great narrator.

Morris, Thomas D. *Southern Slavery and the Law, 1619–1860*. Chapel Hill, NC: University of North Carolina Press, 1996. Detailed survey of the legal structures that supported slavery in the slave states of the South.

Murdock, Harold. *Bunker Hill: Notes and Queries on a Famous Battle*. Boston: Houghton Mifflin Company, 1927. A marvelous antiquarian's exploration of the nooks and crannies of a famous revolutionary battle.

Newmyer, R. Kent. *John Marshall and the Heroic Age of the Supreme Court*. Baton Rouge: Louisiana State University Press, 2001. A detailed legal history of the Marshall Court and the cases Marshall used to fashion a central national identity and economic system.

Oakes, James. *The Ruling Race: A History of American Slaveholders*. New York: Random House, 1982. An innovative presentation of competing theories of how slaveowners justified the enslavement and ownership of blacks and the moral stresses that led some to evangelical Protestantism and others to secession.

Onuf, Peter S. *Statehood and Union: A History of the Northwest Ordinance.* Bloomington, IN: Indiana University Press, 1987. A study of how the Confederation Congress dealt with the status and organization of the western territory it won from Great Britain in the Revolution.

Rahe, Paul Anthony. *Republics Ancient and Modern: Classical Republicanism and the American Revolution.* Chapel Hill, NC: University of North Carolina Press, 1992. A staggeringly thorough survey of the political nature and structure of republican governments and their example for the Founding Fathers.

Rakove, Jack N. *The Beginnings of National Politics: An Interpretive History of the Continental Congress.* New York: Knopf, 1979. Portrait of the Continental Congress as a practical, problem-solving body, not so much driven by faction as by the novelty of the dilemmas it faced and the solutions it was politically possible to reach.

Remini, Robert Vincent. *Andrew Jackson and the Course of American Democracy, 1833–1845.* New York: Harper & Row, 1984. The third and final volume of Remini's tremendous survey of the life of Andrew Jackson.

———. *Andrew Jackson and the Course of American Empire* (New York: Harper & Row, 1977).

———. *Andrew Jackson and the Course of American Freedom, 1822–1832* (New York: Harper & Row, 1981).

———. *The Battle of New Orleans.* New York: Viking, 1999. A detailed but face-paced description of the battle that made Andrew Jackson a national hero.

———. *Henry Clay: Statesman for the Union.* New York: W.W. Norton, 1991. The best biography of Clay.

———. *John Quincy Adams*. New York: Times Books, 2002. A brief biography of one of the most gifted, but one of the most politically unfortunate, presidents.

Richardson, Robert D. *Emerson: The Mind on Fire*. Berkeley, CA: University of California Press, 1995. Great biography that links Emerson to the surge of Romanticism in Europe and America.

Rogin, Michael Paul. *Fathers and Children: Andrew Jackson and the Subjugation of the American Indian*. New York: Knopf, 1975. Psychological study of Andrew Jackson that roots his murderous hostility toward Indians in a deep psychic need to see political relationships from the viewpoint of a dominant, patriarchal father.

Schlesinger, Arthur M. *The Age of Jackson*. Boston: Little, Brown, 1945. A classic and admiring survey of Jackson's presidency, casting Jackson in the role of "man of the people" presiding over an early version of the New Deal.

Schoelwer, Susan Prendergast. *Alamo Images: Changing Perceptions of a Texas Experience*. Dallas, TX: Southern Methodist University Press, 1985. History of how our public image of the Alamo as a "shrine" developed in art and architecture.

Schwartz, Seymour I. *The French and Indian War, 1754–1763: The Imperial Struggle for North America*. New York: Simon & Schuster, 1994. Surveys the battles and strategies that gave Great Britain dominance in North America and around the globe.

Sheriff, Carol. *The Artificial River: The Erie Canal and the Paradox of Progress, 1817–1862*. New York: Hill & Wang, 1996. A detailed analytical study of the origins, construction, and functions of the Erie Canal.

Silbey, Joel. *The Partisan Imperative: The Dynamics of American Politics before the Civil War*. New York: Oxford University Press, 1985. Argues for the crucial role played by personal identification with party and the degree to which party loyalty inflamed political contests in the early republic.

Smith, Timothy L. *Revivalism and Social Reform: American Protestantism on the Eve of the Civil War.* Baltimore: Johns Hopkins University Press, 1957, 1980. The classic account of the involvement of evangelical revivalists with social reform movements from 1840 to 1861.

Stampp, Kenneth M. *The Peculiar Institution: Slavery in the Antebellum South.* New York: Knopf, 1956. This book single-handedly rewrote the priorities for understanding slavery and ended a long era in which slavery was looked on as a benign institution.

Steele, Ian K. *Warpaths: Invasions of North America.* New York: Oxford University Press, 1993. A military history of European invasion that argues for the ingenuity and skill of the Indians in rising to meet and defeat European organization and technology.

Taylor, Alan. *American Colonies.* New York: Viking, 2001. Ambitious survey of the entire Americas as colonies, beginning with prehistory and concluding with the Russian and British explorations of Alaska and the Pacific Northwest.

Thomas, Hugh. *The Slave Trade: The Story of the Transatlantic Slave Trade.* New York: Simon & Schuster, 1997. A vast, sprawling narrative, extended over four continents and four centuries, of the traffic in African slaves and its eventual suppression.

Tuveson, Ernest Lee. *Redeemer Nation: The Idea of America's Millennial Role.* Chicago: University of Chicago Press, 1968. A study of America's self-image as divinely ordained to preach a gospel of democracy to the world as a precursor to a golden age of millennial happiness.

Wallace, Anthony F. C. *The Death and Rebirth of the Seneca.* New York: Knopf, 1970. An anthropologist's interpretation of the Handsome Lake religious revival among the Seneca of upstate New York and the suggestion of a paradigm of "revitalization" for understanding the renewal and revival of cultures.

———. *Rockdale: The Growth of an American Village in the Early Industrial Revolution*. New York: Knopf, 1978. Focuses on one mill town in southeastern Pennsylvania to demonstrate the creative and unpredictable mixture of commercial values and evangelical Protestant religion in fostering a community that opposed slavery and eagerly expected the millennium.

Watson, Harry L. *Liberty and Power: The Politics of Jacksonian America*. New York: Hill and Wang, 1990. A short but skillful survey of the shifting tides of political conflict in Jackson's America, with special attention to the underlying cultural values represented by these conflicts.

White, G. Edward. *The Marshall Court and Cultural Change, 1815–1835*. New York: Oxford University Press, 1991. In-depth survey of the legal philosophy and critical decisions of John Marshall and the Supreme Court.

Wilentz, Sean. *Chants Democratic: New York City and the Rise of the American Working Class, 1788–1850*. New York: Oxford University Press, 1984. Chronicles the development of a property-less urban working class and its political organization.

Winslow, Ola Elizabeth. *Jonathan Edwards, 1703–1758: A Biography*. New York: Macmillan, 1940. A Pulitzer Prize winner at its publication and still the finest biography of Edwards available.

Wolf, Stephanie. *As Various as Their Land: The Everyday Lives of Eighteenth-Century Americans*. New York: Harper Collins, 1993. A charming but shrewd survey of the "ordinary" lives of colonial Americans in the home, at work, and in their community.

Wright, Robert. *The Continental Army*. Washington, DC: Center of Military History, 1986. Highly detailed military analysis of the structure and doctrine of Washington's army.

Wright, Ronald. *Stolen Continents: The Americas through Indian Eyes Since 1492*. Boston: Houghton Mifflin, 1992. A powerfully written "alternative" history of the European conquest of the Americas from the point of view of five Indian tribes—the Aztec, Maya, Inca, Cherokee, and Iroquois.

Document Collections:

Allen, W. B., ed. *George Washington: A Collection*. Indianapolis, IN: Liberty Press, 1988. Outstanding single-volume anthology of Washington's writings, mostly letters.

Belz, Herman, ed. *The Webster-Hayne Debate on the Nature of the Union*. Indianapolis, IN: Liberty Fund, 2000. Complete texts of Webster's debates in the Senate with Robert Hayne over the tariff, plus speeches from Thomas Hart Benton, Edward Livingston, and others.

DePauw, Linda G., et al., eds. *Journal of William Maclay*, vol. 9 of the *Documentary History of the First Federal Congress of the United States of America*. Baltimore: Johns Hopkins University Press, 1988. A first-person account of the inner workings of the first Congress under the Constitution.

Dunn, Richard S., and Laetitia Yaendle, eds. *The Journal of John Winthrop, 1630–1649*. Cambridge, MA: Harvard University Press, 1996. The running commentary Winthrop kept from 1629 until close to his death on the founding of the Massachusetts Bay colony; also available in an abridged edition.

Forbes, Allyn B., ed. *The Winthrop Papers*. Boston: Massachusetts Historical Society, 1929–1947, five volumes (1498–1649). Complete compilation of the letters and papers of three generations of Winthrops in England and America.

Freeman, Joanna B., ed. *Alexander Hamilton: Writings*. Library of America, 2001. Best one-volume collection of Hamilton's writings and major state papers as secretary of the treasury.

Howe, Daniel Walker, ed. *The American Whigs: An Anthology*. New York: Wiley, 1973. The only collection of Whig political writings.

Hyneman, Charles S., and Donald Lutz, eds. *American Political Writings during the Founding Era, 1760–1805*. Indianapolis, IN: Liberty Press, 1983, two volumes. A broad collection of American political pamphlets, sermons, and treatises, with the first volume devoted to the revolutionary period and the second, to the Constitution and early republic.

Johnson, Thomas, and Perry Miller, eds. *The Puritans: A Sourcebook of Their Writings*. New York: Harper & Row, 1938, rev. ed., 1963. The most convenient source for a broad sampling of Puritan writing, organized topically in two volumes.

Kline, Mary Jo, ed. *The Political Correspondence and Public Papers of Aaron Burr*. Princeton: Princeton University Press, 1983, two volumes.

Lence, Ross. *Union and Liberty: The Political Philosophy of John C. Calhoun*. Indianapolis, IN: Liberty Fund, 1992. Fourteen of Calhoun's most important writings, including his protests against the "Tariff of Abomination" and the Compromise of 1850.

Oberg, Barbara et al, editors. *The Papers of Thomas Jefferson*. Princeton: Princeton University Press, 1950-, 30 volumes.

Peterson, Merrill D., ed. *The Portable Thomas Jefferson*. New York: Penguin, 1975. The best single-volume collection of Jefferson's papers and letters.

Richardson, James D. ed. *A Compilation of the Messages and Papers of the Presidents, 1789–1897*. Washington, DC: Government Printing Office, 1896–1899. Provides the texts of presidential proclamations, inaugural addresses, annual messages to Congress, and veto messages, from George Washington to William McKinley.

Soderlund, Jean R., ed. *William Penn and the Founding of Pennsylvania, 1680–1684: A Documentary History*. Philadelphia: University of Pennsylvania Press, 1983. Culled from the larger papers of the William Penn project, this single volume collects the most important documents concerning Penn and the creation of the Pennsylvania colony.

Stout, Harry S., gen. ed. *The Works of Jonathan Edwards*. New Haven: Yale University Press, 1957– . A comprehensive edition of Edwards's writings and papers, including sermons, philosophical and theological books, correspondence, and "miscellanies"; currently at 19 volumes.

Syrett, Harold C., et al., eds. *The Papers of Alexander Hamilton*. New York: Columbia University Press, 1961–1981, 27 volumes.

The History of the United States, 2nd Edition

Scope (Lectures 37–48):

Lectures 37 through 48 of this course focus on sectional conflict during the middle decades of the 19th century. They divide into three groups: the first three lectures dealing with escalating political tensions between slaveholders and non-slaveholders from the early 1850s through the election of Abraham Lincoln and the outbreak of war in 1860–1861; the next six, with the four years of the Civil War; and the final three, with the era of Reconstruction.

The lectures on the period 1852–1861 emphasize the failure of established institutions to cope with such volatile issues as the Fugitive Slave Act of 1850 and the extension of slavery into the federal territories, highlighting the process by which Americans in the North and the South increasingly came to expect the worst from each other. The sectional splits in major Protestant denominations, such as the Baptists and Methodists; the collapse of the second-party system of Whigs and Democrats; and the Supreme Court's seeming championing of the southern position on slavery extension in the Dred Scott case of 1857 contributed to a situation in which sectionalism flourished. The Kansas-Nebraska Act of 1854, the caning of Massachusetts Senator Charles Sumner in the Senate chamber in 1856, John Brown's raid on Harpers Ferry in 1859, and the Republican triumph in 1860, which gave an overtly sectional party control of the presidency, marked milestones on a path toward a breakup of the Union.

That breakup came in the winter and spring of 1860–1861 with the secession of 11 slave states and the creation of the Confederate States of America. The six lectures devoted to the war years, 1861–1865, assess the relative strengths and weaknesses of each side, trace the ebb and flow of military campaigning, discuss the quality of military leadership, examine the forces that brought emancipation to the fore, and describe the impact of the conflict on the respective home fronts. These lectures illuminate the many connections between the military and civilian spheres and emphasize that U.S. victory was far from a certainty until the last winter of the conflict. This group of lectures also underscores the immense scope of the war, its shattering human and material cost, what it resolved and did not resolve, and its implications for political and economic development in the postwar years.

The postwar era witnessed a seismic political struggle in the North over who would set the terms under which former Confederate states would be restored to full partnership in the Union. The lectures on Reconstruction explore the break between President Andrew Johnson and Republicans in Congress, the reasons behind Johnson's impeachment, passage of the 14th and 15th Amendments to the Constitution, and the establishment and functioning of congressional Reconstruction in the South. This portion of the course counters the still-popular idea, promulgated by the immensely successful film *Gone with the Wind* and other films and works of fiction, that the postwar years saw the white South subjected to unparalleled political corruption under Republican-led state governments. It closes with an examination of the Compromise of 1877, which brought an end to Reconstruction, and a consideration of whether Reconstruction should be reckoned as a lost opportunity for black Americans. ■

Sectional Tensions Escalate
Lecture 37

We call the late 1850s the "antebellum" period—the end of the antebellum period—meaning "ante," before, and "bellum," war. People then didn't use that expression, of course. They didn't know that they were living in a time just before a war would erupt.

The fugitive slave law poisoned sectional relations in the wake of the Compromise of 1850. Harriett Beecher Stowe wrote *Uncle Tom's Cabin* to protest the law. The 1852 book became a bestseller on both sides of the Atlantic. Many in the North applauded Stowe's critique of slavery. The South reacted angrily, banning the book in some places and offering a number of ineffective proslavery novels in response.

The Anthony Burns case stirred northern opposition to the fugitive slave law. Burns escaped from Virginia to Boston in 1854 but was returned to slavery after Franklin Pierce's Democratic administration employed federal power. Several northern states responded by passing new personal liberty laws designed to frustrate the return of fugitive slaves. The South deplored northern efforts to use state power to hinder enforcement of federal law. The issue of fugitive slaves thus witnessed northern advocacy of states' rights and southern demands for more central power.

The second American party system fractured between 1852 and 1856. The system had pitted national Democratic and Whig parties against one another since the 1830s. Internal party tensions regarding slavery weakened the Whigs in 1852. The Democrats nominated Franklin Pierce, a northern "Doughface" who strongly supported southern positions regarding slavery. The Whigs fought bitterly before nominating Winfield Scott after 53 ballots. Many southern Whigs supported the pro-southern Pierce, who won by a large margin and carried all but two southern states.

Passage of the Kansas-Nebraska Act of 1854 influenced both parties and rescinded the Missouri Compromise. The act's call for popular sovereignty in the territories alienated Whigs in the slaveholding South. Many antislavery northern Whigs also left the party. The Democratic Party became more pronounced in its southern leanings.

The American, or Know-Nothing, Party briefly seemed destined to replace the dying Whigs. The American Party attracted voters distressed by the flood of new Catholic immigrants and won some national and local success in 1854–1855 before succumbing to internal stresses related to slavery by 1856.

Stephen A. Douglas opposed the proslavery Lecompton Constitution for Kansas in 1857.

The Republican Party, founded on opposition to the extension of slavery, emerged as the principal rival to the Democrats by 1856. The party attracted some Know-Nothings and many Free-Soil Democrats. Sectionalism dominated the election of 1856. The Democrats nominated James Buchanan, another northern Doughface. The Republicans nominated John C. Frémont, an antislavery man famous for leading army explorations in the West. The Know-Nothings nominated former president Millard Fillmore. Buchanan won with a strongly sectional vote. He carried all but one slave state (Fillmore carried Maryland) and did well in parts of the Lower North. Frémont carried New England and much of the Upper North.

Sectional strife over slavery already had taken a toll on some of the Protestant denominations. The Methodists divided in 1844. Methodists originally had held a strong stance against slavery, but the church had accommodated its southern members for many years. The Methodist Episcopal Church, South, was founded in 1845 with a strong defense of slavery as a positive good.

The Baptists divided in 1845; the national convention's refusal to appoint slaveholding missionaries triggered the split. Southern churches organized the Southern Baptist Convention in Augusta, Georgia.

The Presbyterians avoided a formal division in the 1840s but suffered from sectional divisions. By 1837, "Old School" and "New School" Presbyterians reflected sectional tensions in the church. New School membership was centered in the free states. Southernerns were predominantly Old School. In May 1861, the Old School Presbyterians divided along sectional lines.

The Episcopal Church did not divide. Church leaders stressed political realities rather than raising highly charged theological points. For the most part, the Episcopal Church in the Confederacy closely resembled the national church. The Catholic Church remained largely aloof from debates about slavery.

"Bleeding Kansas" placed sectional animosities on grim display. The Kansas-Nebraska Act had sought to finesse the question of extending slavery into the territories by allowing residents to decide for themselves whether to accept the institution. Stephen A. Douglas had pushed for this doctrine of popular sovereignty. The doctrine alienated anti-extensionists in the North and pro-extensionists in the South.

> **Anti-extensionists in the North and pro-extensionists in the South squared off against one another in Kansas, and not just rhetorically: They moved into Kansas and began killing each other.**

Violence erupted in Kansas between proslavery and antislavery elements. President Pierce sided with proslavery forces in Kansas. Senator Charles Sumner of Massachusetts was caned on the floor of the Senate in 1856 after delivering a speech critical of the proslavery forces in Kansas. The question of slavery in Kansas was not resolved by the end of the decade. President James Buchanan supported the proslavery Lecompton Constitution for Kansas in 1857, which Congress eventually voted against. Stephen A. Douglas opposed it, thereby ending his chances of carrying the South as a presidential candidate in 1860. Buchanan's support for admission of Kansas as a slave state marked him as a thoroughly pro-southern Democrat. ■

Suggested Reading

William J. Cooper, *The South and the Politics of Slavery, 1828–1856.*

David Herbert Donald, *Charles Sumner and the Coming of the Civil War.*

James M. McPherson, *Battle Cry of Freedom: The Civil War Era*, chaps. 3–5.

David M. Potter, *The Impending Crisis, 1848–1861*, chaps. 5–10, 12.

Albert J. Von Rank, *The Trials of Anthony Burns.*

Questions to Consider

1. Did the North and South have good reasons to fear each other's influence on the course of national affairs?

2. Would a serious crisis have been possible in the absence of slavery?

Drifting Toward Disaster
Lecture 38

We left off, in our last lecture, with the discussion of the violence in Kansas Territory that erupted between proslavery and antislavery advocates. The Kansas-Nebraska Act had proved to be one of the most divisive pieces of legislation ever passed by the United States Congress.

Three events in particular contributed to escalating sectional tensions: The Supreme Court's *Dred Scott* decision in 1857; the Illinois senatorial contest between Abraham Lincoln and Stephen A. Douglas in 1858; and John Brown's raid on Harpers Ferry, Virginia, in 1859. The Court rendered a landmark decision in the *Dred Scott* case, which had enormous impact on sectional feelings in the North and South. The history of the case stretched back several years. It concerned a slave who had taken up residence in a free state and proceeded to sue for his freedom. Both the composition of the Court and President James Buchanan were important factors in the case. The Court's ruling had two important elements: Dred Scott was not a citizen, and Congress could not keep slavery out of the territories.

The response to the decision was heated. Many in the North, and especially in the Republican Party, reacted angrily. Most of the South applauded the decision. The Court emerged from the case tarnished; it had joined the list of national institutions plagued by sectional strife. Political parties already had been compromised as institutions capable of muting sectional problems.

Some northerners considered an alliance between East and West. The eastern and western non-slave states had many economic ties. Many northerners saw the South as a block to national economic development. The Republicans called for a Homestead Act, a tariff, and various internal improvements.

The Lincoln-Douglas debates in the 1858 Illinois senatorial election had national implications. The candidates and their issues presented a clear choice to voters. A series of famous debates featured disagreement over issues related to slavery. Douglas sought to finesse the issue of slavery's expansion into

> **Events from *Dred Scott* through John Brown's raid, though immensely disruptive in terms of sectional discord, had not brought the nation to the brink of war.**

the territories. Lincoln addressed the morality of slavery and expansion and advocated the ultimate extinction of slavery, although he rejected the label of abolitionist.

The election had enormous impact on Lincoln's and Douglas's careers. Douglas's positions in the debates weakened him as a presidential candidate, while Lincoln emerged onto the national stage.

John Brown's raid on Harpers Ferry sent shock waves through the nation. Brown had been a violent and controversial foe of slavery. A believer in immediate emancipation, he hoped the raid would ignite a general slave uprising in the South. Brown failed in his immediate goal of freeing the slaves, but the raid had significant impact. News of the raid polarized the nation. Many people in the North cheered Brown's actions; the raid spread fear of slave insurrection through the South. He and six of his followers were tried and executed in Virginia.

The nation was not yet at the brink of war. Still, an atmosphere of distrust set the context for the campaign of 1860. ∎

Suggested Reading

David Herbert Donald, *Lincoln*, chaps. 8–9.

Harold Holzer, ed., *The Lincoln-Douglas Debates*.

James M. McPherson, *Battle Cry of Freedom: The Civil War Era*, chaps. 6–7.

David M. Potter, *The Impending Crisis, 1848–1861*, chaps. 11–15.

Questions to Consider

1. What does reaction to John Brown's raid in the North suggest about the depth of antislavery sentiment outside the slaveholding states?

2. What national institutions could have broken the cycle of increasing sectional antipathy?

The Coming of War
Lecture 39

> In this lecture, we will analyze the campaign; examine the secession of the seven states of the Lower South and the establishment of the Confederate States of America; discuss northern attitudes toward the Lower South's departure from the Union; and close with analysis of the crisis at Fort Sumter.

The 1860 presidential campaign was waged by four candidates on four different platforms. The Democratic Party fractured during the campaign: The regular Democrats nominated Stephen A. Douglas and affirmed their support for popular sovereignty. The southern minority nominated John C. Breckinridge.

The Republican Party, meeting in Chicago, selected a moderate candidate: Several principal contenders failed in early ballots. Lincoln's supporters crafted a winning strategy that united several regions outside the South. The platform accepted slavery where it existed but called for barring it from the federal territories. The Constitutional Union Party attempted to avoid the issue of slavery. John Bell of Tennessee won that party's nomination. The platform ignored slavery and called for support of the Constitution and the Union.

The campaign offered the spectacle of a nation in trauma. All four candidates professed devotion to the Union. Lincoln won easily in the Electoral College, carrying every northern state except New Jersey. Lincoln's opponents polled roughly 60 percent of the popular vote. The election prompted heated reactions. Many southerners considered the Republican triumph a threat to slavery. Those who voted for Lincoln insisted that the South must abide by the verdict of the ballot box.

The Lower South reacted decisively to Lincoln's election. Although Secessionist sentiment was not unanimous in the seven states, beginning with South Carolina, seven states left the Union between December 20, 1860, and

February 1, 1861. Secessionists mounted strong arguments in favor of the constitutionality of secession.

The secessionists established a new slaveholding republic called the Confederate States of America. The Montgomery convention produced essentially moderate work. The Confederate and United States Constitutions offer an interesting comparison. Though they are very similar, the former specifically called for state sovereignty and protected the institution of slavery. The convention selected Jefferson Davis as provisional president. Was secession a revolution? The delegates insisted that they were returning to the principles of 1776.

> **On April 15, Lincoln called for 75,000 volunteers to suppress the rebellion, and that is the key call that sent the Upper South out of the Union.**

The nation reacted to news of secession in various ways. Northern sentiment was initially divided. President-elect Lincoln remained aloof. Efforts at compromise failed.

The crisis at Fort Sumter precipitated the outbreak of war. Lincoln faced a volatile situation when he took office in March 1861. Seven states had left the Union, and other slave states might follow. Northern opinion was hardening against the Deep South and secessionists.

Lincoln's first inaugural address set a stern tone. It upheld the Republican platform from the election of 1860 and promised to leave slavery alone in the South, while advocating its prohibition in the territories. It placed the onus of saving or dismantling the nation on the South. It also placed Fort Sumter in the national spotlight. Lincoln's decision to resupply Fort Sumter triggered violence. Lincoln discussed the issue with his cabinet and other advisers. Davis and his advisers also debated how best to deal with Fort Sumter before deciding to fire on the federal garrison.

The bombardment of Fort Sumter in April 1861 brought immediate action. On April 15, Lincoln called for 75,000 volunteers to suppress the rebellion.

Four states of the Upper South seceded in the wake of Lincoln's call for volunteers. ■

Suggested Reading

William C. Davis, "A Government of Our Own": *The Making of the Confederacy*.

James M. McPherson, *Battle Cry of Freedom: The Civil War Era*, chaps. 7–8.

David M. Potter, *The Impending Crisis, 18481–1861*, chaps. 16–20.

Kenneth M. Stampp, *And the War Came: The North and the Secession Crisis*, 1860–61.

Emory M. Thomas, *The Confederate Nation, 1861–1865*, chap. 3.

Questions to Consider

1. What does the election of 1860 tell us about whether the American people believed there were true differences between the North and South?

2. Can you imagine a modern election in which the candidate of either the Democratic or Republican Party did not appear on the ballot in several states (as was the case with Republicans in 1860)?

3. Did the secessionists of the Lower South make a good case that they were the heirs of the American revolutionary generation?

4. Would secession have been likely in 1860–1861 without the presence of slavery?

The First Year of Fighting
Lecture 40

> The firing on Fort Sumter and Lincoln's call for 75,000 volunteers set the stage for a transfer of sectional disputes from the political arena to the military arena. This lecture will stress that either side could have won the war and will offer an analysis of the strengths and weaknesses that each brought to the conflict.

The United States and the Confederacy each had strengths and weaknesses as they prepared for war. The United States enjoyed several key advantages. It held approximately a five-to-two advantage in military-age manpower, its manufacturing far outstripped that in the Confederacy, and it began the war with a regular army and navy. The Confederacy also possessed important strengths. It did not have to conquer the United States to win. Its armies would defend home ground—three-quarters of a million square miles. Its geographic size would pose a daunting obstacle to U.S. forces.

Several important factors favored neither side. The quality of military leadership was approximately equal; Lincoln and Davis both proved to be effective commanders-in-chief. And the responses of England and France remained to be seen.

Both sides hoped to gain the support of the border slave states. Kentucky sought unsuccessfully to remain neutral before opting to remain in the Union. A divided Missouri declined to secede but witnessed bitter guerrilla warfare. It sent about three times as many soldiers to the North as it did to the South. Maryland spurned secession but harbored significant pro-southern sentiment. Delaware did not flirt seriously with secession. A new border state was created when several dozen counties broke away from Virginia to form the new state of West Virginia.

Strategic planning and the battle of First Bull Run dominated the initial year of the war. The two sides pursued very different national strategies. The Confederacy sought to defend its borders, knowing that a tie was as

> In his typically audacious fashion, Lee was not thinking of simply holding his ground in northern Virginia. He was going to be thinking much more offensively.

good as a win strategically. Winfield Scott's Anaconda Plan, which proposed to split the Confederacy in two, provided a blueprint for U.S. victory.

First Bull Run, or Manassas (July, 21, 1861), gave the Confederacy an initial victory, which chastened the United States and encouraged the Confederacy. The campaign's strategy and tactics anticipated later battles.

The United States achieved mixed success with major offensives in the first half of 1862. Union forces gained the upper hand in the western theater. U.S. Grant's capture of Forts Henry and Donelson opened key river routes into the Confederacy. Grant's success at Shiloh in early April solidified Union gains in Tennessee. In two days at Shiloh, more Americans were shot than in all previous American battles to that time.

The Confederacy eventually prevailed at the Second Battle of Bull Run, August 1862.

Confederates blunted U.S. efforts in the eastern theater. Robert E. Lee's victory in the Seven Days campaign in June and July turned back George B. McClellan's offensive against Richmond. There were even more casualties than at Shiloh. Lee followed up his success at Richmond with a victory at Second Bull Run (Manassas) in August of 1862. ■

Suggested Reading

Bruce Catton, *Terrible Swift Sword*, chaps. 1–7.

Douglas Southall Freeman, *Lee's Lieutenants*, vol. 1; vol. 2, chaps. 1–7.

Hattaway, Herman, and Jones, Archer, *How the North Won: A Military History of the Civil War*, chaps. 1–7.

James M. McPherson, *Battle Cry of Freedom: The Civil War Era*, chaps. 9–13, 15.

Emory M. Thomas, *The Confederate Nation*, chaps. 4–5.

Questions to Consider

1. Reviewing the factors covered in this lecture, how would you assess each side's chances for victory?

2. Is it possible to gauge accurately the impact of such intangibles as fighting to defend home and hearth?

Shifting Tides of Battle
Lecture 41

This lecture continues the military narrative for the 15 months between the summer of 1862 and the autumn of 1863, a period that confirmed for soldiers and civilians on both sides that the war would indeed be very long and bitter—much longer and much more bitter than anyone had imagined.

The year between the summer of 1862 and the summer of 1863 convinced Americans on both sides that the war would be long and bitter. This lecture traces some of the major military campaigns of this year, underscoring the enormous swings of morale behind the lines in the North and South as each side won victories and suffered defeats.

The Confederacy mounted a broad strategic counteroffensive in the autumn of 1862. Lee invaded Maryland in September. He hoped to achieve a range of goals: to hold the military initiative, to provision his army in the North, to help Democrats in the impending election, and to impress the Europeans. The campaign crested in Lee's defeat at the battle of Antietam on September 17, 1862, the bloodiest day in U.S. history.

Out West, the Confederates were also mounting an offensive, this one under Braxton Bragg, which moved through Tennessee into Kentucky. Bragg invaded Kentucky in September and, on October 8, fought what proved to be a tactical stalemate at Perryville. Just as Lee hoped that Marylanders would rally to his standard, Bragg also hoped to regain a lot of the ground lost in the very early campaigning in Tennessee.

Confederate general Robert E. Lee.

Bragg also had a political motive: He hoped Kentucky would rally to the Confederacy. The Confederates retreated after the battle of Perryville. It was not nearly as bloody a battle as Antietam, but at the end of the battle, Bragg decided to retreat from Kentucky, making it very much like Antietam in that regard.

Were these two autumn campaigns a turning point? The military effects slightly favored the United States—the Confederates retreated. But the United States failed to exploit its successes. Antietam assisted U.S. diplomatic efforts. Lee's failure convinced the British to back away from supporting the Confederacy. Lincoln used Antietam as a springboard to issue his preliminary proclamation of emancipation on September 22, 1862. Now the United States was officially opposed to slavery.

But the United States suffered a grim season of fighting in the winter of 1862 and the spring of 1863. The western theater yielded a mixed verdict. The battle of Stones River (Murfreesboro), December 31, 1862–January 2, 1863, brought stalemate in Tennessee. U. S. Grant's initial movements against Vicksburg ended in failure.

It seemed very likely to many people—including Abraham Lincoln—by August of 1864, that the United States' effort to force those seceded states back into the Union might fail.

Lee won two major victories in the eastern theater. The battle of Fredericksburg in December 1862 presented Lincoln with a crisis, and the battle of Chancellorsville in May 1863 aggravated drooping Union morale. These campaigns greatly affected the two home fronts. The United States suffered from internal turmoil. Many people opposed conscription and emancipation. Antiwar political activity reached a peak with the Copperheads. The Confederacy took heart from Lee's victories. Lee and his army emerged as the great Confederate rallying point. Opposition to conscription and other government actions did not overbalance hope for Confederate independence.

The United States wove a tapestry of success in the summer and autumn of 1863: George G. Meade defeated Lee at Gettysburg on July 1–3. Lee's invasion of Pennsylvania won initial success, but the Union army turned back the Confederates in the largest battle of the war, in which more than 50,000 men were killed, wounded, or missing in battle. Ulysses. S. Grant showed determination after a string of early failures and captured Vicksburg on July 4. The capture of Vicksburg gave the United States control of the Mississippi River.

Grant defeated Bragg at Chattanooga on November 24–25. Bragg's victory at Chickamauga in September had threatened Union control of Chattanooga. Grant's victory severed a vital rail connection between the eastern and western Confederacy.

Was the summer of 1863 the war's decisive turning point? Lee's string of victories was reversed, but Union victory that summer wasn't assured. Gettysburg seems much more conclusive from our perspective than it did at the time. ■

Suggested Reading

Bruce Catton, *Never Call Retreat*, chaps. 1–5.

———, *Terrible Swift Sword*, chap. 7.

Douglass Southall Freeman, Lee's Lieutenants, vol. 2, chaps. 9–37; vol. 3, chapters 1–10.

Hattaway, Herman, and Jones, Archer, *How the North Won: A Military History of the Civil War*, chaps. 8–14.

James M. McPherson, *Battle Cry of Freedom: The Civil War Era*, chaps. 17, 19, 21–22.

Questions to Consider

1. Should the Confederacy have avoided invasions of the United States?

2. How broad a chronological context is necessary to gauge the impact of individual military campaigns?

Diplomatic Clashes and Sustaining the War
Lecture 42

This lecture will look first at diplomacy: an arena dominated by Confederate efforts to secure formal recognition from Great Britain and France, and the Lincoln administration's countermoves. The lecture also will examine the enormous difficulty and cost of fielding and maintaining large armies.

This lecture shifts the focus from the battlefield to the home front. The U.S. and Great Britain devoted considerable attention to diplomacy with the European powers. Cotton dominated early Confederate diplomatic planning. Confederates had expected British dependence on cotton to be decisive, but British development of other sources of cotton, in Egypt and India, defeated Confederate expectations.

The U.S. naval blockade complicated diplomatic affairs. The blockade did not meet the letter of international law, so the Confederacy expected Great Britain to refuse to accept the legality of the blockade. Much to the Confederates disappointment, Britain did not challenge the federal blockade because the Royal Navy almost never met the letter of international law itself.

The closest that Britain and the U.S. came to armed conflict was in November of 1861, when a U.S. warship stopped the British vessel Trent and seized two Confederate diplomats. But the worst diplomatic crisis actually occurred in the autumn of 1862, when Britain's prime minister was advised to try to mediate an end to the American war because it appeared the Confederates were winning. Britain's foreign secretary said that if Britain failed to mediate an end to the war, they ought to recognize the Confederacy as an independent state. France was ready to follow Great Britain's lead.

But news of two factors—the North's success in the battle of Antietam topped off by Lincoln's preliminary Emancipation Proclamation—dealt a major blow to Confederate hopes for European recognition. Considering Lincoln's

Confederate soldiers. Slavery allowed the Confederacy to mobilize a higher percentage of its white military-age males than the Union could.

proclamation, it became obvious that antislavery Britain would never ally itself with the overtly slaveholding Confederate States of America.

Taking a step back, let's consider the challenges of supplying two huge American armies during the Civil War. The two nations labored diligently to fill their ranks. The Confederacy struggled with a shallow pool of white manpower, but slavery allowed the Confederacy to mobilize most of its white military-age males. Confederate conscription legislation in 1862–1864 yielded men and controversy by arbitrarily extending enlistment periods and the draft age.

The United States worked with a much larger pool of possible recruits. The United States also resorted to a controversial draft, in March of 1863. Black men supplied much-needed manpower after 1863. Was it a rich man's war and a poor man's fight? Both armies, in fact, were composed of a good cross-section of the population.

The two sides financed their war efforts through various means. The Confederacy used taxes, bonds, and paper money to fund the war. It never achieved a sound fiscal footing; various factors led to a severe spiral of inflation. The United States proved far more successful in financing its war. It also used taxes, bonds, and paper money—but in far different proportions. The United States avoided terrible inflation.

> **Overall, the Confederacy proved able to produce most of what it needed, and to produce it in such a way as to place its armies on pretty much equal footing with United States armies in the field.**

Both sides proved quite effective in supplying their armies. The U.S. economy easily produced adequate war-related material. The Confederacy used innovative means to produce necessary goods. The Confederates usually operated at a material disadvantage, but not a decisive one. U.S. armies were often somewhat better supplied. The Union example anticipated how the United States would supply its armies in later wars. ■

Suggested Reading

D. P. Crook, *The North, the South, and the Powers, 1861–1865*.

Howard Jones, U*nion in Peril: The Crisis over British Intervention in the Civil War*.

James M. McPherson, *Battle Cry of Freedom: The Civil War Era*, chaps. 12, 14, 18, 20, 22.

Phillip Shaw Paludan, "A People's Contest": *The Union and the Civil War, 1861–1865*, pt. 2.

Emory M. Thomas, *The Confederate Nation*, chap. 8.

Questions to Consider

1. Can you imagine any circumstances under which Britain or France would have sent the type of aid to the Confederacy that France had given to the colonies during the American Revolution?

2. Do you believe a smaller pool of manpower or the disparity in resources was more damaging to the Confederacy?

Behind the Lines—Politics and Economies
Lecture 43

This lecture continues our attention to the home fronts, offering a comparative look at politics and economics in the United States and the Confederacy. ... [It also] highlights the fact that both the United States and the Confederacy dealt with political problems in the course of the war, but did so in very different ways.

The United States maintained a vigorous two-party system, even waging the heated 1864 presidential contest in the midst of war, while the Confederacy self-consciously shunned formal party structures. The war brought enormous dislocation to the Confederate home front. Political divisions appeared early and persisted throughout the war, although the Founders sought to avoid party politics.

There were various sources of political division. Pockets of strong unionism remained in most states. Supporters of states' rights aligned against those who supported stronger central authority. Ironically, the southern government was the most intrusive central government in U.S. history until the middle of the 20th century.

The Confederate notion that they could do without parties didn't really pan out. They had never named formal parties as the United States did, but what they developed were pro– and anti–Jefferson Davis factions. They were "states' rights" versus "willingness to tolerate more central power" factions, but much of it centered on Davis. Pro– and anti–Jefferson Davis factions grew inside and outside Congress. The vice president, Alexander Stephens, opposed Davis bitterly.

The Confederate economy weakened as the war progressed, and the transportation infrastructure suffered enormous damage. The problem wasn't so much lack of production but lack of transportation. Their inability to manufacture rolling stock and replacement rails further weakened the railroads. Severe shortages and spiraling inflation also caused economic hardship for much of the Confederate population, with inflation creating a barter economy in many places. By war's end, a barrel of flour cost $1,000 (soldiers were paid $18 a month).

Confederates reacted in different ways. Conscription, economic hardship, and the presence of U.S. armies caused many people to give up on the war effort. At least 105,000 deserted from the army during the war. Thousands of refugees struggled to rebuild their lives. Most people did their best and continued to support the Confederate cause. If not for this support, the Confederacy would have collapsed much sooner.

> **The grief shared by families both North and South was certainly identical. If you lose a husband, brother, son, or nephew, it doesn't matter whether you lived in Oneida, New York, or whether you lived in Fredericksburg, Virginia.**

The northern home front experienced a far different type of war. The Republicans and Democrats maintained a robust two-party system. The Republicans displaced the Democrats as the dominant party, and factions within the party contended for supremacy. Most Republicans agreed on broad policies to win the war, but the radical wing pushed harder for emancipation. Abraham Lincoln (a moderate) moved closer to their position over time.

The Democrats sought a proper wartime role. War Democrats supported the Lincoln administration on key issues. Peace Democrats questioned most of the Republican policies. Virtually all Democrats adamantly opposed emancipation, saying that the war was a struggle to restore the Union.

The election of 1864 served as a referendum on the war and emancipation. A series of critical Union victories propelled Lincoln to an election victory over George B. McClellan. Nearly 80 percent of soldiers cast their ballots for the Republicans.

The northern economy proved able to provide guns and butter in ample quantities. The agricultural sector outperformed the prewar economy in many ways—production of wheat, corn, and beef all increased. Some parts of the manufacturing sector suffered, while many others proved highly successful. In addition, the transportation network expanded and improved. While the infrastructure in the South was failing, it was being extended in the North.

The war also brought about a radical shift of wealth from the South to the North. The war allowed Republicans to enact legislation that pointed toward a modern capitalist colossus, and Congress created a more modern national banking system by issuing national bank notes. Three acts in particular were instrumental in the North's success:

- The Homestead Act (1862) opened western lands to many small farmers. Eighty million acres would be given out under the act.

- The Land-Grant College Act (1862) laid the foundation for universities that would offer practical training for engineers, farmers, and others.

- The Pacific Railroad Act, supported by federal loans, set the stage for transcontinental transportation links.

Although the impact of the war on the two sides was enormously different, the North and South shared one major experience: the feelings of grief for lost friends and family. ■

Suggested Reading

Richard E. Beringer, Herman Hattaway, Jones, Archer, and William N. Still, Jr., *Why the South Lost the Civil War*.

Leonard P. Curry, *Blueprint for Modern America: Nonmilitary Legislation of the First Civil War Congress*.

Drew Gilpin Faust, *Mothers of Invention: Women of the Slaveholding South in the American Civil War*.

Gary W. Gallagher, *The Confederate War*, chaps. 1–2.

James M. McPherson, *Battle Cry of Freedom: The Civil War Era*, chaps. 14, 18, 20, 23, 26.

Mark Neely, Jr., *The Union Divided: Party Conflict in the Civil War North*.

Phillip Shaw Paludan, "A People's Contest," chaps. 4–7, 10.

Heather Cox Richardson, *The Greatest Nation of the Earth: Republican Economic Policies during the Civil War*.

Questions to Consider

1. What might the United States have looked like in the late 19th century if the Republicans had lost the election of 1864?

2. Was military defeat or disaffection behind the lines more important in bringing ultimate Confederate failure?

African Americans in Wartime
Lecture 44

This lecture continues our explorations of topics removed from the principal military narrative of the war. It examines African Americans in the United States and in the Confederacy, with an emphasis on the fact that they, more than any other group of Americans, experienced profound change between 1861 and 1865.

Most obviously, the war killed the institution of slavery, under which more than 4 million black people lived and suffered when the war erupted. This lecture examines the experiences of African Americans in the North and the Confederacy, addressing, among other topics, black soldiers in U.S. military forces, the experience of hundreds of thousands of black refugees in the South, the weakening of the bonds of slavery in much of the Confederacy, and Confederate debates over emancipation late in the conflict.

The war resulted in freedom for enslaved black Americans but failed to answer a number of questions regarding the social and political status of the freed people. The ultimate question is, was it a war for union or freedom in 1861–1862?

Most northerners considered it a war for union. There was a strong belief in the mission of America as a beacon of freedom. Democrats supported fighting for union but strongly opposed fighting for black freedom. The Republican Party as a whole also saw the war as a struggle to restore the Union.

Black and white abolitionists and some radical Republicans argued that it was preeminently a war for emancipation and that only in such a war could America be a model for the world. However, Abraham Lincoln occupied a unique position. He had to do everything possible to keep the majority of northerners behind the war effort. The heavily Democratic and anti-emancipation border states loomed large in 1861–1862. Lincoln personally supported gradual, compensated, state-controlled emancipation.

District of Columbia Company E, 4th U.S. Colored Infantry, at Fort Lincoln.

The United States took halting steps toward emancipation early in the war. Congress ended slavery in the territories and the District of Columbia and struck at slavery in the Confederate states with the Confiscation Acts (1862).

Several generals also played a role in the process of bringing emancipation to the fore by attacking slavery. Benjamin Butler, for one, refused to return "contrabands" in 1861. And John Charles Frémont declared slaves held by rebels in Missouri free in 1861. In 1862, David Hunter declared slaves along the south Atlantic coast free. But Lincoln ordered Frémont and Hunter to rescind their orders because he was still worried about the border states and Democrats in the North.

Slaves continued to push the process forward by fleeing to Union lines and forcing the U.S. government to clarify their status. In all, about half a million African Americans fled during the war.

The Emancipation Proclamation of January 1, 1863, placed freedom at center stage. Lincoln took into account several factors in deciding to issue his proclamation:

- The border states had proved utterly intransigent.

- Northern Democrats gave no evidence of embracing emancipation.

- The proclamation would weaken the Confederate war effort.

- Many northerners stood ready to embrace a harder type of war.

The proclamation, justified by Lincoln as a war measure, had enormous impact. But it freed slaves only in the Confederacy and only in those areas not under U.S. military control. It divided northern white opinion in the short term. Some foreign observers described Lincoln's action as meaningless, but England and France backed away from the Confederacy, and the Confederacy reacted angrily.

Over the long term, the proclamation helped place black men in U.S. uniforms, deny black labor to the Confederacy, and swing European opinion to the Union side. In January 1865, the 13th Amendment, which banned slavery, narrowly passed in Congress and affirmed Lincoln's position. It was ratified after the war.

Nearly 200,000 black men served in U.S. military forces, with the northern opinion gradually supporting the idea of black soldiers. Most northerners and even many Democrats had the cynical attitude that it was better to risk black men's lives than white men's lives. They figured that fewer white soldiers might die if black soldiers served in large numbers.

Black soldiers also faced a struggle for equal treatment in the army. They initially earned less pay, and they were often relegated to noncombatant duty. Their performance in combat in such battles as Port Hudson, Milliken's Bend, and New Market Heights helped overcome prejudice. And by being in the military service, black men were able to establish their claims to citizenship.

The war had a major impact on African Americans in the Confederacy as well. Slave labor freed a high proportion of white men to fight, thereby keeping the economy running. African Americans also filled noncombatant roles in the Confederate army. The war weakened the institution of slavery in the Confederacy: The absence of white men loosened control on farms and plantations, and white refugees often could not maintain close control over slaves. Thousands of southern slaves fled and joined the U.S. army.

> **What wasn't answered was whether the freed black people were going to be equal. That was a question that would be left to Reconstruction.**

In 1864–1865, Confederates debated whether to arm slaves. Supporters said it was better to do so and win the war than not to do so and face Union victory. Opponents said that arming slaves called into question everything the Confederacy had been trying to safeguard. If slaves will make good soldiers, how can you pretend they're not really people and are so different from white people? The debate raged through the autumn of 1864 and into the spring of 1865, but in the end, the Confederate Congress voted to arm as many as 300,000 slaves—with no promise of freedom.

The war was a watershed for African Americans. The 13th Amendment killed slavery. Three and a half million slaves were freed in the Confederacy and another half million were liberated in the border states. The question of equality was left for later debate. ■

Suggested Reading

Ira Berlin et al., eds., *Free at Last: A Documentary History of Slavery, Freedom, and the Civil War*.

Robert F. Durden, *The Gray and the Black: The Confederate Debate on Emancipation*.

Joseph T. Glatthaar, *Forged in Battle: The Civil War Alliance of Black Soldiers and White Officers*.

James M. McPherson, *Battle Cry of Freedom: The Civil War Era*, chaps. 10–11, 16, 28.

Clarence L. Mohr, *On the Threshold of Freedom: Masters and Slaves in Civil War Georgia*.

Questions to Consider

1. Some historians have commented that slaves gained "nothing but freedom" from the war. How would you judge the importance of emancipation in the lives of African Americans of the mid-19th century?

2. What does the Confederate debate over arming slaves suggest about the impact of the war on slavery in the South?

The Union Drive to Victory
Lecture 45

The outcome of the war remained uncertain as late as the summer of 1864. Union morale reached its nadir during July and August, prompting Abraham Lincoln to doubt that he and the Republicans would be victorious in the November elections.

Successes at Atlanta and in the Shenandoah Valley in September and October turned the tide decisively in favor of the Union, and Lincoln's reelection guaranteed that the war would be prosecuted vigorously to the end. Grant was promoted to general-in-chief in March 1864, and the northern people believed they finally had a champion who could defeat Lee. Grant put together a grand blueprint for strategic victory, moving with his men to fight Lee while sending William T. Sherman to capture Atlanta. However, despite the hardships of a difficult winter, the Confederates retained high expectations about Lee's ability to win victories.

U.S. morale plummeted between May and early August of 1864. Sherman failed to capture Atlanta immediately, and the first phase of the confrontation in Virginia between Lee and Grant yielded no striking northern success. Casualties reached unprecedented levels, the Confederate capital in Richmond seemed as safe as ever, and secondary northern operations failed. The two sides lost 100,000 men in the campaign before they got to Petersburg in June.

Civilians watched the campaigns closely. Confederates believed the Republicans would lose in the fall 1864 elections if southern armies avoided major defeats. Many in the North doubted that the Confederacy could be subdued.

The tide turned decisively between late August and early November: Admiral Farragut won the battle of Mobile Bay in August; in early September, Sherman captured Atlanta; and Philip H. Sheridan defeated Confederates in the Shenandoah Valley in September and October. Thus the Republicans won a smashing victory in the November elections.

A final round of military campaigns ended the war. Sherman marched through Georgia and the Carolinas in 1864–1865, moving in a 60-mile swath and leaving destruction in his wake. Grant laid siege to Lee at Petersburg, June 1864–March 1865, causing Petersburg to fall on April 3 and Richmond to be captured.

In April 1865, Lee retreated from Petersburg to Appomattox, where he surrendered on April 12. Grant, at Lincoln's behest, offered very generous terms. But Lincoln's assassination on April 14 dampened northern enthusiasm for victory. Assassin John Wilkes Booth was tracked down and killed, and four alleged co-conspirators were hanged.

> **The question of the permanence of the Union was settled forever. The United States was—and would remain—a single nation, within which the states occupied a secondary place.**

Robert E. Lee's surrender at Appomattox Courthouse is generally considered the end of the Civil War.

The war extracted an enormous human and material cost. More than 620,000 soldiers died: 360,000 in the North; 260,000 in the South. In all, 1.1 million were killed and wounded. The Confederate economy lay in ruins, with the total cost to the South at about $4 billion. Two-thirds of assessed wealth was destroyed on the southern landscape, much of which bore deep scars. Both governments had expended unprecedented sums of money.

The war permanently answered several questions. The inviolability of the Union had been guaranteed, and slavery was dead with the adoption of the 13th Amendment in 1865. The superiority of central power over local and state government had been demonstrated. Meanwhile, other important issues remained unresolved. For example, what would the former Confederate states have to do to regain full partnership in the Union, and would black Americans achieve full equality in the restored nation? ■

Suggested Reading

Bruce Catton, *Never Call Retreat*, chaps. 5–7.

Douglas Southall Freeman, *Lee's Lieutenants*, vol. 3, chaps. 11–37.

Gary W. Gallagher, *The Confederate War*, chaps. 3–4.

Hattaway, Herman, and Jones, Archer, *How the North Won: A Military History of the Civil War*. Chaps. 15–20.

James M. McPherson, *Battle Cry of Freedom: The Civil War Era*, chaps. 24–28, epilogue.

Phillip Shaw Paludan, "A People's Contest," conclusion.

Edward Steers, Jr., *Blood on the Moon: The Assassination of Abraham Lincoln*.

Questions to Consider

1. Can you think of another bitter civil war that ended without executions or other severe punishments for the losers? How do you account for the North's leniency?

2. Would you call the Civil War a "total" war? A "modern" war?

Presidential Reconstruction
Lecture 46

With this lecture, we begin a three-part discussion of the turbulent period of Reconstruction. Our coverage will extend from 1863–1877, with a heavy emphasis on the 12 years following Appomattox.

Debates in the North over how best to bring the Confederate states back into the Union began while the war still raged. Lincoln and Congress each sought to control the process, and this struggle between the executive and legislative branches continued when Andrew Johnson assumed the presidency following Lincoln's assassination.

Several questions dominated much of the debate:

- How drastic would be the required changes in southern society?

- What place would black people have in the reconstructed South?

- Would the president or Congress have the greater influence in setting policy?

- Would the moderate or radical Republicans gain the upper hand?

Lincoln had offered his 10 Percent Plan in December 1863. It included a lenient offer of amnesty to Confederates who would take the oath of allegiance and accept slavery's abolition, exempting some Confederate officials from its generous terms. It set a low bar for establishing state governments that Lincoln would recognize. When 10 percent of the voting population pledged its loyalty, a new government could be established in a Confederate state. Louisiana, Tennessee, and Arkansas eventually took advantage of Lincoln's plan.

Congress called for a harsher peace with the Wade-Davis Bill of July 1864. It set more stringent requirements for loyalty—50 percent rather than 10 percent—and required an oath pledging that one had always supported the United States. It outlined a far more difficult process to set up new governments. Lincoln killed the bill with a pocket veto, prompting a stern rebuke in the form of Congress's Wade-Davis "Manifesto."

Andrew Johnson continued presidential reconstruction following Lincoln's assassination. He initially spoke harshly about how he would treat southern traitors. But in May 1865, he offered a lenient plan. He did so without calling Congress into a special session or talking with Republican leaders.

Johnson offered amnesty to almost all former Confederates. He envisioned setting up new governments in southern states without the participation of black men, and he pardoned thousands of ex-Confederates who were exempted from his general offer of amnesty.

> "In short, the Democratic Party may be described as a common sewer into which is emptied every element of inhumanity and barbarism which has discolored the age."—Governor Oliver Morton of Indiana

Southern states responded defiantly. Many ex-Confederates won election to state governments. Some states enacted "Black Codes" that denied African Americans basic rights and legal protections, while some states hesitated to ratify the 13th Amendment abolishing slavery.

Congress and Johnson faced a crisis in 1866, when Republicans in Congress tried to assert their power. They set up a Joint Committee on Reconstruction that was dominated by moderates, and they passed a civil rights bill and extended the life of the Freedmen's Bureau. Republicans also passed and sent to the states for ratification the 14th Amendment, which gave citizenship, but not the vote, to African Americans and guaranteed them equal protection under the laws.

Johnson fought back unsuccessfully. He vetoed the Civil Rights Bill and the Freedmen's Bureau extension (both were overridden), and he opposed the 14th Amendment as unconstitutional. Johnson's hope for a new national conservative party withered and died when the Republicans swept the 1866 off-year elections. ■

Suggested Reading

Herman Belz, *Reconstructing the Union: Theory and Practice during the Civil War*.

Dan T. Carter, *When the War Was Over: The Failure of Self-Reconstruction in the South, 1865–1867*.

David Herman Donald, Jean Harvey Baker, and Michael F. Holt, *The Civil War and Reconstruction*, chaps. 26–28.

Eric Foner, *Reconstruction: America's Unfinished Revolution, 1863–1877*, pts. 1–6.

William C. Harris, *With Charity for All: Lincoln and the Restoration of the Union*.

William Lee Rose, *Rehearsal for Reconstruction: The Port Royal Experiment*.

Brooks D. Simpson, *The Reconstruction Presidents*, chaps. 1–3.

Questions to Consider

1. What role would the radical Republicans likely have played in the absence of intransigence on the part of the former Confederate states?

2. Did much of the wrangling between Johnson and Congress have more to do with traditional tensions between rival branches of government rather than with the merits of Reconstruction policy?

Congress Takes Command
Lecture 47

The Republicans had triumphed in 1866, and now they were going to move into another phase of their relationship with Johnson that would leave them completely triumphant. The elections of 1866 showed that the North was fully behind the 14th Amendment, but four southern states would have to ratify it before it became law.

Radical Republicans assumed greater power after the elections of 1866. Reacting stubbornly following the elections, Johnson urged southern states to oppose the 14th Amendment. Only Tennessee ratified it. Moderate Republicans responded by moving closer to the radical position.

Congress engaged in a flurry of action in 1867. It passed the first and second Reconstruction Acts (over Johnson's vetoes). These acts divided the old Confederacy (except Tennessee, which had rejoined the Union) into five military districts. They also mandated new constitutions in the southern states and required states to ratify the 14th Amendment before readmission. Congress also passed the Tenure of Office Act (over Johnson's veto), limiting presidential authority over removal of some appointed officials.

The confrontation between Congress and the president culminated in the impeachment of Johnson in February 1868. Johnson's vetoes and continued resistance alienated most Republicans. Radical Republicans called for impeachment when Johnson removed Secretary of War

Ulysses S. Grant, president of the United States from 1869 to 1877.

Edwin M. Stanton without senatorial approval (under the Tenure of Office Act). Moderate Republicans at first hesitated but fell in line when radicals made their case. The 126–47 vote for impeachment in the House followed strict party lines.

Johnson's lawyers mounted an able defense. They questioned whether Johnson was guilty of any crimes for which the Constitution allows impeachment. And they questioned whether he had violated the Tenure of Office Act. The Senate, needing a two-thirds majority, failed to convict by a single vote, 35–19. Some moderates and conservatives did not want to set the precedent of a conviction.

Reconstruction proceeded in the South while Johnson and Congress dueled. Voters were registered: 735,000 blacks and 635,000 whites were enrolled, making 5 of the 10 southern states black majorities. New state constitutions were written, and seven states ratified the constitutions and set up governments that ratified the 14th Amendment in 1868. By 1869–1870, all former Confederate states had been readmitted.

> The *New York Times* spoke for many in April 1870 when it put it this way: "Let us have done with Reconstruction. The country is sick and tired of it. Let us have peace."

The election of 1868 served as a referendum on Republican Reconstruction policies. The election, along with ratification of the 15th Amendment, seemed to signal the end of Reconstruction. Democrats, of course, attacked Reconstruction. They nominated Oration Seymour of New York to run against Republican nominee Ulysses S. Grant. The parties waged a vicious, sometimes violent campaign. The newly created Ku Klux Klan intimidated voters, black and white, across the South. Grant won the presidency, and Republicans retained control of Congress.

The Republicans turned to black suffrage after the election. They drafted the 15th Amendment, prohibiting states from denying the franchise to black men. Eleven of 21 northern states still denied the right to vote to blacks. The final three unreconstructed states ratified the 15th Amendment as a condition of readmission to the Union, and the amendment became law in 1870. Many Republicans and others in the North considered Reconstruction as having ended. ■

Suggested Reading

David Herman Donald, Jean Harvey Baker, and Michael F. Holt, *The Civil War and Reconstruction*, chaps. 29–32.

Eric Foner, *Reconstruction*, pts. 7–9.

Brooks D. Simpson, *The Reconstruction Presidents*, chaps. 4–5.

Hans L. Trefousse, *Impeachment of a President: Andrew Johnson, the Blacks, and Reconstruction*.

Questions to Consider

1. How did Andrew Johnson's intransigent opposition to expanding black civil and political rights eventually work to the advantage of African Americans?

2. Did radical Reconstruction mark a logical expansion of, or a departure from, the principal Union goals set during the Civil War?

Reconstruction Ends
Lecture 48

In this lecture, we'll encounter the deeply flawed, but amazingly tenacious, view of Republican Reconstruction in the South as a time when corrupt state governments—dominated by carpetbaggers, scalawags, and their African American allies—ran roughshod over the white South.

For many decades, Republican Reconstruction evoked images of corrupt state governments running roughshod over the white South. These images applauded the efforts of the Ku Klux Klan and other similar groups to "liberate" the South from Republican rule. And books and films, such as *Gone with the Wind*, have perpetuated this myth.

The reality of southern Republican rule offers a far different picture. The level of corruption there was roughly comparable to that of northern state and municipal governments. Carpetbaggers and scalawags were not especially venal or corrupt, and black politicians never dominated southern politics. Although black voters constituted 80 percent of the Republican voters in the South, white politicians dominated the party. Only 16 African Americans were elected to Congress; none was elected governor of a state. Only in South Carolina did black politicians hold a significant number of governmental positions.

The Republican efforts to build a strong base in the South were hindered because the party had no roots among white voters and was attempting to unite groups with no history of common effort. Democrats exploited these Republican weaknesses to recapture, or "redeem," southern state governments.

Republican state governments in the South actually compiled a creditable record. They enacted social, judicial, and governmental reforms and faced terrorist opposition from such groups as the Ku Klux Klan (though convictions of Klan members were rare).

The election of 1872 witnessed a realignment of the parties. By 1871–1872, several factors led to a movement to unseat Grant as the Republican nominee in the North: Rumors of Republican corruption in the South, empathy for white southerners on the part of many white northerners who believed that enough had been done to bring the nation back together, and charges of corruption against his administration.

There was a lot of corruption in the Grant administration, but Grant himself was not corrupt. This corruption hurt the image of the Republican Party, and there was a movement in the North to unseat Grant among a group who called themselves Liberal Republicans. This group broke with Grant and nominated Horace Greeley. But Grant won a clear victory, with 56 percent of the popular vote. This result showed that the North was not ready to forgive the South.

> [The United States] could have seen that a more equal, biracial society was in place, that Reconstruction marked the end of a period where black people were freed, but they were denied almost everything else.

Republicans lost ground in the years following Grant's reelection. The Panic of 1873 hurt them as the ruling party, and a growing number of northern voters decided that Reconstruction had lasted long enough. In 1874, Democrats won control of the House of Representatives. And by 1875, Republicans controlled only four southern state governments.

In the state elections of 1875, Democrats put in operation the "Mississippi Plan," which entailed economic and social pressure on the 10–15 percent of white Mississippians who called themselves Republicans, in an effort to bring them over into the Democratic Party. It also entailed brutal intimidation of black voters. White Democrats held carefully orchestrated "riots," as they called them, whenever Republicans gathered at political picnics and other political speaking occasions.

The election of 1876 and the Compromise of 1877 signaled the end of Reconstruction. Disputed voting returns in Louisiana, South Carolina, and Florida cast the electoral verdict in doubt. Republican Rutherford B. Hayes needed all three states to win; Tilden would win with any one of the three. An electoral commission voting along straight party lines gave all three states and the election to Hayes. The Compromise brought an end to the dispute. Hayes made promises to the South, including withdrawal of the last federal troops, and Democrats agreed to Hayes's election. ■

Suggested Reading

David Herman Donald, Jean Harvey Baker, and Michael F. Holt, *The Civil War and Reconstruction*, chaps. 30–34.

Eric Foner, *Reconstruction*, pts. 9–12.

Questions to Consider

1. Is it possible to detect legacies of the Reconstruction era in contemporary American society?

2. Should we view Reconstruction as an overall success or as a lost opportunity?

Maps (Lectures 37—48)

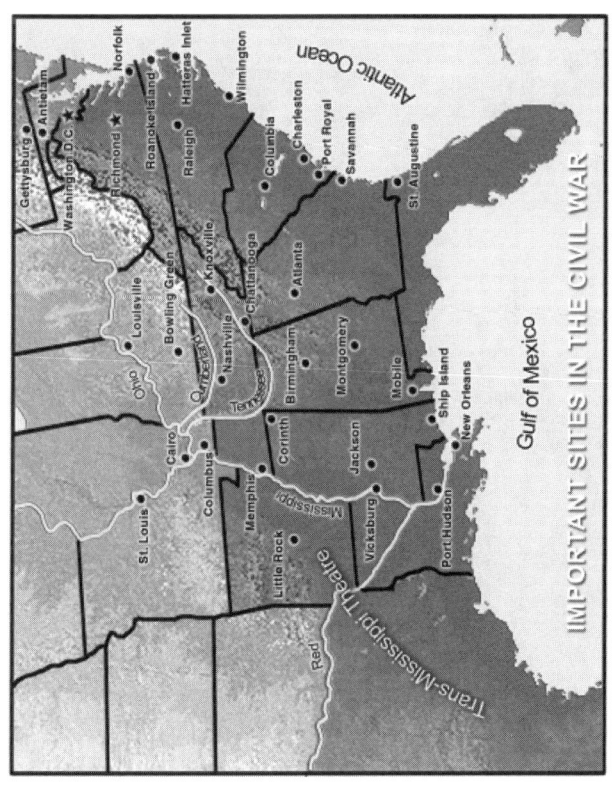

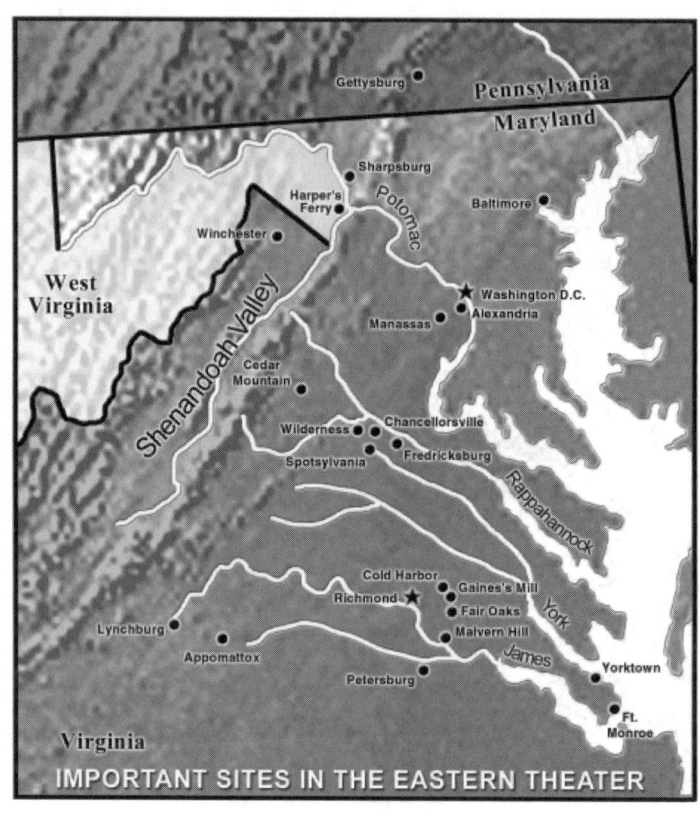

Timeline (Lectures 37–48)

March 1852 .... Publication of Harriet Beecher Stowe's *Uncle Tom's Cabin* makes many previously unengaged northerners sensitive to the issue of slavery.

Nov. 1852 .... Whig party fields its last serious presidential candidate, signaling breakdown of the second-party system; Franklin Pierce elected as Democratic president.

May 30, 1854 .... Kansas-Nebraska Act becomes law; doctrine of popular sovereignty as applied to the territory inflames sectional tensions.

May–June 1854 .... Anthony Burns case intensifies northern opposition to the Fugitive Slave Law.

May–July 1854 .... Political groups in various states adopt the name Republican Party, launching what would become the Democratic Party's rival in the third-party system.

1854–1855 .... Rise and decline of the Know-Nothing Party.

May 22, 1856 .... Abolitionist Senator Charles Sumner of Massachusetts caned by Preston Brooks of South Carolina on the floor of the Senate after delivering his "Crime against Kansas" speech.

Nov. 1856 .... Democrat James Buchanan elected president.

March 6, 1857 .... The Supreme Court's Dred Scott decision opens federal territories to slavery and outrages many people in the North.

Timeline (Lectures 37–48)

Aug.–Sept. 1857 .... Beginning of economic "panic" that causes widespread hardship.

Jan. 1858 .... Kansas voters reject proslavery Lecompton Constitution; although President Buchanan urges Congress to admit Kansas to the Union under the Constitution, his efforts eventually fail.

Aug.–Oct. 1858 .... Abraham Lincoln and Stephen A. Douglas meet in a series of debates in the Illinois senatorial election; Douglas wins the election but damages his reputation in the South, while Lincoln attains national stature.

Oct. 16–18, 1859 .... John Brown's raid on Harpers Ferry intensifies sectional tensions; state of Virginia hangs Brown on December 2.

Summer 1860 .... A series of fires in Texas spreads rumors of slave insurrection across the South.

Nov. 1860 .... Abraham Lincoln elected as the first Republican president.

Dec. 20, 1860 .... South Carolina secedes from the Union.

Jan. 9–Feb. 1, 1861 .... The remaining six states of the lower South secede (Mississippi, Jan. 9; Florida, Jan. 10; Alabama, Jan. 11; Georgia, Jan. 19, Louisiana, Jan. 26; Texas, Feb. 1).

Feb. 4–March 11, 1861 .... A convention of delegates from the seven seceded states meeting in Montgomery, Alabama, writes a constitution and selects Jefferson Davis and Alexander H. Stephens as provisional president and vice president of a new slaveholding republic called the Confederate States of America.

March 4, 1861	Lincoln's first inaugural address declares that the "momentous issue of civil war" lay in the hands of secessionists.
April 12–13, 1861	Confederate bombardment results in the surrender of Fort Sumter.
April 15, 1861	Lincoln calls for 75,000 volunteers to suppress the rebellion.
April 17–June 8, 1861	Four states of the upper South secede in response to Lincoln's call for volunteers (Virginia, April 17; Arkansas, May 6; North Carolina, May 20; Tennessee, June 8).
May 24, 1861	Benjamin F. Butler declares fugitive slaves at Fort Monroe, Virginia, "contraband of war" and refuses to return them to their Confederate owners.
July 21, 1861	Battle of First Manassas, or Bull Run, yields a flashy Confederate victory that builds confidence in the South and convinces many northerners that the war will be long and hard to win.
Aug. 6, 1861	Congress passes the First Confiscation Act, freeing slaves who had been employed in the Confederate war effort.
Nov. 8, 1861	Confederate diplomats James M. Mason and John Slidell are removed from the British vessel *Trent*, precipitating a diplomatic crisis between the United States and Great Britain.
Feb. 6–16, 1862	U. S. Grant captures Fort Henry on the Tennessee River and Fort Donelson on the Cumberland River.

Feb. 25, 1862	President Lincoln signs the Legal Tender Act, which creates national treasury notes soon dubbed "greenbacks."
March 16, 1862	U.S. Congress abolishes slavery in the District of Columbia, with compensation to loyal owners.
April 6–7, 1862	U. S. Grant wins the battle of Shiloh, completing a series of Union triumphs that deny the Confederacy control of major sections of Tennessee.
April 16, 1862	C.S. Congress passes the first national Conscription Act in American history; acts passed on September 27, 1862, and February 17, 1864, supplement the original legislation.
April 25, 1862	New Orleans falls to Union forces under David G. Farragut, giving the United States control of the lower Mississippi River.
May 15, 1862	U.S. Congress passes the Homestead Bill.
June 17, 1862	U.S. Congress passes the Land Grant College Bill (Morrill Act).
June 19, 1862	U.S. Congress prohibits slavery in the territories.
June 25–July 1, 1862	The Seven Days battles reverse a tide of Union military success as Robert E. Lee drives George B. McClellan away from Richmond.
July 17, 1862	U.S. Congress passes the Second Confiscation Act, which frees all slaves of owners who support the Confederacy.

July 22, 1862 .... Lincoln tells his cabinet that he intends to issue an emancipation proclamation.

Aug. 28–30, 1862 .... Robert E. Lee wins a victory over John Pope's Army of Virginia at the battle of Second Manassas, or Bull Run.

Sept. 17, 1862 .... Union victory at the battle of Antietam, or Sharpsburg, ends Robert E. Lee's first invasion of the North.

Sept. 22, 1862 .... Lincoln issues his preliminary Emancipation Proclamation.

Oct. 8, 1862 .... Battle of Perryville marks the climax of a Confederate invasion into Kentucky by armies under Braxton Bragg and E. Kirby Smith; the Confederates withdraw from the state after the battle.

Nov. 4, 1862 .... Democrats score gains in the northern off-year elections.

Dec. 13, 1862 .... Robert E. Lee defeats Ambrose E. Burnside at the battle of Fredericksburg.

Dec. 31, 1862–Jan. 2, 1863 .... Battle of Stones River, or Murfreesboro, fought in middle Tennessee, resulting in the retreat of Braxton Bragg's Confederate army and the beginning of six months of inactivity on this front.

Jan. 1, 1863 .... Lincoln issues his Emancipation Proclamation.

Feb. 25, 1863 .... U.S. Congress passes the National Banking Act.

March 3, 1863 .... U.S. Congress passes the Enrollment Act, which institutes a national draft; the Union will issue four calls under this legislation, in July 1863 and March, July, and December 1864.

May 1–4, 1863	Robert E. Lee defeats Joseph Hooker (who had replaced Ambrose E. Burnside as commander of the Army of the Potomac in late January 1863) in the battle of Chancellorsville.
June 20, 1863	West Virginia joins the Union as a new state.
July 1–3, 1863	George G. Meade's victory in the battle of Gettysburg ends Robert E. Lee's second invasion of the North.
July 4, 1863	Confederate army at Vicksburg surrenders to U. S. Grant.
July 13, 1863	Anti-draft riots begin in New York City and rage for several days.
Nov. 23–25, 1863	Union victory at the battle of Chattanooga lifts Confederate siege and opens the way for a campaign against Atlanta.
Dec. 8, 1863	Lincoln issues his Proclamation of Amnesty and Reconstruction as a blueprint for restoring the Union; this first presented the president's "10 Percent Plan" for Reconstruction.
March 12, 1864	U. S. Grant named general-in-chief of Union forces; plans simultaneous offensives designed to pressure Confederate military forces on a broad front.
May 5–6, 1864	Battle of the Wilderness opens the Overland campaign between U. S. Grant and Robert E. Lee.

May 7, 1864	William Tecumseh Sherman begins his Atlanta campaign against Joseph E. Johnston's Army of Tennessee.
June 15, 1864	U.S. Congress makes pay for black and white soldiers equal.
July 2, 1864	The Wade-Davis Bill passes the U.S. Senate, presenting an alternative to President Lincoln's 10 Percent Plan for Reconstruction; Lincoln kills it with a pocket veto on July 4, and supporters of the bill answer with the Wade-Davis Manifesto criticizing the president's actions.
Aug. 5, 1864	David G. Farragut's Union fleet wins the battle of Mobile Bay, closing the last major Confederate port on the Gulf of Mexico.
Sept. 2, 1864	Sherman's Union forces enter Atlanta, providing a critical Union victory that virtually guaranteed President Lincoln's reelection in November.
Sept. 19–Oct. 19, 1864	Climactic phase of the 1864 Shenandoah Valley campaign, during which Philip H. Sheridan wins decisive victories over Jubal A. Early's Confederate army.
Nov. 1, 1864	New Maryland state constitution abolishing slavery takes effect.
Nov. 7, 1864	Jefferson Davis proposes enrolling slaves in the Confederate military and freeing all who served faithfully; this touches off an acrimonious debate that continues for several months.

Nov. 8, 1864	Abraham Lincoln reelected and Republicans gain large majorities in both Houses of Congress and do well in northern state races.
Nov. 16–Dec. 21, 1864	Sherman's army makes its famous "March to the Sea" from Atlanta to Savannah, leaving a wide path of destruction in its wake.
Jan. 11, 1865	Missouri state constitutional convention abolishes slavery.
Jan. 31, 1865	U.S. House of Representatives approves constitutional amendment abolishing slavery.
Feb. 22, 1865	Amendment to Tennessee's state constitution abolishes slavery.
March 3, 1865	Bureau of Refugees, Freedmen, and Abandoned Lands (Freedmen's Bureau) established in the U.S. War Department.
March 13, 1865	C.S. Congress authorizes President Davis to recruit slaves as soldiers (but not to offer them freedom if they serve).
April 2, 1865	Confederate government abandons Richmond; Robert E. Lee's army begins retreat westward.
April 9, 1865	Lee surrenders to U. S. Grant at Appomattox Courthouse.
April 14, 1865	Lincoln shot in Ford's Theater; he dies the next morning.
May 10, 1865	Jefferson Davis is captured near Irwinville, Georgia.

May 29, 1865 .... Andrew Johnson issues proclamations offering amnesty to most former Confederates and naming a provisional governor in North Carolina charged with beginning the process of Reconstruction; many Republicans in Congress react negatively to Johnson's actions.

Summer–autumn 1865 .... Former Confederate states take advantage of Johnson's leniency, including several states that enact "Black Codes" discriminating against African Americans.

Dec. 18, 1865 .... The 13th Amendment is ratified, abolishing slavery throughout the United States.

April 9, 1866 .... Congress passes the Civil Rights Bill over President Johnson's veto.

May–July 1866 .... Riots against African Americans and white Republicans in Memphis and New Orleans result in scores of deaths and underscore the willingness of former Confederates to resort to violence.

June 13, 1866 .... Congress passes 14th Amendment and sends it to the states for ratification; defined all native-born or naturalized persons (white or black) as citizens; prohibited states from denying any person's "life, liberty or property without the due process of law"; and guaranteed all persons the "equal protection of the laws."

July 16, 1866	Congress extends the life of the Freedmen's Bureau over President Johnson's veto.
Autumn 1866	Republicans win elections handily, ensuring a three-to-one majority in the next Congress; President Johnson's effort to create a National Union Party ends in abject failure.
March 2, 1867	Congress passes first Military Reconstruction Act over President Johnson's veto; 10 states of the former Confederacy are divided into 5 military districts. Congress passes Tenure of Office Act over President Johnson's veto; Johnson prohibited from removing appointees without Senate approval.
March 23, 1867	Congress passes second Military Reconstruction Act over President Johnson's veto; federal military commanders will take the lead in implementing the process of forming new state governments.
Feb. 24, 1868	House of Representatives impeaches President Johnson by a vote of 126 to 47; action precipitated by Johnson's attempt to remove Secretary of War Stanton in defiance of the Tenure of Office Act, but the underlying cause is Republican weariness with Johnson's vetoes and other efforts to undermine congressional Reconstruction.

March 30–May 26, 1868	President Johnson's trial in the Senate; final vote to acquit 35 to 19, a single vote short of the two-thirds majority required for conviction.
June–July 1868	Alabama, Arkansas, Florida, Louisiana, North Carolina, and South Carolina readmitted to the Union; each has ratified the 14th Amendment and otherwise met congressional criteria for readmission, and their members of Congress are soon seated.
July 21, 1868	Congress passes concurrent resolution declaring the 14th Amendment ratified.
Nov. 1868	Republican candidate U. S. Grant elected president in race against Democrat Horatio Seymour of New York.
May 10, 1869	Final spike driven connecting the Union Pacific and Central Pacific Railroads at Promontory Point, Utah Territory; the United States has its first transcontinental rail line.
Jan.–March 1870	Mississippi, Virginia, and Texas rejoin the Union, having ratified the 15th Amendment as one of the conditions for readmission.
March 23, 1870	15th Amendment achieves final ratification.
Feb. 24, 1871	Georgia rejoins the Union, the last of the former Confederate states to do so.

April 20, 1871	Ku Klux Klan Act gives President Grant the power to suspend writ of habeas corpus and employ federal troops to suppress armed resistance to federal law; reaction to increasing violence directed against white and black Republicans by the Klan and other terrorist groups.
Nov. 1872	U. S. Grant reelected to a second term in race against Horace Greeley, who had run as the candidate of the liberal Republicans and the Democrats.
Sept. 1873	Economic panic begins when Jay Cooke's banking firm declares bankruptcy; within two years, 18,000 businesses fail and unemployment soars to almost 15 percent.
Nov. 1874	Democrats gain control of the House of Representatives in off-year elections.
1875	Mississippi comes under white conservative rule via the "Mississippi Plan," a program of planned violence and intimidation designed to prevent black and white Republican voters from casting ballots; seven other former Confederate states already have been "redeemed," that is, returned to white conservative control: Tennessee (1869), Virginia and North Carolina (1870), Georgia (1871), and Arkansas, Alabama, and Texas (1874).

Nov. 1876	Results from presidential canvass disputed in three unredeemed southern states (Florida, Louisiana, and South Carolina) and in Oregon; Democrat Samuel J. Tilden carries the popular vote over Republican Rutherford B. Hayes and needs electoral votes from just one of the three disputed states to win the election.
Jan. 26, 1877	Congress creates a commission to examine the disputed returns; the 15-member commission has 8 Republicans and 7 Democrats.
March 2, 1877	The commission announces votes of 8 to 7 in favor of awarding the electoral votes from all four disputed states to Hayes, thus electing him by a vote of 185 to 184.
March 5, 1877	Hayes inaugurated president, having agreed to the "Compromise of 1877" that gives certain concessions to the Democrats and the South in return for their accepting a Republican victory in the presidential race; Hayes soon withdraws the last federal troops from the South.

Glossary (Lectures 37–48)

blockade: A force of naval vessels placed to intercept shipping into or out of an enemy's ports.

bounty: A cash payment by the national, state, or local government designed to attract volunteers to the armed forces.

contraband: Material belonging to an enemy subject to seizure by a belligerent power in time of war. During the Civil War, the term most often applied to slaves in the Confederacy who made their way to Union lines.

earthworks: Fortifications constructed of dirt, sand, and other materials (a term often used interchangeably with *breastworks* or *field works*).

entrenchments: Defensive works prepared either in the field or as part of more permanent fortifications around cities or other crucial positions (also often called, simply, *trenches*).

fire-eaters: Outspoken advocates of southern rights who took extreme positions regarding the protection of slavery. Many of them, such as Edmund Ruffin, played a prominent role in the secession movement.

flank: The end of a line of troops on the field of battle or in a fortified position. To *flank* an enemy's position involves placing troops on its side or rear. A *flanking march* is a maneuver designed to give the troops in motion either a tactical or a strategic advantage.

fleet: A group of naval warships and support vessels operating as a unified force.

flotilla: Similar to a fleet but usually consisting of a smaller number of vessels.

guerrilla: A combatant who operates in small units or bands beyond the control of major organized military forces. These men often carried out raids and small attacks behind enemy lines.

logistics: Military activity dealing with the physical support, maintenance, and supply of an army.

martial law: Temporary government of civilians by military authorities, typically involving the suspension of some civil liberties.

muzzleloader: A shoulder weapon that is loaded at the muzzle, or front of the barrel.

noncommissioned officers: Those who hold the ranks of sergeant and corporal.

partisan: A combatant operating in small groups beyond the control of major military forces. Sometimes used interchangeably with *guerrilla*, but during the Civil War, partisans often were viewed as better disciplined and less likely to commit outrages against civilians or enemy soldiers.

popular sovereignty: The doctrine that provided for the voters in a federal territory to decide whether they would accept slavery (rather than having Congress decide for them). An attempt to find a middle ground between those who wanted to exclude slavery from all territories and those who wanted it protected by Congress, the doctrine figured prominently in the Compromise of 1850 and the Kansas-Nebraska Act.

quartermaster: The military department responsible for the supply of clothing, shoes, and other equipment.

specie: Coined money, usually gold or silver. Specie payments are payments in coin, or the redemption of paper money on demand with coin equivalent.

strategy: The branch of warfare involving the movement of armies to (1) bring about combat with an enemy under favorable circumstances or (2) force the retreat of an enemy.

tactics: The branch of warfare involving actual combat between attackers and defenders.

trains: The wagons accompanying armies that carried food, forage, ammunition, and other supplies (not to be confused with railroad rolling stock).

transport: An unarmed vessel carrying troops or supplies.

volley: The simultaneous firing of their weapons by a number of soldiers in one unit.

works: A generic term applied to defensive fortifications of all types.

Biographical Notes (Lectures 37–48)

Banks, Nathaniel Prentice (1816–1894). One of the most prominent Union political generals, he served throughout the Civil War without achieving any distinction on the battlefield. No match for Stonewall Jackson in the Shenandoah Valley in 1862, he similarly came to grief during the 1864 Red River campaign.

Barton, Clara (1821–1912). The most famous northern nurse, her excellent work at Antietam and elsewhere earned her the nickname "Angel of the Battlefield." Appointed head nurse of Benjamin F. Butler's Army of the James in 1864, she is most famous as the founder of the American Red Cross.

Beauregard, Pierre Gustave Toutant (1818–1893). One of the ranking officers in the Confederacy, he presided over the bombardment of Fort Sumter in April 1861; led the southern army at the opening of the battle of First Bull Run, or Manassas; and later held various commands in the western and eastern theaters.

Bell, John (1797–1869). Tennesseean who ran as the presidential candidate of the Constitutional Union Party in 1860. A former Whig with moderate views, he gave lukewarm support to the Confederacy after Lincoln's call for 75,000 volunteers to suppress the rebellion.

Booth, John Wilkes (1838–1865). Member of the most celebrated family of actors in the United States and a staunch southern sympathizer. He first planned to kidnap Abraham Lincoln, subsequently deciding to assassinate him. He mortally wounded the president on April 14, 1865, and was himself killed shortly thereafter by pursuing Union cavalry.

Bragg, Braxton (1817–1876). A controversial military figure who led the Confederate Army of Tennessee at Stones River, Chickamauga, and Chattanooga. Intensely unpopular with many of his soldiers and subordinates, he finished the war as an adviser to Jefferson Davis in Richmond.

Breckinridge, John Cabell (1821–1875). Vice president of the United States under James Buchanan and the southern Democratic candidate for president in 1860, he served the Confederacy as a general and secretary of war. He fought in the eastern and western theaters, winning the battle of New Market in May 1864.

Brown, John (1800–1859). Abolitionist whose violent activities during the mid-1850s in Kansas Territory and raid on Harpers Ferry in October 1859 gained him wide notoriety. He was hanged after his capture at Harpers Ferry, becoming a martyr to many in the North.

Buchanan, James (1791–1868). Long-time Democratic politician who was elected president in 1856 and watched helplessly as the nation broke up during the winter of 1860–1861. During the last months of his presidency, he sought without success to find a way to entice the seceded states back into the Union.

Buell, Don Carlos (1818–1898). Union army commander in the western theater in 1861–1862 who fought at Shiloh and led the northern forces at Perryville. Reluctant to conduct vigorous campaigns against the Confederates, he was relieved of command in the autumn of 1862.

Burns, Anthony (1834–1862). Born a slave in Virginia, Burns escaped to Boston in 1854 and soon stood at the center of a famous fugitive slave case. Arrested and held for return to Virginia under the Fugitive Slave Law, he inspired an outpouring of antislavery sentiment in Boston and elsewhere in the North. Re-enslaved for a time, he eventually was freed, attended Oberlin College, and spent the last part of his life as a Baptist minister in Canada.

Burnside, Ambrose Everett (1824–1881). Union general best known for commanding the Army of the Potomac at the battle of Fredericksburg in December 1862. His wartime career also included early service along the North Carolina coast and later action with Grant's army in 1864.

Butler, Benjamin Franklin (1818–1893). Union general who coined the term "contraband" for runaway slaves in 1861 and commanded the army that approached Richmond by moving up the James River during U. S. Grant's grand offensive of May 1864. A prewar Democrat who supported John C. Breckinridge in 1860, he became a radical Republican during the war.

Cooke, Jay (1821–1905). A brilliant financier who raised hundreds of millions of dollars for the Union war effort through the sale of government bonds. Sometimes accused of receiving special treatment from the Lincoln administration, he had powerful defenders who insisted that his actions helped keep northern armies in the field.

Crittenden, John Jordan (1787–1863). Politician from Kentucky who worked hard to avoid the breakup of the Union in 1860–1861. He proposed reinstating the Missouri Compromise line, called for a national convention to discuss the secession crisis, and later, worked hard to keep Kentucky in the Union.

Davis, Henry Winter (1817–1865). Maryland politician who won election at various times under the banners of the Whig; American, or Know-Nothing; and Republican parties. As a member of the House of Representatives from Maryland in 1864, he opposed Lincoln's lenient plans for Reconstruction and cosponsored, with Senator Benjamin F. Wade of Ohio, the Wade-Davis Bill and the Wade-Davis Manifesto.

Davis, Jefferson (1808–1889). Colonel during the war with Mexico, secretary of war under Franklin Pierce, and prominent senator from Mississippi in the 1840s and 1850s, he served as the Confederacy's only president. His nationalist policies triggered great political debate among Confederates.

Dix, Dorothea Lynde (1802–1887). An antebellum advocate of improved care for the mentally ill, she served as superintendent of Union army nurses during the war. She rendered solid service, despite a personality that often placed her at odds with both subordinates and superiors.

Douglas, Stephen Arnold (1812–1861). Prominent senator from Illinois in the 1850s who favored the doctrine of popular sovereignty and ran unsuccessfully as the regular Democratic candidate for president in 1860.

Douglass, Frederick (1817 or 1818–1895). Born a slave, he escaped to freedom in 1838, became an abolitionist and newspaper editor, and by 1860, was the most prominent African American leader in the United States. He pressed tirelessly to add freedom as a northern war aim.

Early, Jubal Anderson (1816–1894). Confederate general who compiled a solid record as an officer in the Army of Northern Virginia. He ended the war a disgraced figure in the Confederacy because of his defeats in the 1864 Shenandoah Valley campaign.

Farragut, David Glasgow (1801–1870). The most famous Union naval figure of the war, he was promoted to rear admiral in 1862 (the first officer to hold that rank). He led naval forces in successful operations against New Orleans in 1862 and Mobile Bay in 1864.

Frémont, John Charles (1813–1890). Famous as an antebellum western explorer, he ran as the first Republican candidate for president in 1856 and served as a Union general in Missouri and Virginia during the war. While commanding in Missouri in 1861, he attempted to free the state's slaves by issuing a proclamation that abolitionists applauded but Lincoln ordered him to rescind.

Grant, Ulysses S. (1822–1885). The most successful Union military commander, serving as general-in-chief for the last fourteen months of the war and twice winning election as president during the postwar years.

Halleck, Henry W. (1815–1872). An important Union military figure who presided over striking successes in the western theater in 1862, served as general-in-chief of the Union army in 1862–1864, and was demoted to chief of staff when Grant assumed the top military position in March 1864.

Hood, John Bell (1831–1879). Confederate commander best known for his unsuccessful defense of Atlanta against William Tecumseh Sherman's army and the disastrous campaign in Tennessee that culminated in the battle of Nashville in mid-December 1864.

Hooker, Joseph (1814–1879). Union general nicknamed "Fighting Joe" who commanded the Army of the Potomac at the battle of Chancellorsville. Replaced by George G. Meade during the Gettysburg campaign, he later fought at Chattanooga and in the opening phase of the 1864 Atlanta campaign.

Hunter, David (1802–1886). A Union general who, as commander along the South Atlantic coast, tried to free all slaves in his department in May 1862, only to see Lincoln revoke his order. He later led an army in the Shenandoah Valley in 1864.

Jackson, Thomas Jonathan (1824–1863). Nicknamed "Stonewall" and second only to Lee as a popular Confederate hero, he was celebrated for his 1862 Shenandoah Valley campaign and his achievements as Lee's trusted subordinate. He died at the peak of his fame, succumbing to pneumonia after being wounded at the battle of Chancellorsville.

Johnson, Andrew (1808–1875). A Democratic politician from Tennessee, he was the only U.S. senator from a seceding state who kept his seat after the firing on Fort Sumter. Elected Lincoln's vice president in 1864, he pursued a lenient Reconstruction program after Lincoln's death, fought bitterly with radical Republicans in Congress, and narrowly avoided removal from office after being impeached in 1868.

Johnston, Albert Sidney (1803–1862). A prominent antebellum military figure from whom much was expected as a Confederate general. He compiled a mixed record in the western theater before being mortally wounded on April 6, 1862, at the battle of Shiloh.

Johnston, Joseph Eggleston (1807–1891). A Confederate army commander who served in both Virginia and the western theater. Notoriously prickly about rank and privileges, he feuded with Jefferson Davis and compiled a record demonstrating his preference for defensive over offensive operations.

Lee, Robert Edward (1807–1870). Southern military officer who commanded the Army of Northern Virginia for most of the war and became the most admired figure in the Confederacy.

Lincoln, Abraham (1809–1865). Elected in 1860 as the first Republican to hold the presidency, he provided superior leadership for the northern war effort and was reelected in 1864 before being assassinated at Ford's Theater on the eve of complete Union victory.

McClellan, George Brinton (1826–1885). One of the most important military figures of the war, he built the Army of the Potomac into a formidable force and led it during the Peninsula campaign, the Seven Days battles, and at Antietam. Often at odds with Lincoln because of his unwillingness to press the enemy, he was relieved of command in November 1862 and later ran as the Democratic candidate for president in 1864.

McDowell, Irvin (1818–1885). Military officer who commanded the Union army at the battle of First Bull Run, or Manassas. The remainder of his wartime career was anticlimactic.

Meade, George Gordon (1815–1872). Union general who fought in the eastern theater, commanding the Army of the Potomac at Gettysburg and throughout the rest of the war. U. S. Grant's presence with the army after April 1864 placed Meade in a difficult position.

Pierce, Franklin (1804–1869). Democratic politician elected to the presidency in 1852. A "northern man of southern principles," he favored the proslavery side in the heated political debates regarding the extension of slavery into the Kansas Territory in 1854–1856.

Pope, John (1822–1892). Union general who won several small successes in the western theater before being transferred to the eastern theater to command the Army of Virginia. His defeat at the battle of Second Bull Run, or Manassas, in August 1862 ended his important service during the war.

Scott, Dred (1795[?]–1858). Slave who stood at the center of legal proceedings that culminated in 1857 in the Supreme Court's landmark *Dred Scott v. Sanford* decision. The Court declared that as an African American, Scott was not a citizen and, therefore, could not institute a suit. The Court held the Missouri Compromise unconstitutional and seemingly opened all federal territories to slavery.

Scott, Winfield (1786–1866). One of the great soldiers in U.S. history, he performed brilliantly in the war with Mexico and remained the ranking officer in the army at the outbreak of the Civil War. He devised the Anaconda Plan in the spring of 1861, a strategy that anticipated the way the North would win the conflict.

Sheridan, Philip Henry (1831–1888). Ranked behind only Grant and Sherman as a Union war hero, Sheridan fought in both the western and eastern theaters. His most famous victories came in the 1864 Shenandoah Valley campaign; at the battle of Five Forks on April 1, 1865; and during the Appomattox campaign.

Sherman, William Tecumseh (1820–1891). Union military officer who overcame early-war difficulties to become Grant's primary subordinate. An advocate of "hard" war, he is best known for his capture of Atlanta and "March to the Sea" in 1864.

Stanton, Edwin McMasters (1814–1869). Politician from Ohio who served as secretary of war under Abraham Lincoln and Andrew Johnson. Johnson's demand for Stanton's resignation helped trigger impeachment proceedings against the president in early 1868.

Stephens, Alexander Hamilton (1812–1883). A moderate Democrat from Georgia who supported Stephen A. Douglas in the 1860 presidential campaign and embraced secession reluctantly, he served throughout the war as vice president of the Confederacy. Increasingly at odds with Jefferson Davis over issues related to growing central power, he became an embittered public critic of the president and his policies.

Stevens, Thaddeus (1792–1868). Radical Republican congressman from Pennsylvania who chaired the House Ways and Means Committee. He favored harsh penalties for slaveholding Confederates and pushed to make emancipation a major focus of the Union war effort.

Stowe, Harriett Beecher (1811–1896). Author and reformer from Connecticut whose revulsion at the Fugitive Slave Act prompted her to publish *Uncle Tom's Cabin*, a bestselling novel that proved immensely influential in promoting antislavery sentiment in the United States.

Sumner, Charles (1811–1874). Radical Republican senator from Massachusetts who was caned on the floor of the Senate by Congressman Preston Brooks of South Carolina after delivering his famous "Crime against Kansas" speech in 1856. During the war, he chaired the Senate Committee on Foreign Affairs and consistently pressed for emancipation.

Taney, Roger Brooke (1777–1864). Chief Justice of the Supreme Court (1835–1864), he antagonized abolitionists with the Dred Scott decision in 1857. During the war, he sought to curb Abraham Lincoln's power to suspend the writ of habeas corpus, opposed northern conscription, and argued that governmental assaults on civil liberties posed a greater threat to the nation than secession of the southern states.

Vallandigham, Clement Laird (1820–1871). Congressman from Ohio and a leading Copperhead who staunchly opposed emancipation and most of the rest of the Republican legislative agenda. Exiled to the Confederacy by Lincoln in 1863, he returned to the United States and helped draft the peace platform at the 1864 Democratic national convention.

Wade, Benjamin Franklin (1800–1878). Radical Republican senator from Ohio who chaired the Joint Committee on the Conduct of the War, urged Abraham Lincoln to dismiss George B. McClellan, and called for the emancipation of all slaves. In 1864, he co-authored the Wade-Davis Bill and the Wade-Davis Manifesto that attacked Lincoln's actions relating to Reconstruction.

Bibliography (Lectures 37–48)

Essential Reading

Berlin, Ira, et al., eds. *Free at Last: A Documentary History of Slavery, Freedom, and the Civil War*. New York: The New Press, 1992. Reprinted in paperback. A basic collection of primary testimony relating to black participation in the Civil War. The editors provide excellent introductory essays to sections dealing with black military service, the process of emancipation, and the transition from slave to free labor in the Upper and Lower South.

Donald, David Herbert, Baker, Jean Harvey, and Holt, Michael F. *The Civil War and Reconstruction*. New York: W. W. Norton, 2001. A thoroughly revised edition of a classic text, this volume offers a great deal of factual and interpretive detail.

Foner, Eric. *Reconstruction: America's Unfinished Revolution, 1863–1877*. New York: Harper & Row, 1988. Reprinted in paperback. This standard survey includes material on wartime Reconstruction.

Gallagher, Gary W. *The Confederate War*. Cambridge, Mass.: Harvard University Press, 1997. Reprinted in paperback. A concise treatment that focuses on popular will, nationalism, and military strategy in the Confederacy.

Hattaway, Herman, and Jones, Archer. *How the North Won: A Military History of the Civil War*. Urbana: University of Illinois Press, 1983. Reprinted in paperback. The best one-volume military history of the Civil War, this study pays rigorous attention to all theaters and places campaigns and battles in a broad political context.

McPherson, James M. *Battle Cry of Freedom: The Civil War Era*. New York: Oxford University Press, 1988. Reprinted in paperback. Equally well written and researched, this Pulitzer Prize–winning analytical narrative is the best one-volume treatment of the subject. It gives full attention to the background of the conflict, as well as to the military and nonmilitary aspects of the war.

Paludan, Philip Shaw. *"A People's Contest": The Union and the Civil War, 1861–1865*. New York: Harper & Row, 1988. The best one-volume treatment of the nonmilitary side of the northern war experience, this volume emphasizes how the conflict pushed the North toward modern nationhood.

Potter, David M. *The Impending Crisis, 1848–1861*. New York: Harper & Row, 1976. Reprinted in paperback. A fine analytical narrative of the political events and sectional controversies that preceded the Civil War.

Thomas, Emory M. *The Confederate Nation, 1861–1865*. New York: Harper & Row, 1979. Reprinted in paperback. A superior one-volume history of the subject, well researched and well written.

Supplementary Reading

Notes: Some of the following books may be out of print. Internet sites such as www.abebooks.com and www.amazon.com may be helpful in locating copies.

Belz, Herman. *Reconstructing the Union: Theory and Policy during the Civil War*. Ithaca, N.Y.: Cornell University Press, 1969. A detailed analysis of congressional legislation, presidential proclamations, and wartime debate relating to bringing the seceded states back into the Union.

Beringer, Richard E., Hattaway, Herman, Jones, Archer, and Still, William N., Jr. *Why the South Lost the Civil War*. Athens: University of Georgia Press, 1986. A detailed study that attributes Confederate defeat to disaffection, war weariness, doubts about slavery, and religion rather than to northern military might and industrial superiority.

Carter, Dan T. *When the War Was Over: The Failure of Self-Reconstruction in the South, 1865–1867*. Baton Rouge: Louisiana State University Press, 1985. An excellent treatment of the southern response to Andrew Johnson's Reconstruction program.

Catton, Bruce. *Never Call Retreat*. Garden City, N.Y.: Doubleday, 1965. Reprinted in paperback. The third volume of Catton's engagingly written

"Centennial History of the Civil War," a trilogy that ranges widely across the military and political landscape of the conflict.

———. *Terrible Swift Sword*. Garden City, N.Y.: Doubleday, 1963. Reprinted in paperback. The second volume of the "Centennial History of the Civil War."

Cooper, William J. *The South and the Politics of Slavery, 1828–1856*. Baton Rouge: Louisiana State University Press, 1978. Reprinted in paperback. A well-written narrative that places slavery at the center of antebellum southern politics.

Crook, D. P. *The North, the South, and the Powers: 1861–1865*. New York: John Wiley and Sons, 1974. A good brief overview of the diplomatic history of the war.

Curry, Leonard P. *Blueprint for Modern America: Nonmilitary Legislation of the First Civil War Congress*. Nashville: Vanderbilt University Press, 1968. Examines the Republican legislation that influenced the social, economic, and political development of the nation for the rest of the century.

Davis, William C. *"A Government of Our Own": The Making of the Confederacy*. New York: The Free Press, 1994. Reprinted in paperback. A detailed and engagingly written narrative of the Montgomery convention at which the Confederacy was established.

Donald, David Herbert. *Charles Sumner and the Coming of the Civil War*. New York: Alfred A. Knopf, 1961. Reprinted in paperback (together with Donald's *Charles Sumner and the Rights of Man* in a two-volumes-in-one edition). The first volume of Donald's two-volume biography of Sumner, this superbly written narrative provides numerous insights into abolitionism, sectionalism, and national politics.

———. *Lincoln*. New York: Simon & Schuster, 1995. Reprinted in paperback. The best one-volume life of Lincoln, written by a two-time winner of the Pulitzer Prize for biography.

Durden, Robert F. *The Gray and the Black: The Confederate Debate on Emancipation*. Baton Rouge: Louisiana State University Press, 1972. Quotes extensively from wartime testimony in examining the bitter debate over whether to enroll slaves in the Confederate army.

Faust, Drew Gilpin. *Mothers of Invention: Women of the Slaveholding South in the American Civil War*. Chapel Hill: University of North Carolina Press, 1996. Reprinted in paperback. A well-written, prize-winning examination of the ways in which upper-class southern women were influenced by, and reacted to, a conflict that severely disrupted their lives and society.

Freeman, Douglas Southall. *Lee's Lieutenants: A Study in Command*. 3 vols. New York: Scribner's, 1942–1945. Reprinted in paperback. These compellingly written volumes are the classic treatment of the Army of Northern Virginia's high command. Few studies have exerted as much influence on the military history of the Civil War.

Gillette, William. *Retreat from Reconstruction: A Political History, 1867–1878*. Baton Rouge: Louisiana State University Press, 1979. A detailed discussion of the last decade of Reconstruction that finds a waning commitment to black rights among white northerners.

Glatthaar, Joseph T. *Forged in Battle: The Civil War Alliance of Black Soldiers and White Officers*. New York: The Free Press, 1989. Reprinted in paperback. An excellent scholarly examination of the military experiences and battlefield record of the black soldiers who made up almost 10 percent of the Union army.

Harris, William C. *With Charity for All: Lincoln and the Restoration of the Union*. Lexington: University Press of Kentucky, 1998. The fullest modern treatment of wartime reconstruction, this study argues that Lincoln would have allowed southern states a large voice in the process even after the end of the war.

Holzer, Harold, ed. *The Lincoln-Douglas Debates: The First Complete, Unexpurgated Text*. New York: HarperCollins, 1993. A useful edition of the famous debates that set Lincoln on the road to national prominence.

Jones, Howard. *Union in Peril: The Crisis over British Intervention in the Civil War*. Chapel Hill: University of North Carolina Press, 1992. This excellent treatment of Anglo-American diplomatic affairs during the first 20 months of the conflict highlights the degree to which military operations influenced British leaders.

Mohr, Clarence L. *On the Threshold of Freedom: Masters and Slaves in Civil War Georgia*. Athens: University of Georgia Press, 1986. Reprinted in paperback. The best study of slavery in a Confederate state, this work emphasizes the ways in which the war weakened the hold of master over slave.

Neely, Mark, Jr. *The Union Divided: Party Conflict in the Civil War North*. Cambridge, Mass.: Harvard University Press, 2002. A provocative work that argues against the prevailing idea that the North's two-party system helped the Union war effort.

Rable, George C. *But There Was No Peace: The Role of Violence in the Politics of Reconstruction*. Athens: University of Georgia Press, 1984.

———. *Civil Wars: Women and the Crisis of Southern Nationalism*. Urbana: University of Illinois Press, 1989. Reprinted in paperback. Impressive research and clear writing are two of this important book's many strengths.

Richardson, Heather Cox. *The Death of Reconstruction: Race, Labor, and Politics in the Post-Civil War North, 1865–1901*. Cambridge, Mass.: Harvard University Press, 2001. A revisionist study that argues class dynamics in the North played a critical role in bringing the end of Reconstruction.

———. *The Greatest Nation of the Earth: Republican Economic Policies during the Civil War*. Cambridge, Mass.: Harvard University Press, 1997. A good study of the Republican Party's economic ideology and the process by which much of it was translated into wartime legislation.

Rose, Willie Lee. *Rehearsal for Reconstruction: The Port Royal Experiment*. Indianapolis: Bobbs-Merrill, 1964. Reprinted in paperback. A classic treatment of the transition from slavery to freedom for black people on the South Carolina Sea Islands.

Simpson, Brooks D. *The Reconstruction Presidents*. Lawrence: University Press of Kansas, 1998. This well-researched and provocatively argued book includes two chapters on Lincoln and wartime reconstruction.

Stampp, Kenneth M. *And the War Came: The North and the Secession Crisis, 1860–1861*. Baton Rouge: Louisiana State University Press, 1950. Reprinted in paperback. An influential study of the shifting attitudes toward the South among northerners during the period between Lincoln's election and the firing on Fort Sumter.

Steers, Edward, Jr. *Blood on the Moon: The Assassination of Abraham Lincoln*. Lexington: University Press of Kentucky, 2001. A careful treatment that lays to rest a host of myths about the Lincoln assassination.

Trefousse, Hans L. *Impeachment of a President: Andrew Johnson, the Blacks, and Reconstruction*. New York: Fordham University Press, 1999 (reprint of 1975 edition). An even-handed, scholarly exploration of Johnson's impeachment and trial.

Von Rank, Albert J. *The Trials of Anthony Burns: Freedom and Slavery in Emerson's Boston*. Cambridge, Mass.: Harvard University Press, 1998. A compelling treatment of the most famous fugitive slave case of the 1850s.

The History of the United States, 2nd Edition

Scope (Lectures 49–84):

America industrialized rapidly in the late 19th century, and was one of the world's three leading industrial powers (along with Germany and Britain) by 1900. Its citizens already had the adventurous outlook, the tradition of hard work, and the entrepreneurial initiative that are vital to successful industrialization. A legal situation amenable to maximum economic growth and widespread faith in capitalism further aided the Industrial Revolution. The Americans were lucky in having plentiful natural resources at their disposal. Immense forests provided wood for cheap construction everywhere east of the Mississippi. Coal fields in Pennsylvania, Kentucky, and West Virginia fueled industry's steam-powered machinery, while ore from the great Minnesota ranges provided the raw material for the iron and steel industry. Oil fields in western Pennsylvania, Ohio, and later, Oklahoma, Texas, and California fed another rapidly growing industry.

Railroads, built in the East from 1830, were extended across the Mississippi after the Civil War. The first transcontinental road was completed in 1869, reducing the coast-to-coast journey from a matter of months, as it had been in the 1840s, to just three days by 1900. Completion of a dense nationwide railroad network between 1869 and 1900 facilitated companies' national marketing campaigns. It also permitted improvements in diet, because fresh foods grown in southern California and Florida could be brought quickly to market in the northern cities, even during the winter.

The scale of American businesses grew rapidly, too, enabling the oil, coal, iron and steel, railroad, food, and meat-packing industries to enjoy economies of scale. The downside of this growth was that businesses became anonymous. Workers trapped in low-paying, dangerous, and monotonous jobs became resentful and organized trade unions. The late 19th century witnessed a rapid growth in unions, especially among skilled workers who could not easily be replaced with strikebreakers, and a succession of strikes. Ferocious retaliation by employers, who used armed detectives and, when possible, state militiamen, made industrial disputes ugly and bloody. Employers also tried to "divide and conquer" by hiring workers from many different ethnic groups, recent immigrants who would be less likely to make common cause against them and whose many languages would make organization difficult.

Railroads were vital not only to industry but also to settlers on the Great Plains in the 1870s and 1880s. Trains brought in wood, coal, and other necessities that settlers lacked locally, while carrying away from the area its massive annual grain harvests. The cumulative effect of Plains settlement was to create a great yearly food surplus (one of the constants of 20th-century life) and to end the danger of famine. For each particular farmer, the steady fall in grain prices caused hardship, which was accentuated by the railroads' local monopoly as sole available carrier and by a steady deflation through the late 19th century. Plains farmers attempted to join southern tenant and sharecropping farmers in the Populist Party, whose mushroom growth in the 1880s and 1890s was never successfully rewarded with electoral successes.

The rapid growth of America's industrial and agricultural productivity made the nation wealthy and created the possibility of a more aggressive foreign policy. Some politicians, notably Theodore Roosevelt, favored the creation of an American colonial empire to rival those of Britain, France, Portugal, Germany, and Belgium. The disintegration of Spain's Caribbean and Pacific empire presented an opportunity. America went to war against Spain in 1898 and became the dominant power in Cuba and the Philippines. It also influenced the Panamanian revolution and the building of an ocean-to-ocean canal there between 1903 and 1914. The debate over foreign policy acquired a new urgency when the First World War began in 1914. At first, President Woodrow Wilson argued that America must remain neutral "in thought and deed" so that it could broker a reasonable peace. Before long, however, American businesses were trading heavily with the British and French, while the Royal Navy prevented them from trading with Germany. Germany retaliated with unrestricted submarine warfare against American shipping, which in turn prompted an American declaration of war. That decision, along with the Russian Revolution, made 1917 one of the most momentous years of the 20th century. The weaknesses of the Versailles Treaty by which World War I ended, and the American decision not to participate in the League of Nations, laid the foundations of an even more disastrous war 20 years later.

Whatever its international role, America continued to generate new technology and to grow wealthier than any nation in world history. The 1920s witnessed the perfection of modern mass-production techniques and the development of "welfare capitalism," by which employers attended to their workers' social needs, as well as to their productive powers, as a way of forestalling workers' radicalism. By 1929, however, productivity had outstripped America's capacity to consume, because incomes were still unequally distributed. The Wall Street Crash of that year was followed by a devastating economic depression, worse than any earlier fluctuation in the American economy. By 1933, banks were failing and factories lay silent, even though surrounded by men who desperately needed work. A handful of Americans, struck by this incongruity and convinced that capitalism was no longer a viable economic system, turned to Communism. Millions more, however, supported the New Deal, a series of policies by which a new president, Franklin Roosevelt, attempted to rescue the American system. The New Deal's many agencies gave the federal government a more intrusive and powerful role than ever before in the regulation of the economy. It was not successful in ending the Great Depression, but it restored confidence in the business system, introduced such innovative programs as Social Security, and ensured that trade unions would enjoy the same legal protections as business.

The onset of the Second World War brought the Depression to an end, which it did by escalating demand for exports and prompting rapid American mobilization. Roosevelt, like Wilson, tried at first to stay out of the conflict—he faced an influential isolationist faction at home. The Japanese attack on Pearl Harbor in 1941, however, made American participation in the war, against both Japan and its German partner, inevitable. America, allied with Winston Churchill's Britain and Josef Stalin's Soviet Union, had defeated Hitler's Germany by May of 1945, after the D-Day invasion of France and heavy aerial bombardment of German cities. The invention of a secret weapon, the atomic bomb, also enabled American forces to defeat Japan in August 1945.

No sooner had the war ended in the complete defeat of their enemies than the allies, America and Russia, fell out. The contrast in their political and economic systems, and the American fear that Soviet Communism would spread remorselessly until it dominated the world unless stopped forcibly, fueled the antagonism. The Soviets' refusal to let the newly liberated nations of Eastern Europe elect democratic governments seemed to the new American leader, President Truman, characteristic of their aggressive designs. In consequence, America decided not to withdraw from international affairs after the Second World War as it had after the First. Instead, it became the leader of the Western democracies in a new bipolar world.

The Cold War standoff between America and the Soviet Union persisted until 1989, bringing them to the brink of war in 1962 (during the Cuban missile crisis) but restraining them with the knowledge that each had nuclear weapons sufficient to annihilate the other. The demands of a big military establishment contributed to economic buoyancy throughout most of the era. Fears that the Great Depression would return with the end of war proved groundless. The United States in the 1950s and 1960s became, in the words of economist John Kenneth Galbraith, the "affluent society," in which an opulent consumer lifestyle came within reach of nearly everyone, even factory workers' families.

The great exception to the spread of American prosperity was the large African American community. Ever since the end of Reconstruction, it had endured the most precarious economic and political condition. To be black in the South was to suffer under government-supported policies of racial segregation. Black Americans throughout the late 19th and early 20th centuries had moved from the rural South to the urban North as industrialization spread. There, too, however, they had faced severe racial discrimination. The Civil Rights movement of the 1950s and 1960s was, therefore, vitally important in transforming their civic status. It led to the laws of 1964 and 1965 by which all forms of government-approved racial discrimination were abolished. The movement was not able to end the economic disadvantages against which many African Americans continued to struggle, however, and the intractability of that problem persisted up to and beyond the millennium.

Not only the Civil Rights movement but many other social movements contributed to the turbulence of the 1960s in America. In pursuit of its Cold War policy of preventing the spread of Communism, the nation went to war in Vietnam but found itself unable to prevail against tenacious low-tech foes in jungle warfare. The long, costly war became bitterly unpopular at home and the antiwar movement contributed to an unprecedented "generation gap" in millions of families. Numerous groups, meanwhile, imitated the Civil Rights movement by claiming that they, too, were minorities and that they suffered discrimination unjustly; first women in the new feminist movement, then Native Americans, Hispanic Americans, and homosexuals. America was socially fractured by these experiences, while its government lost prestige, a loss greatly exacerbated by the Watergate scandal that forced President Nixon to resign in disgrace in 1974.

President Carter spoke of a "national malaise" in 1978 to a nation mired in disillusionment, inflation, and economic stagnation. His successor, the former film star Ronald Reagan, was eager to restore national vitality and determined to escalate the Cold War confrontation with an immense peacetime military buildup. This controversial policy may have contributed to the collapse of the Soviet Union and its empire of Eastern European satellites in 1989, another of the crucial years of the century. The fall of the Berlin Wall and the peaceful triumph of democracy in the former Soviet sphere laid to rest the 20th-century menace of Communism and left America as the world's sole superpower.

War against Iraq and ethnic genocide in the former Yugoslavia showed that the New World Order was anything but a utopia of peace and good will. America had to decide whether to maintain its worldwide commitments or retreat to its historic isolationist posture. Cautiously, and with care to prevent another Vietnam morass, it maintained its commitments. Richer than ever in the 1990s but still suffering from the chronic exclusion of its urban, minority, and Native American "underclass" from the general prosperity, America remained vulnerable. A domestic terrorist destroyed the federal government's building in Oklahoma City in 1995, while foreign terrorists destroyed the New York World Trade Center in 2001. The future of the nation, like earlier futures, continued to hold out great promise but also present great challenges. ■

Industrialization
Lecture 49

In the late 19th century, the scale of American industry increased dramatically. John D. Rockefeller in the oil industry, and Andrew Carnegie in the iron and steel business, built massive corporations, integrating vertically and horizontally until they dominated entire sectors of the economy.

Rockefeller and Carnegie and their fellow entrepreneurs were daring, intensely focused on business opportunities, and ruthless, yet idealistic about transforming the world for the better. They were lucky in being able to exploit immense American reserves of crude oil, iron ore, and coal—another aspect of American exceptionalism—and talented in building nationwide marketing networks.

With the help of a generation of brilliant inventors, including Thomas Edison and Alexander Graham Bell, and a succession of improvements in manufacturing, the United States had established itself as one of the three world leaders in industry by 1890, rivaling Britain and Germany.

First of all, we have the iron and steel business, which was central to American industrialization. The manufacture of metal objects had already been going on for many, many centuries. Small-scale iron and steel production had been familiar, particularly, making tools and making weapons for literally hundreds of years. In the early part of the 19th century, though, British industrialists had begun to accelerate the scale on which that was done.

America was well supplied with the basic raw materials: iron ore, limestone, and coal, and American entrepreneurs enhanced the scale and efficiency of production, as the career of Andrew Carnegie (1835–1919) demonstrates. He began life as a poor immigrant. His attention to detail, coupled with a vision of great possibilities, contributed to his success. He also modernized steel production and greatly expanded U.S. exports.

Along with iron and steel, a second vital commodity in American industrialization was oil. Before 1860, whales were the principal source of oil. But whaling was dangerous and unpredictable. By the 1850s, the price of whale oil was rising sharply because of the overuse of the whale fisheries. This was when rock oil production began.

George Bissell and Edwin Drake discovered that oil could be procured by drilling (with a salt drill) at Titusville, Pennsylvania, in 1859. The oil rush was comparable to the California gold rush, and John D. Rockefeller (1839–1937) built his empire on oil refining. The scale of his operations enabled him to buy out competitors. He controlled 85–90 percent of the market. Like Carnegie, he was an expert organizer. He was a pioneer of vertical integration, or controlling the entire production process from exploration to marketing.

> **By the 1890s, the United States had caught up with its great rivals, Britain and Germany, and in the early 20th century was easily going to surpass them as the world's predominant industrial power.**

Although Rockefeller was also a sober, God-fearing workaholic and Baptist Sunday-school teacher, he lived in constant fear that supplies might run out at any time. Only in 1901 did discoveries in Texas allay his fears.

Rockefeller's company, Standard Oil, pioneered universal marketing and distribution. Red "Standard" wagons were synonymous with quality. The origins of the auto industry (in the 1890s) created still more demand for Rockefeller's product.

As industrialization accelerated, society became accustomed to the idea of successive improvements and inventions. Thomas Alva Edison (1847–1931) was among the inventor-geniuses of the era. Painstaking and meticulous, he made a science of developing and testing new possibilities in his laboratory at Menlo Park, New Jersey. His invention of the electric light bulb (1879) would revolutionize the use of time. And his gramophones (1877) and moving pictures (1896) laid the foundations for the 20th-century entertainment industry. He held 1,328 patents at the time of his death. Alexander Graham Bell rivaled Edison's ingenuity. The telephone (1876) began to overcome previously insuperable boundaries of space.

Congress and the Supreme Court created a highly favorable environment for rapid economic growth. Industrial strikes became common as a severe class division developed, but they rarely succeeded.

The great entrepreneurs lived ostentatious lives in the spotlight of publicity. Some contemporaries nicknamed them "robber-barons" and criticized their dishonest practices. Many lived in Manhattan mansions or in the millionaires' colony of Newport, Rhode Island.

They also became philanthropists. Carnegie's *Gospel of Wealth* (1889) argued for the social responsibilities of the rich. He founded a network of more than 2,000 free libraries in Britain and America. And the Rockefeller Foundation and other bequests endowed education and cultural projects. Such people established the principle that philanthropy is an important part of American life.

By 1890, America had caught up with Britain in industrial productivity despite a much later start. By 1900, many of its big industries were dominated by "immortal" corporations rather than individual owners. ■

Suggested Reading

Andrew Carnegie, *Autobiography*.

Matthew Josephson, *The Robber-Barons*.

Martin Melosi, *Thomas A. Edison and the Modernization of America*.

Daniel Yergin, *The Prize: The Epic Quest for Oil, Money, and Power*.

Questions to Consider

1. What factors favored the rapid growth of American industry?

2. Which was more important in the industrial giants' success: luck or skill?

Transcontinental Railroads
Lecture 50

> The first transcontinental railroad, planned in the 1850s, but delayed by the Civil War, was built between 1866 and 1869 by the Central Pacific Railroad Company, moving east from Sacramento, California, and by the Union Pacific Railroad, moving west from Omaha, Nebraska, both companies heavily subsidized with land grants and direct cash payments from the federal government.

The Central Pacific builders in particular, many of them Chinese immigrants, had to overcome horrific obstacles in crossing the Sierra Nevada Mountains; tunneling near the summit took three years. Both companies faced daunting technical and supply challenges because distances were so great. Completion of the railroad, however, cut travel time from the Mississippi to the West Coast from three months to about one week. The line was joined by four other transcontinentals in the following decades; spur lines between them gradually created a comprehensive national network and facilitated settlement in areas of the Plains and Mountain states that had previously been too remote.

Railways had been pioneered in Britain but caught on quickly in America in the 1830s. Railways' low-friction environment enables one locomotive to pull many times its own weight in cars. The track has to be well engineered; curves must be gentle; and gradients, slight, so initial costs were immense. But by accelerating industrialization and personal mobility, the railways also gave the Union a crucial advantage in the Civil War.

Congress authorized the Union Pacific to build westward from the Missouri and the Central Pacific to build eastward from Sacramento. Construction began in earnest in 1866. The Union Pacific made rapid progress over the level Great Plains. Work gangs were composed of Irish immigrants and Union army veterans. The first locomotive crossed the ice of the frozen Missouri River before there was even a bridge.

The "End of the Track" became a moving tent city. Every few days, the whole little miniature city would move along, and their barkeepers and brothel keepers were there, professional gamblers trying to win money off the men who'd been paid for their work. To feed the enormous crew of railroad builders and protect them against the Indian attacks, buffalo hunters were also hired.

By 1890, all but the most perishable goods could literally be sold anywhere in America.

The Central Pacific confronted horrific technical difficulties in the Sierra Nevada Mountains. Chinese work gangs provided the manual labor. Before the age of dynamite, nitroglycerine and blasting powder were used to clear rock. Minimizing grades on the Donner Pass route required years of blasting and tunneling. Some days, crews progressed no more than a single foot, and the Nevada and Utah deserts beyond the mountains created water-supply problems.

When the two lines met at Promontory Point, Utah, on May 10, 1869, transcontinental travel times diminished drastically, from three months to a week, and the telegraph contributed to railroad safety. Later improvements included Westinghouse air brakes (1869), rotary snow plows (1884), and all-steel carriages (1904). Railroads were the first American industry that ran in spite of the weather, pushing seasonal concerns to the background.

Luxurious rail travel thrived between 1870 and 1950, and the railroads were a major boost for tourism, especially in the West. Railroads also facilitated commercial farmers' settlement of the Great Plains and the creation of nationwide marketing networks. The railroads were the lifeline of isolated Plains communities. They brought wood, coal, and manufacturers to farmers. They also shipped bulk farm produce back East.

Corporations designed national advertising and marketing plans. Railroad companies subsidized farmers' settlements, advertising as far away as Europe. By 1890, all but the most perishable goods could be sold anywhere in America within a week of being manufactured. Plus, the development of refrigerated trains in the 1890s began to overcome the perishability problem.

Railroads transformed nearly every aspect of American life between 1830 and 1890, while binding together the two coasts and bringing all citizens into closer proximity. ■

Suggested Reading

Stephen Ambrose, *Nothing Like It in the World: The Men Who Built the Transcontinental Railroad.*

Robert Athearn, *Union Pacific Country.*

Sarah Gordon, *Passage to Union: How the Railroads Transformed American Life, 1829–1929.*

John Stilgoe, *Metropolitan Corridor.*

Questions to Consider

1. How were railroads and other elements of the Industrial Revolution linked?

2. Were the greatest challenges to the railroads technical or political?

The Last Indian Wars
Lecture 51

The technological disparity between the Plains Indians and the whites was so immense that the coming of settlers, with the railroads, made continuation of the Indians' independent life impossible. In the 1870s, the whites hunted almost to extinction the buffalo herds on which the Indians lived, partly for food and hides, and partly as a way of undermining the Indians' livelihood.

White settlers' eagerness for land made treaties hard to enforce, especially when news of gold discoveries in such treaty lands as the Black Hills of South Dakota set off new gold rushes. The Sioux, Cheyenne, and other Plains tribes were warrior societies who lived to fight and ought not to be romanticized. They were able to settle their differences briefly and win a signal victory against George Custer at Little Bighorn in 1876. In reaction, however, the U.S. Army intensified its campaign against them and broke all resistance within a year. After that, the settlement and development of the West were only briefly threatened by isolated campaigns, such as that against the Apache Geronimo in 1886.

Plains Indians, Sioux, Cheyenne, Arapaho, and others were hunters and gatherers whose way of life depended on the great buffalo herds but was already deeply affected by the whites. Their way of life had changed when they domesticated feral horses. Horses increased their mobility and hunting options. Francis Parkman's *The Oregon Trail* described their nomadic hunting life before 1850.

The Indians' participation in the fur trade brought them weapons that could give them decisive advantages over their enemies. They could use guns but could not make or repair them. Neither could they make powder and ammunition. But, very often, the arrival of the whites brought smallpox, measles, and other illnesses to which the Indians had no immunity, and this would wipe out tribes completely. Like Francis Parkman, another enterprising American, artist George Catlin, recorded the Plains Indians' way of life before they died out.

U.S. government policy alternated between trying to destroy Native American peoples and trying to make treaties with them. Influential figures, including General William T. Sherman, favored destroying the Plains Indians. Large-scale buffalo hunting by the whites undermined the Indians' independent existence. Each side, whites and Indians, attacked the other, usually over land disputes. White settlers' greed and fear sometimes led to unprovoked attacks, such as the Sand Creek Massacre of 1864.

Benevolent feelings toward the Indians were common back East but rare on the frontier. The Carlisle School and the Lake Mohonk (New York) conferences were philanthropic attempts to safeguard Indians' rights and adapt them to American civilization.

Treaties proved difficult to enforce, because the army was prejudiced in favor of the whites. For example, the Black Hills of South Dakota was established as a reservation by a treaty of 1868. But when George Armstrong Custer led an expedition into the Black Hills in 1874 and reported gold discoveries, gold hunters flooded the area, in violation of the treaty, and the army's efforts to evict them were halfhearted.

Crazy Horse and Sitting Bull concentrated their forces against the army in the summer of 1876. Sitting Bull had a powerful vision of victory. And Custer underestimated the size of the force arrayed against his troop of the 7th Cavalry. His command was annihilated at the Battle of the Little Bighorn in eastern Montana. Black Elk's reminiscences give us a glimpse of that battle. The army responded with intensified efforts to destroy armed resistance. By campaigning through the winter, it overpowered the remaining Indian bands.

Congress passed a law in 1887 called "The Dawes Severalty Act," and it was designed to hasten the Indians' transformation into small-scale American farmers.

Scattered conflicts with other groups persisted in the late 1870s and late 1880s, but Indians won no further significant victories against the Americans. Chief Joseph of the Nez Perce, stripped of his lands in the Wallowa Valley,

Idaho, led a 1,500-mile retreat in 1879. Geronimo, chief of the Chiracahua Apaches, was captured in 1886 after years of raiding on the Arizona-Mexico border.

The Ghost Dance cult (1888–1890) convinced Paiutes, Sioux, and other groups that the ghost-dance shirt made them immune to bullets. Nervous soldiers shot into their assembly at Wounded Knee, South Dakota, in December 1890, killing 200.

Indian reservation policy, intended as a temporary expedient until the Indians were assimilated into society, became a permanent feature of the American West. ■

Suggested Reading

Dee Brown, *The American West*.

Larry McMurtry, *Crazy Horse*.

John G. Neihardt, *Black Elk Speaks*.

Francis Parkman, *The Oregon Trail*.

Questions to Consider

1. Why were the whites so unscrupulous in their treatment of the Indians through most of American history?

2. What factors gave the American army decisive advantages when it went to war against the Indians?

Farming the Great Plains
Lecture 52

> The railroads made large-scale settlement and farming of the Plains possible. Without them, distances were just too great, and besides, the area lacked wood, which was vital for fuel and building materials. Trains could now bring in massive quantities of wood from Michigan and Wisconsin, while shipping out the surplus grain that the farmers were very soon able to produce.

The Homestead Act, passed during the Civil War in 1862, encouraged ordinary farmers to acquire land at almost no cost, and those who could overcome the loneliness, prairie fires, insect infestations, extremes of climate, and incessant winds were able to build prosperous lives. The Act granted a 160-acre quarter section to any family that occupied and improved the land for five years.

They were so successful that, by 1890, they were growing massive annual surpluses, driving down the cost of food throughout the Western world and eliminating the danger of famine in America once and for all. Throughout this period, the Homestead Act was abused by land speculators. It never worked effectively beyond the 100th meridian, where drought conditions prevailed. John Wesley Powell's ambitious alternative based on rational allocation of scarce water resources was never fully adopted.

Many families began with subsistence farming but switched to commercial farming as soon as possible, sending bulk shipments of grain back East by rail and importing wood, coal, and other necessities. Towns developed along the railroads, dominated by great grain elevators. Rapid improvements in farm machinery made Plains farming possible. The hard steel blade of the John Deere plow enabled farmers to cut through the dense prairie sod, and the McCormick reaper reduced the number of men needed for the harvest.

Farmers and cattle ranchers often competed for land. The great cattle trails from Texas to the early railheads, such as Abilene, Kansas, preceded the farmers. Another technological development, barbed wire (1874), had important consequences for the transformation of the Plains, spelling the end of the open range.

Settlers, from back East and from abroad, had to overcome several formidable hardships of Plains farming. First, the lack of wood forced them to build sod houses. Their thickness contributed to moderating temperature extremes. Windows and doors often had to be ordered from Sears, Roebuck. Also, the lack of wood created a need for enormous quantities of buffalo chips to keep warm.

In addition, Plains winters were extremely harsh. Furthermore, ecological upheavals threatened farmers' security. For example, grasshoppers thrived on settlers' crops and sometimes destroyed entire districts. Prairie fires also regularly swept the Plains, as they had done for generations.

Variations in rainfall destroyed farms in marginal areas, especially beyond the 100th meridian. Settlers' hopes that "rain follows the plow" were ill-founded, and attempts at "rainmaking" (*pluviculture*) were unreliable.

Isolation and loneliness defeated some settlers. Ole Rolvaag's *Giants in the Earth* (1927) depicts a Norwegian farmer's wife descending into madness from loneliness. And Western historian Wallace Stegner's *Beyond the Hundredth Meridian* (1954) evokes the material and psychological hardships of the life.

The first group of Americans to experiment with irrigation farming in a systematic way was the Mormon settlers of Salt Lake City.

The success of Plains farming permanently transformed the conditions of food production in America. Abundance of cattle, wheat, and corn drove down prices for American consumers, while improving the quality of their diet. Refrigerated railroad cars after 1880 also increased working-class people's access to fresh meat and vegetables. Low prices for their produce tempted individual farmers to expand their production further but worsened the problem of overproduction.

The system of a rectangular land survey had always had drawbacks. West of the 100th meridian, these drawbacks were disabling. Nature itself does not think in squares. And low rainfall made 160 acres insufficient land for a subsistence farm in the High Plains.

John Wesley Powell's *Report on the Arid Regions* (1878) suggested a new approach to land use in the High Plains and Great Basin. The key commodity was water, access to which should be the principal consideration. He proposed farms of 2,560 acres, 20 of which should be intensively irrigated. ∎

Suggested Reading

Dee Brown, *The American West*.

Willa Cather, *My Antonia*.

Hamlin Garland, *Main Traveled Roads*.

Ole Rolvaag, *Giants in the Earth*.

Wallace Stegner, *Beyond the Hundredth Meridian*.

Questions to Consider

1. Why were settlers willing to face the severe hardships of the Great Plains as homestead farmers?

2. Were farming and cattle ranching compatible with each other?

African Americans after Reconstruction
Lecture 53

> When Reconstruction ended in 1876, southern "Redeemers," often ex-Confederates, took over political control of the South. They promoted the idea of the New South, modern and industrialized, with limited success, but it was still a South based very heavily on racial discrimination. They disfranchised freedmen in much of the South, and then passed legislation to enforce racial segregation.

Realizing that agriculture alone was no longer adequate as an economic base, leaders promoted the idea of the New South, modern and industrialized, with limited success. Henry Grady's famous "New South" speech of 1886 argued for industrial and commercial progress. New industries included textile mills, industrial tobacco manufacturing, large-scale lumbering, coal mining, and steelmaking.

But the South was based on racial discrimination. Jim Crow legislation denied African Americans the vote. They disfranchised freedmen in much of the South, then passed legislation to enforce racial segregation. Black subordination was underlined by periodic lynchings. The federal government's decision to withdraw from the area and the decline of radical Republicanism meant that the white elite was able to rule unchallenged for much of the next 80 years.

Most African Americans lived by sharecropping, but the cotton they grew was no longer a boom crop and tended to bring in less money from year to year, condemning many of them to a cycle of debt and dependency. A former slave, Booker T. Washington, became the first great black leader of the post-slavery era, preaching self-help, sobriety, religion, and education in the hope that the creation of an industrious population would mitigate the rigors of segregation. At the dawn of the 20th century, W. E. B. DuBois proposed a more militant alternative strategy of racial improvement.

The grandfather clauses (Louisiana, 1898) excluded from the franchise men whose grandfathers had not voted in 1867. The black vote fell from 130,000 after Reconstruction to 5,300 in 1900. And poll tax qualification for the vote excluded many other poor blacks. Literacy tests had the same effect. "Understanding clauses" permitted many illiterate whites to vote.

State governments established systematic racial segregation (*Jim Crow*) in most southern states in the 1880s and 1890s. The Supreme Court upheld this legislation in *Plessy v. Ferguson* (1896). Only one Supreme Court Justice, John Marshall Harlan, a former slaveowner, dissented from the majority verdict. Redeemer governments economized on education, especially that of African Americans, so about half of African Americans in the South were illiterate. Jim Crow legislation denied African Americans the vote. State governments rarely intervened to prevent lynchings, which enforced segregation by terror. About 200 lynchings per year occurred during the 1890s and about 100 per year during the next decade.

> **It was clearly the case that the NAACP between then and the 1950s was to play a vital role in overcoming racial segregation.**

The majority of African Americans became sharecropping farmers. They rented land from estate owners in return for a share of the crop. The local store advanced them credit for seeds, tools, and food during the year, but at inflated prices. At the time of settling up, the sharecropper often found that his debt was greater than his profit from the sale of cotton.

Cotton prices were going down on the world market from year to year, making it ever more difficult for sharecroppers to get out of debt. During the Civil War, Britain, one of the best customers, had begun growing cotton in India, part of its empire, instead of relying on American supplies. Deflation also drove prices down.

Black leaders debated the most suitable reaction to these appalling circumstances. Booker T. Washington (1856–1915) favored accommodation to segregation. Born a slave, he became a famous educator as president of Tuskegee Institute. His speech at the Cotton States Exposition in Atlanta (1895) accepted the reality of segregation. He believed that black industry and sobriety would alleviate the worst aspects of segregation. His autobiography, *Up from Slavery* (1901), recounts his own personal struggles.

Massachusetts-born W. E. B. Dubois (1868–1963) disagreed and helped found the National Association for the Advancement of Colored People (NAACP) in 1909. His book *The Souls of Black Folk* (1903) is a classic study of the segregated South. He stresses the double consciousness of African Americans. They are possessed of two selves: the Negro and the American. He favored the intensive education of the "talented tenth" and a policy of "ceaseless agitation" against segregation. He was a founding member of the NAACP and editor of its journal, *The Crisis*, for 25 years. ■

Cotton pickers at work. After Reconstruction, most African Americans in the South earned their living by sharecropping cotton.

Suggested Reading

W. E. B. DuBois, *The Souls of Black Folk*.

Otto Olsen, *Reconstruction and Redemption in the South*.

Booker T. Washington, *Up from Slavery*.

C. Vann Woodward, *The Strange Career of Jim Crow*.

Questions to Consider

1. Which was the more serious problem for African Americans after Reconstruction: racial discrimination or economic hardship?

2. Why did Booker T. Washington and W. E. B. DuBois disagree?

Men and Women
Lecture 54

Middle-class Americans, men and women, emphasized the differences between the two sexes in the late 19th century, in the belief that each of the sexes had its own special proper sphere of activity. Men—muscular, rational, intellectual—should work hard in the outside world … .Women—delicate, intuitive, religious—should create the home as a haven of peace, love, and security.

The men were considered less endowed with natural morality. They were expected to work hard in the outside world, building an agricultural, industrial, and commercial civilization. Men went out to do combat in the world, so the idea ran, and returned at day's end to an ideal home environment tended by a woman.

Because middle-class men did office work rather than farming or heavy labor, they were in danger of becoming "soft." The YMCA, founded in Britain in the 1840s, pioneered "muscular Christianity." Its foremost proponent was Theodore Roosevelt.

It was thought that women should create the home as a haven of peace, love, and security, in which to bring up their children in a good and godly atmosphere. They were supposed to be nurturers and moral guardians of each new generation.

Despite these theories, the majority of women were too poor not to work, but those who labored in farms and factories aspired to live according to the ideal. Doctors believed that rigorous education for women would lead to hysteria, especially when pregnant, and that granting them political rights would make them mannish, threatening differences embedded in nature itself. The single biggest source of employment for those who had to work was domestic service. Others became teachers, nurses, and department store clerks.

Female reformers had to overcome strongly held ideas of gender differences or use them on behalf of their plans. Frances Willard, longtime leader of the Women's Christian Temperance Union, emphasized making the world more "homelike" by ridding it of the alcohol menace. Her lecturing style and setting emphasized the home virtues. She was dismayed by such militant women as Carry Nation, known for attacking saloons with an axe.

Even the early advocates of votes for women, Elizabeth Cady Stanton and Susan B. Anthony, argued from the assumption of women's difference from men—that they could bring their nurturing virtues into the political world and, thus, purify and ennoble it. And pioneers of women's higher education were careful to stress their colleges' roles as moral chaperones and guardians and the wholesomeness of their curricula.

Because it was widely feared that women who got too much education might become unhinged, Vassar monitored its students' movements carefully. Ellen Richards, the first woman to graduate from MIT, pioneered scientific education for women but tried to make it conform to prevailing notions of propriety.

A younger generation of women, coming to maturity at the very end of the 19th century, challenged the limits of this theory.

Occasionally, ideas about gender differences came to women's aid in unexpected ways. Lizzie Borden's defense is a notorious example. Accused of murder (1892) and with no real alibi, she was trained to act during the trial as a frail, delicate female—and was acquitted.

A younger generation of women challenged the limits of "women's sphere" in the late 19th and early 20th centuries. Settlement House pioneer Jane Addams argued that gender-role separation had directed middle-class women down an evolutionary blind alley. Her work at Hull House enabled her to overcome years of ill health.

Margaret Sanger argued for a new frankness about sex and the need to educate women about contraception. She had to overcome a tradition of reticence and the effects of the Comstock laws, anti-obscenity legislation passed in 1872. ■

Suggested Reading

Ben Barker Benfield, *Horrors of the Half-Known Life*.

Ann Douglas, *The Feminization of American Culture*.

Ellen DuBois, *Feminism and Suffrage*.

Estelle Friedman and John D'Emilio, *Intimate Matters: A History of Sexuality in America*.

Questions to Consider

1. Why were so many middle-class women content to accept ideals of emphatic gender difference?

2. Why were more women involved in the temperance movement than in appealing for the right to vote?

Religion in Victorian America
Lecture 55

Victorian religion in America was less doctrinal and more sentimental than its Puritan antecedents. Jesus as a friend and companion, rather than God as an angry judge, dominated popular religion, while traveling revivalists, like Dwight Moody, emphasized the simple promise of divine love for all who turned away from sin.

Preachers in the *social gospel* tradition, such as Washington Gladden, urged Christians to think about the salvation of society, not just individual souls. They also tried to help the poor and reform grim urban conditions and worked in the temperance movement to outlaw alcohol.

The majority of Americans were Protestants, but a swelling tide of immigration from Ireland, Italy, and Poland was bringing large numbers of Catholics into America, while Jewish populations arrived from Germany (Reformed) and Russia (Orthodox). America's principle of religious freedom and church-state separation allowed other religions to flourish and soon showed doubters (especially numerous anti-Catholics) that the nation could accommodate religious pluralism.

Women's religious literature about a middle-class heaven and about Jesus as a sensitive friend and helper flourished. Elizabeth Stuart Phelps's *The Gates Ajar* (1868) and *The Story of Jesus Christ* (1897) are classics of the genre. Other invocations of Jesus include Charles Sheldon's *In His Steps* (1896) and Lew Wallace's *Ben Hur* (1880).

Protestants, who had earlier favored plain buildings, began to create decorative churches with more stained glass and Gothic architecture, and to include choral music in their services. Popular preachers began to emphasized a free-will conversion rather than the old predestinarian theology. And Dwight Moody, who worked in the Chicago slums, was the era's most popular evangelist.

Protestantism began to divide into liberal and evangelical branches. Protestants confronted intellectual problems in different ways. Darwinian biology contradicted the Genesis creation story in the important matter of the age of the Earth. And historical-critical methods had shone new light on the Bible, suggesting that perhaps the book was a compilation of writings composed in different times and places.

Liberal Protestants tried to adapt Christianity to modern intellectual trends. Those who accepted the fruits of modern intellectual life were divided over the *social gospel* question.

Influential thinkers in this period accepted and emphasized different ideas in their work. Henry Ward Beecher was content with economic orthodoxy and Social Darwinism and rejected the liberal Protestants beliefs. Walter Rauschenbusch and Washington Gladden argued for the social gospel, the collective improvement of society. And George Herron argued for Christian Socialism and accused America of being a fallen nation.

The American Catholic Church was predominantly Irish but became more ethnically diverse in the late 19th and early 20th centuries. Irish famine victims had swelled the population in the 1840s and 1850s. Archbishop John Hughes of New York and other leaders feuded with the city over religion and public education. The third plenary synod of Baltimore decided in 1884 to create an independent Catholic school system.

Italian, Slavic, and Polish immigrants diversified the Catholic population after 1870. Bishops fought to prevent *Cahensley-ism*, the creation of ethnically distinct parishes.

Catholic intellectual life was dominated by ex-Protestant converts. Isaac Hecker founded the Paulist Fathers. And Orestes Brownson's journals helped shape Catholic opinion on a wide range of religious, social, and political issues.

Jewish immigration contributed to American religious diversity. German Jewish immigrants usually joined Reform synagogues. Isaac Meyer Wise's reforms created controversy, and he argued that many of the old rituals should be abandoned. The Conservative movement tried to preserve more of the Jewish heritage than Wise had.

Eastern European Jewish immigrants brought an unchanged Orthodoxy from Poland, Russia, and Austria-Hungary, while intra-Jewish tensions were offset by charitable impulses.

In the 20th century, as American medicine improved dramatically, the attractions of Christian Science commensurately diminished.

America's homegrown religions continued to thrive. Mormons began to adapt to Victorian values. Legislation against polygamy culminated in the *Reynolds* case (1879). A new revelation to Wilford Woodruff brought the practice to an end. Charles Taze Russell foresaw the end of the world and created the Jehovah's Witnesses in 1880 to prepare for it. Mary Baker Eddy's Christian Scientists denied the reality of the material world. ■

Suggested Reading

Nathan Glazer, *American Judaism*.

Charles Morris, *American Catholic: The Saints and Sinners Who Built America's Most Powerful Church*.

Mark Noll, *History of Christianity in the United States and Canada*.

Elizabeth Stuart Phelps, *The Gates Ajar*.

Charles Sheldon, *In His Steps*.

Lew Wallace, *Ben Hur*.

Questions to Consider

1. Why did the Protestant churches begin to split into liberal and evangelical sections?

2. Why was adaptation to America difficult for Catholic immigrants?

The Populists
Lecture 56

> Southern cotton farmers, sharecroppers, black and white alike, were becoming chronic debtors by the late 1880s as prices continued to fall. Midwestern farmers also found conditions turning steadily against them. ... They decided by the early 1890s that the only solution to their problems was to form their own political party, and legislate for better conditions.

Railroad shipping rates were too high, buying vital new farm machinery was forcing them into debt, and prices for their crops were falling, preventing them from repaying their creditors. They were victims of their own success as producers. The enormous western grain harvests drove down the price of food. Individual farmers were tempted to plant more corn and wheat as unit costs fell, but that worsened the overall situation.

Southern cotton farmers, mostly sharecroppers, produced big annual harvests that had to compete with Indian and Egyptian cotton on the world market. Their prices too were low. They tried an array of cooperative marketing schemes to bypass predatory banks and elevator owners but decided by the early 1890s that they should turn to politics to legislate for better conditions.

Farmers were vulnerable to these economic trends. The amount of money in circulation did not keep pace with the rise in population and productivity, which caused deflation. Many farmers were heavily in debt for land and machinery purchases, and repayment was particularly difficult in

William Jennings Bryan, Democratic and Populist leader who ran three times, unsuccessfully, for the U.S. presidency.

deflationary conditions. Farmers usually had to sell immediately after harvest, when prices tended to be lowest. Furthermore, the local railways were monopolies, and although railroads and grain elevator companies were indispensable, they began to seem predatory.

Outwitted by their opponents' economic and legal stratagems, farmers turned to direct political action in the early 1890s. They created organizations, first social and economic, later political, to reform conditions. The Granger movement (founded in 1867) brought together prosperous farmers for mutual social and educational assistance. And the Independent National or "Greenback" Party campaigned for inflationary currency legislation in the 1870s and early 1880s.

> **Farming, from being the principal national activity, shrank to become one of the many special interests of an increasingly industrial nation.**

Farmers' alliances in the 1880s also organized poor farmers. They tried to set up cooperative marketing arrangements to bypass grain elevator companies. Members campaigned for state laws regulating railroad rates. Meetings took on the character of religious revivals. Black farmers' alliances, segregated at first, faced the same economic conditions and tried to make common cause with the whites.

Thus the Populist Party was built on an unlikely alliance between these two constituencies; unlikely in the South because it crossed the color line and unlikely between the two areas because it linked Union veterans from Midwestern farms with Confederate veterans from the South.

The People's Party was created in 1892 and held its convention in Omaha. Ignatius Donnelly of Minnesota wrote the party's platform, which tried, unsuccessfully, to woo urban working-class voters. Among other things, the party supported direct election of senators, free coinage of silver, a graduated income tax, an eight-hour workday for industrial workers, and a ban on immigration. Many members theorized that a conspiracy of British, Jewish, and Yankee bankers had deliberately created the depression of the 1890s, worsening the farmers' plight.

The Populists' 1892 presidential candidate was James Weaver, a former Union army general. He won one million votes and carried four states: Nevada, Colorado, Idaho, and Kansas. The American two-party system is sensitive to emerging social and political forces and incorporates their issues. As the Populists began to focus on "free silver," the Democratic Party took up the issue, too.

In 1896, the Populists tried to secure the services of William Jennings Bryan, the "Boy Orator of the Platte." Bryan was the Democratic Party candidate, whose "Cross of Gold" speech electrified his party's Chicago convention. Populists met two weeks later in St. Louis and disputed over whom to choose as their presidential candidate. They also chose Bryan, meaning that he ran on two tickets. The compromise decision for a Bryan-Watson ticket doomed their electoral prospects.

Their political zeal took on religious overtones for a while, and they enjoyed local and state-level successes in the early 1890s, but they were never able to build a stable party structure nationwide and, thus, were unable to win national elections. Their failure to attract William Jennings Bryan as their candidate in 1896 annihilated the Populists' plan to displace permanently one of the two major parties.

The Republican candidate, William McKinley, won the election over the Democrats and Populists, on behalf of a "sound money" policy. Populism failed because it was never able to overcome the gulf between the farmers and the industrial workers.

Many of the issues confronting Populist farmers continued to plague their successors. Tenancy and sharecropping became more common; farmer ownership, less so. Overall, American farming was beset by overproduction throughout most of the 20th century. Southern sharecropping remained widespread, and segregation continued.

Eventually, farming became less central to national life. The percentage of the population working as farmers shrank steadily and is now barely three percent. Farmers became one of many special-interest lobbies (very successfully), rather than the backbone of the entire population. By 1920, more than half of all Americans lived in cities. ■

Suggested Reading

Frank Baum, *The Wizard of Oz*.

Lawrence Goodwyn, *The Populist Moment*.

Richard Hofstadter, *The Age of Reform*, sections I–III.

C. Vann Woodward, *Tom Watson: Agrarian Rebel*.

Questions to Consider

1. Were currency reforms and inflation adequate solutions to the farmers' troubles?

2. Why were the Populists unable to build an electoral majority?

The New Immigration
Lecture 57

[The] late 19th century in Europe was full of stories about America, most of them exaggerating its wealth and opportunities to anyone brave enough to risk the Atlantic crossing. Worsening conditions for European farmers prompted many of them to emigrate to the American frontier, especially from Scandinavia, Britain, and Germany.

Some people came to America in search of better opportunities; others, because of persecution or economic crisis at home. By 1900, more than a million people a year were emigrating to America.

Immigrants from Britain came in search of better opportunities and adapted relatively easily. They had no language barrier to overcome. Many already possessed industrial skills relevant to American conditions. Many were subsidized by railroad companies, as settlers to northern and western states.

Immigrants from Russia, Italy, and China faced many more serious problems. Some were forced to flee persecution. Others migrated in response to changes in the world economy, as with Italian citrus growers.

Throughout most of the 19th century, America welcomed immigrants, a sentiment embodied in the poem by Emma Lazarus (1883) engraved on the Statue of Liberty. The cost of transportation prevented the poorest people from making the journey. Steamships made the voyage, and even return migration, feasible. Custom-built ships and "steerage" fares reduced costs and increased safety.

Migrants to New York arrived at Castle Garden (built in 1855) and, later, Ellis Island (1892). New arrivals were subject to health checks for trachoma, mental illness, and lameness and could be turned back. Nine of every 10 were admitted, however, and could often join family and friends who had arrived earlier.

Immigrants tended to cluster together on first arrival, creating ethnic enclaves in the cities and, sometimes, in rural communities. In New York and other cities, ethnic groups jostled side by side as they adapted to American life. Intense localism gradually gave way to the idea of a common national origin. All had to struggle with the English language. American customs and industrial work rhythms were alien. Rural residents found clock time disturbingly different from the usual cycle of natural time. Immigrants often had to compromise or modify their religious traditions.

America's success in assimilating people from all over the world is one of the nation's very, very greatest achievements.

Immigrants invented and adapted old traditions in the New World. The St. Patrick's Day parade is an invention of Irish immigrants in America, not an import from Ireland. Chop suey and pizza were unknown in China and Italy.

Assimilation and success led to dispersal in the second and third generations. Economic opportunity was not as golden as naive immigrants had anticipated,

Immigrants at Ellis Island. The site today has been converted into a museum of immigration.

but it was nonetheless real. Public schooling and "Americanization" programs intensified rates of assimilation. World War I marked a crescendo of Americanization, public schools taught in English only, and sometimes also highly responsive student groups.

Inter-group prejudice and discrimination were real but less intense than in most of the Old World. Asian immigrants in California suffered the most acute discrimination in the late 19th and early 20th centuries. Black migrants from the rural South experienced comparable problems of adjustment and adaptation.

American confidence in the "melting pot" began to falter in the 1910s and 1920s. Anti-immigrant *nativists* feared the newcomers. They were alleged to bring in dangerous political ideas. American anarchists were nearly all foreign born; Socialists often came from abroad. Foreigners brought in Catholicism, too. The idea that immigrants really were the "wretched refuse" of Europe frightened advocates of *eugenics*, those who hoped to encourage reproduction of the "fittest."

Laws of 1921 and 1924 dramatically cut immigration quotas, except for quotas for immigrants from northwestern Europe. The ethnic enclaves in the cities began to break up as the stream of young immigrants was cut off.

America's success at assimilating people from all over the world is an astonishing achievement. Most multi-ethnic nations have been far less successful. ■

Suggested Reading

Abraham Cahan, *The Rise of David Levinsky*.

Maldwyn Jones, *Destination America*.

Orm Overland, *Immigrant Minds, American Identities: Making the United States Home, 1870–1930*.

Thomas Sowell, *Ethnic America*.

Questions to Consider

1. What obstacles did immigrants have to surmount in adapting to American life?

2. What were the advantages and disadvantages to America itself of an open-immigration policy before 1920?

City Life
Lecture 58

Last time we looked at immigrants coming into America. This time I want to study in more depth the conditions in the cities they inhabited. American cities grew very rapidly in the late 19th and early 20th centuries, concentrating and intensifying industrial life.

The cities were often badly planned or not planned at all, and they became overcrowded, as immigrants and rural migrants poured in to work in the factories and the dockyards and the slaughterhouses. Land values and rents were high in city districts. Jacob Riis's *How the Other Half Lives* (1890) documented deplorable living conditions. Workers needed to live close to the factories. Adequate water supplies and sanitation were rare. In 1885, such cities as Baltimore and New Orleans still had open sewers.

Epidemic disease and fire were also common. Open fires, for cooking and heat, along with gas or kerosene flames for light, made fire universal. Large numbers of animals in cities, especially horses, worsened the risk of disease. Impure food was on sale throughout the later 19th century, until Upton Sinclair's *The Jungle* (1906) prompted the first federal pure food legislation. Also, domestic and industrial sources created high levels of smoke and other pollution. In addition, rivers were used for waste disposal.

City government was dominated by ethnic *machines*, which traded basic services for immigrant voters' loyalty, while enriching their leaders. The Irish-American Tweed Ring and its Tammany Hall successors dominated New York. City bosses did provide services that poor immigrants needed. *Ward-heelers* got to know every inhabitant of a locality and served their immediate needs.

Anglo-Saxon civic reformers periodically tried to stop the corrupt machines. Persuading voters *not* to accept favors proved difficult. The introduction of civil service examinations as a condition of employment contributed to reform. "Muckraking" journalists, such as Lincoln Steffens, exposed the nationwide extent of the problem.

New inventions and new ideas combined to improve urban life between 1870 and 1910. Streetcars enabled cities to spread out. Electrification from about 1890 increased the efficiency and cleanliness of cities and contributed to suburbanization. Streetcars began to be complemented by bicycles and cars after 1900.

Skyscrapers framed with steel girders enabled cities to grow upward. They depended on lightweight materials and Elisha Otis's safety elevator (demonstrated in 1853). Plate-glass windows revolutionized the amount of light that could be admitted into buildings.

> **One of the ways in which the new cities developed an urban identity was through … . major-league sports teams.**

The settlement-house movement brought urbanites the help of privileged, yet concerned, citizens. Chicago's Hull House, founded by Jane Addams (1889), was the model. Settlements offered child care and help for immigrants in adapting to American life. They challenged machine rule.

Urban identity and loyalty developed through sports and the media. The railroad network facilitated the rise of major league sports. Newspapers helped create a sense of urban unity. City boosters understood the importance of good public relations and civic amenities to attract businesses. ■

Suggested Reading

Jacob Riis, *How the Other Half Lives*.

Upton Sinclair, *The Jungle*.

Lincoln Steffens, *The Shame of the Cities*.

Sam Bass Warner, *Streetcar Suburbs*.

Questions to Consider

1. Why did urban reform prove slow and difficult in the late 19th and early 20th centuries?

2. How did technology change the characteristics of urban life between 1870 and 1910?

Labor and Capital
Lecture 59

Most of the new city dwellers were working-class people. We saw the conditions they lived in last time. Now, let's look at how they worked. As the scale in cost of setting up a business increased, working-class men's chances of becoming employers in their own right decreased.

As the scale of industry increased and became impersonal, labor and management often came into conflict. Employers, regarding labor as a cost, wanted to keep wages as low as possible. They sheltered behind the laissez-faire doctrine and sanctity of contract. Most were reluctant to ensure safe working conditions. States that passed safe-work laws suffered the out-migration of employers. Massachusetts lost the textile industry to North Carolina and Georgia, where the abuse of child labor was common.

Humanitarian reformers tried to prevent child labor. Factory children became prematurely aged by overwork. They had little or no opportunity for schooling.

Trade unions developed slowly, overcoming a variety of obstacles, and played a major role in economic life by 1900. Early unions' members lacked a common binding interest. The Noble and Holy Order of the Knights of Labor (founded in 1869) welcomed workers, farmers, and small businessmen. The Haymarket Affair (1886), in which anarchists battled with police, provoked a crisis in the Knights and turned middle-class opinion against organized labor.

Geographical dispersal and work rivalries challenged railroad workers' unity. Strikes could succeed if they enjoyed community support. Conversely, strike-related violence, as with the Great Railroad Strike (1877), eroded middle-class support. Unionization was most effective in highly skilled trades, because skilled laborers were more difficult to replace. Samuel Gompers led the American Federation of Labor (founded in 1886).

> **The battle forth in the interest of starving men, women, and children stands forth in the history of labor struggles as the Great Pullman Strike.— Eugene Debs**

The economic depression of the early 1890s witnessed a climax of violent encounters between employers and unions. Employers tried to prevent unionization. They hired an ethnically diverse workforce, exploiting linguistic barriers and ethnic tensions. Strike leaders were blacklisted, and strikers were replaced by strikebreakers who were often African Americans or immigrants who didn't plan to stay permanently in the country. Employers used private detectives, court injunctions, and state militiamen against strikes.

A steelworkers' union was defeated in the Homestead Strike (1892). Workers and strikebreaking detectives fought a pitched gun battle. The strikers were

The Haymarket Affair, a confrontation between police and protesters in Chicago in 1886. The drama and violence of the Haymarket riot frightened the middle class and made them less sympathetic to the labor movement.

starved out, and their union was broken. They wouldn't have an effective union for another 40 years.

Court injunctions and federal troops defeated a nationwide railroad strike in 1894. It began with a labor dispute in the model town of Pullman, Illinois. The Supreme Court upheld (1895) the use of an injunction against union leader Eugene Debs of the American Railroad Union. Debs founded the American Socialist Party and became its perennial presidential candidate. ■

Suggested Reading

Leon Fink, *Workingmen's Democracy: The Knights of Labor and American Politics*.

Harold Livesay, *Samuel Gompers and Organized Labor in America*.

Nick Salvatore, *Eugene Debs: Citizen and Socialist*.

David Stowell, *Streets, Railroads, and the Great Strike of 1877*.

Questions to Consider

1. Why was it difficult for workingmen to organize trade unions?

2. How did manufacturers justify their anti-union tactics?

Theodore Roosevelt and Progressivism
Lecture 60

> Progressivism is the general name for a group of reform movements of the early 20th century. Progressive reformers tried to increase honesty and efficiency in business and government, to forestall monopolies at the head of the great economy, to Americanize immigrants, and to substitute rational and scientific planning and methods for dependence on tradition and ad hoc methods.

Progressivism was America's first urban-based reform movement. Its adherents were businessmen, managers, and professionals. Some Progressives (most were Anglo-Saxon Protestants) believed their social status was declining. They believed in honesty, efficiency, and expertise. Common sense and hands-on practicality were no longer adequate in the complex industrial world. They believed in democratic solutions to the threat of plutocracy. Among Progressive campaigns were those for the direct election of senators and for the recall of elected officials.

Many were racial supremacists and eugenicists. Building a superior race appeared to them consonant with building a better society. Southern racial segregation intensified under Progressive auspices (including the administration of Woodrow Wilson).

Theodore Roosevelt (1858–1919) embodied early Progressivism. He transformed himself from a weakling into an advocate of hearty manliness. He thought it his duty as a gentleman to get involved in state politics and contest corrupt political machines. A personal crisis in 1884 led to his temporary abandonment of New York and politics in favor of High Plains farming.

Roosevelt believed in purification through violence and was excited by the chance to go to war. He believed America should join the great imperial powers. He led the Rough Riders, a cavalry unit, in the Spanish-American War of 1898. Military success led him to the governor's mansion, the vice presidency, and the presidency of the United States in quick succession.

Roosevelt reinvigorated the role of president. He supervised a new policy toward the environment. He conducted an energetic foreign policy. He became the first American to win the Nobel Peace Prize and supervised the building of the Panama Canal. He made a distinction between good and bad trusts in his anti-monopoly policy. He accepted the need for closer regulation of corporations whose conduct had public consequences. He sometimes took the union side in industrial disputes.

> **It was also under Woodrow Wilson that these two Progressive reforms ... came about: the direct federal election of senators and the creation of a direct federal income tax.**

His successor, William Howard Taft, disappointed Roosevelt. He tried to reenter the White House in 1912, by which time every candidate claimed to be "Progressive." Roosevelt came to regret his announcement, in 1904, that he would leave office after the next election. Taft lacked Roosevelt's flair for good public relations and came into increasing conflict with corporations.

Roosevelt tried to regain the Republican presidential nomination in 1912. The regular party organization was too strong for him. He created the Progressive ("Bull Moose") Party instead. The Bull Moose Party split Republican votes, enabling Woodrow Wilson to win the election of 1912. Wilson was only the second Democrat to be president since the Civil War. He had been a professor, then president, of Princeton University and a reform governor of New Jersey.

Progressivism reached its high water mark in Wilson's first administration. Wilson's policies were reminiscent of Roosevelt's planned "New Nationalism."

Woodrow Wilson, who became president, was inaugurated in 1913, and was only the second Democrat to be president since the Civil War. There had been a long period of Republican dominance ever since then, just broken twice by the two-time election of Grover Cleveland.

Wilson was a southerner. He'd been a professor of political science at Princeton University, and had risen to become the president of Princeton, and then a Progressive reform governor of New Jersey. Ironically, in practice, Woodrow Wilson's early policies were more or less exactly what Roosevelt had said he was going to do had he been elected. That is, Wilson put into action a policy rather like the New Nationalism: He created the federal reserve—a national banking overseer, and he established the Federal Trade Commission in 1914—scrutinizing corporations' manipulations and misconduct, but not forcing them to break up, despite his pledges beforehand.

It was also under Woodrow Wilson that these two Progressive reforms—originally advocated by the Populists and voiced repeatedly in the intervening years—came about: the direct federal election of senators; and the creation of a direct federal income tax—with whose consequences we continue to live right up until the present. ■

Suggested Reading

John Milton Cooper, *The Warrior and the Priest: Woodrow Wilson and Theodore Roosevelt.*

Richard Hofstadter, *The Age of Reform.*

Nathan Miller, *Theodore Roosevelt: A Life.*

Robert Weibe, *The Search for Order: 1877–1920.*

Questions to Consider

1. How did the circumstances of Roosevelt's life make him a successful national leader?

2. Why did Progressivism become popular among so many strata of American society?

Mass Production
Lecture 61

The first Industrial Revolution had been in textiles, in iron and steel manufacture, in railroads, and in oil production, but the second Industrial Revolution, or the elaboration of it, was principally in consumer goods.

The first Industrial Revolution was in textiles, iron and steel, railroads, and oil, but the second was in consumer goods. After 1870, manufacturers turned to mass production of consumer goods. Mid-19th-century manufacturers, such as Isaac Singer (sewing machines) and Samuel Colt (guns), began to mass-produce industrial products that they could sell cheaply, in large numbers, through nationwide advertising campaigns.

Singer, who started from small beginnings, invented the sewing machine in 1853. He also initiated the idea of purchasing on the installment plan. Singer mass-produced sewing machines; Colt mass-produced guns. At first they relied on "fitters" to assemble nearly identical parts.

The first devices with full interchangeability of parts were Albert Pope's bicycles, which enjoyed a popular vogue in the 1890s. Improvements in machine tools and hard steel facilitated Pope's achievement. The American bicycle craze enabled him to enlarge his market, which ranged from the very lavish to the very modest. The bicycle inspired other inventors, including the Wright brothers, who began as bicycle repairmen.

Chicago's slaughterhouses, in which animals on overhead conveyors were systematically killed and dismembered, gave Henry Ford (1863–1947) the idea for a moving assembly line on which automobiles would be systematically assembled. The first cars were individually built luxury items, far too expensive for the average consumer. Ford looked for economies of scale and standardized manufacture.

Ford installed the first moving assembly lines in 1913. By the end of the year, he was producing 200,000 cars a year. He brought down the price of cars and raised his workers' wages, which increased their loyalty and made them potential buyers. Automobile manufacture in the early 20th century accelerated trends in mass production of consumer goods.

> **Advertising developed along with mass production of consumer goods, because it wasn't enough to make these things; you had to make sure that you could then sell them.**

Ford's contemporaries recognized the magnitude of his achievement. Lenin tried to persuade him to supervise the industrialization of post-revolutionary Russia. Aldous Huxley's *Brave New World* uses a calendar that dates years from Ford's time. Manufacturers recognized the importance of human psychology in making mass production succeed.

Scientific management experts controlled more areas of the worker's experience. Frederick Taylor's time-and-motion studies increased

A Model T Ford, a car manufactured by the Ford Motor Company from 1908 through 1927. More than 15 million Model Ts were built in Detroit and Highland Park, Michigan.

efficiency. His texts became the bibles of time-management proponents. His disciple Frank Gilbreth took the principle of time-and-motion studies further, inventing therbligs, a unit of muscular movement that assisted micromanagement policy. Elton Mayo's Hawthorne experiment revealed psychological aspects of employee welfare by testing various environmental factors, such as climate and color.

Advertising developed hand-in-hand with mass production of consumer goods. Classic devices in the industry—such as inducing artificial need or using celebrity endorsements—developed in the 1910s and 1920s. Buying on credit spread alongside advertising. Ford spent $2 million advertising the Model A in its first week. ■

Suggested Reading

Daniel Bell, "Work and Its Discontents: The Cult of Efficiency in America," in *The End of Ideology*, edited by Daniel Bell, pp. 222–262.

Catherine Gourley, *Wheels of Time: A Biography of Henry Ford*.

David Hounshell, *From the American System to Mass Production*.

Robert Kanigel, *The One Best Way: Frederick Winslow Taylor and the Enigma of Efficiency*.

Questions to Consider

1. What were the crucial breakthroughs that made it possible to mass-produce consumer goods?

2. Who benefited from these changes, and who suffered because of them?

World War I—The Road to Intervention
Lecture 62

The First World War was by far the most destructive war that the world had ever seen up to that time. Eventually, about 10 million people died in this war, and it completely wrecked nations.

The United States undertook a more active foreign policy after 1898. The Spanish-American War gave the United States a powerful presence in the Caribbean and the Philippines. The Philippines campaign (1899–1902) caused controversy at home, with atrocities committed on both sides. The Panama revolution and the canal project bore witness to American hemispheric power. American forces intervened in the Mexican revolutionary wars, killing 200 Mexicans in Vera Cruz in 1914.

When the European nations went to war in 1914, America stayed aloof. Sympathy for Britain was strong among President Wilson's cabinet members, however, and the president himself became convinced that Britain's cause was just. American businesses and banks traded heavily with England and France between 1914 and 1917, while farmers enjoyed an immense export boom and high prices for as much food as they could produce.

A German submarine sank the British luxury liner, the *Lusitania*, off Ireland with the loss of 1,200 lives, 124 of them American, causing American public opinion to swing sharply toward a British alliance. The Germans claimed that the *Lusitania* was carrying munitions, in addition to civilian passengers. The British government flatly denied it at the time, although subsequently we've learned that it's true; it was.

President Wilson decided to send a diplomatic note of protest to the German government criticizing this act. He phrased it in such angry language, with the implicit threat that America would join the war on the British side, that the secretary of state begged him not to send it. William Jennings Bryan advised Wilson not to send the note. But when Wilson sent it anyway, Bryan resigned in protest.

Wilson was reelected in 1916 under the slogan "He kept us out of war." But no sooner had he been re-inaugurated than the German decision to declare unrestricted submarine warfare against American ships in the Atlantic led him to declare war against Germany in 1917. Britain, France, Italy, and Russia fought against an alliance of Germany, the Austro-Hungarian Empire, and Turkey. We now know that German claims that it was carrying munitions were true.

The campaigns for 100 percent Americanism, which had already been roaring along to help assimilate immigrants, were intensified.

America's previously small army grew rapidly in 1917 and trained hard, taking the field in large numbers in 1918 under the leadership of General Pershing to forestall a German assault on the western front. Soldiers took newly invented IQ tests. Such was the state of American medical care that 30 percent of recruits were declared to be physically unfit. YMCA purity crusaders were shocked at the immorality of the army camps. Mennonites and Quakers were not allowed to claim conscientious objector status. Many were sent to prison, where they were mistreated and accused of cowardice.

When British dollar reserves were exhausted, American bankers asked the president to extend loans or credits to Britain. Failure to do so would have created economic recession. Wilson and many of his cabinet were pro-British. There was a common belief during the age that the Anglo-Saxon peoples of the United States and Britain shared a common destiny.

For westerners, Europe seemed so far away, and the issues involved so remote, that they didn't support sending their men to war. Wilson was able to consolidate western support by use of the Zimmerman telegram. This intercepted message, sent from Germany to Mexico, promised the return of territories lost by Mexico to the United States in 1847.

Citizens, in general, and clergy, in particular, became enthusiastic for war. Four-minute men, organized by George Creel's Committee of Public Information, gave patriotic fundraising speeches and urged young men to enlist. Congress passed legislation to restrict opponents of the war. Clergy preached blood-curdling pro-war sermons. And state governments and vigilante groups tried to destroy all German vestiges in America. ■

Suggested Reading

Ray Abrams, *Preachers Present Arms*.

John Milton Cooper, *The Warrior and the Priest*.

Gordon, *Woodrow Wilson and World Politics: America's Response to War and Revolution*.

David Ramsay, *Lusitania: Saga and Myth*.

Questions to Consider

1. Why did America's initial intention to stay neutral break down between 1914 and 1917?

2. What were the domestic consequences of American intervention in the war?

World War I—Versailles and Wilson's Gambit
Lecture 63

President Wilson traveled to Versailles near Paris for the 1919 peace talks, while another American, Herbert Hoover, organized famine relief in large parts of devastated Europe.

The years 1917–1918 witnessed a transformation of the geopolitical world. German military successes on the eastern front helped precipitate the Russian Revolution of 1917, with immense consequences for the rest of the 20th century.

America's decision to intervene in World War I was the first great change, ending a long era of its separation from European affairs. The Russian Revolution was the second great change. Lenin's Bolsheviks alone among Russian groups promised an end to the war, in which about five million Russians died. The Treaty of Brest-Litovsk (1918) acknowledged Russian defeat and German gains in Eastern Europe.

Victory on the eastern front enabled Germany to launch a powerful offensive in the west in the spring of 1918. American forces, arriving just in time with a million men by April, helped repel the advance. They played a useful role in the counteroffensives that led to Allied victory by November 11, 1918. American losses were high—more than 100,000 killed—except by comparison with those of the European nations.

President Wilson traveled to Versailles (near Paris) for the 1919

Woodrow Wilson, President of the United States from 1913 to 1921.

peace talks while another American, Herbert Hoover, organized famine relief in large parts of a devastated Europe. Wilson was disillusioned to discover that the victorious leaders, Lloyd-George of England and Clemenceau of France, were more interested in imposing blame and vindictive reparations on Germany than in making the world safe for democracy.

> **It's impossible for us today to look back on the Versailles treaty without the gnawing awareness that its shortcomings ... were laying the foundations for the Second World War.**

A committee of political and academic experts brought by Wilson, the Inquiry, had planned the peace. It ensured that the American negotiators were well supplied with detailed information and maps. Wilson hoped that the Fourteen Points, based on their advice, would be the basis of a non-vindictive treaty. He hoped to make good on his claim that this had been the "war to end all wars" and the war "to make the world safe for democracy." German consent to an armistice on November 11, 1918, was based on the Fourteen Points. The final point established an international League of Nations.

Uneasy about the treaty but hopeful of rectifying its worst features through an international government body, the League of Nations, Wilson was thwarted by the American Senate's refusal to join the League. Fearing loss of sovereignty, the Senate refused to affiliate the United States with the League. The Russian Revolution intensified anti-radical fears in America and prompted the Red Scare, in which many foreign-born Socialists, anarchists, and Communists were summarily deported.

The British and French leaders, Lloyd-George and Clemenceau, were determined to make Germany accept blame and responsibility for the war. Germany felt betrayed by Wilson's acceptance of the western Allies' approach. Some American negotiators also deplored Wilson's retreat, which led to extraordinary demands on the German state and people. Dismayed by the outcome, he accepted it only in the expectation that the League of Nations would correct its worst features.

Turbulent events at home helped to defeat Wilson's hopes:

- The Spanish flu epidemic swept across America (and the world), proving even more lethal than the war itself, killing 22 million people worldwide (625,000 in the United States).

- An anarchist bomb almost killed Attorney General Mitchell Palmer.

- The "Palmer Raids," bypassing all due process for radicals, were his retaliation.

- American Socialism, already weakened by the imprisonment of Debs, was now riven between Socialists and Communists.

Some senators were influenced by Keynes's Economic Consequences of the Peace, which warned of the treaty's shortcomings. Wilson exhausted his strength on an unsuccessful 8,000-mile nationwide tour to promote the treaty and league. He was disabled by a severe stroke during this journey. The weaknesses of the Versailles treaty laid the groundwork for another, even worse war 20 years later. ∎

Suggested Reading

Alfred Crosby, *America's Forgotten Pandemic: The Influenza of 1918*.

Robert H. Ferrell, *Woodrow Wilson and World War I, 1917–1921*.

David M. Kennedy, *Over Here: The First World War and American Society*.

John Maynard Keynes, *The Economic Consequences of the Peace*.

Questions to Consider

1. What were President Wilson's worst mistakes at the conclusion of World War I?

2. What were the short- and long-term consequences of the Russian Revolution?

The 1920s
Lecture 64

As I mentioned previously, laws of 1921 and 1924 restricted immigration from southern and eastern Europe, and banned immigration completely from Asia. There was an openly racial intent in this legislation.

The transformation of America into an ethnically and religiously diverse nation, predominantly urban, caused a backlash in the 1920s. Fear of foreigners contributed to immigration restriction laws in 1921 and 1924, which restricted immigration from southern and eastern Europe and banned immigration from Asia.

Native Protestants' hopes for a morally improved nation, expressed in the Prohibition Amendment to the Constitution, soon soured. Prohibition created ideal conditions for the development of organized crime; so many otherwise respectable citizens violated the alcohol ban that it became unenforceable. It had been the first issue to mobilize large numbers of women in a political campaign.

The moralistic, intolerant side of American Protestantism was exhibited also in a revival of the Ku Klux Klan, which targeted Catholics and Jews as much as African Americans during the 1920s, and contributed to the defeat of America's first Catholic presidential candidate, Al Smith, in 1928.

The Ku Klux Klan aimed to restore virtuous, rural Protestant values. Revived in 1915 at Stone Mountain, Georgia, it advocated white supremacy but was also anti-Catholic and anti-immigrant. Fundamentalists tried to prevent the teaching of evolution in state high schools. Tennessee passed an anti-evolution law in 1925. The Scopes "monkey trial" of 1925 was a courtroom victory but a public relations defeat for the fundamentalists. Al Smith, Democratic presidential candidate in 1928, was an Irish Catholic and could not attract the votes of southern white Protestants.

A brighter side of the 1920s saw high levels of employment; rising real wages; improved city conditions; the rapid spread of cars, refrigerators, and radios among ordinary families; and the maturing of the movie industry (silent until 1927). Hollywood movies became a central part of popular entertainment, and inventive marketing created the first generation of great stars. Rapid technological improvements provided "talkies" after 1927. Healthier cities also witnessed the creativity of such artistic movements as the Harlem Renaissance. The fiction of Sinclair Lewis criticized the new consumerism and the conformity it bred.

> **Certainly, Prohibition did more than anything else to facilitate the rise of organized crime.**

Consumer durable goods became accessible to a rapidly growing middle class. Per capita income was $522 in 1921 and $716 in 1928, far higher than in any other country in the world. America was producing 5.5 million cars per year, and Americans owned five-sixths of all the world's cars.

The Great Migration from the southern countryside to northern cities created urban black enclaves, notably in Harlem, New York. Influential community leaders competed for black audiences. Marcus Garvey and the Universal Negro Improvement Association led a "back to Africa" campaign. W. E. B. DuBois and the NAACP continued the campaign against segregation. Black and white intellectuals joined to enjoy and study the Harlem phenomenon. Alain Locke described and analyzed the "new Negro" in 1925.

The size and reach of the federal government declined through the 1920s. Calvin Coolidge was content to keep government intervention in the economy to a minimum. He won reelection in his own right in 1924. The restraint of the government makes a striking contrast with the immense growth of totalitarian states in Italy and Russia. ∎

W. E. B. DuBois (1868–1963), sociologist and African American leader.

Suggested Reading

Frederick Lewis Allen, *Only Yesterday*.

Jervis Anderson, *This Was Harlem: A Cultural Portrait*.

Norman H. Clark, *Deliver Us from Evil*.

F. Scott Fitzgerald, *The Great Gatsby*.

Questions to Consider

1. How did changes in everyday life affect American women in the 1920s?

2. Who supported Prohibition and why? Who opposed it and why?

The Wall Street Crash and the Great Depression
Lecture 65

The collapse of share prices on the Wall Street stock exchange in the fall of 1929 was traumatic, because it ruined many influential people and destroyed the savings of thousands more, who had let themselves be deceived by false hopes.

Boom conditions in the 1920s eventually led to unrealistic expectations and the creation of speculative bubbles, culminating in the Wall Street crash. The collapse of the Florida land boom in 1926, when land values fell by many times overnight, was a premonition of worse things to come.

Miami grew from 30,000 people in 1920 to 75,000 in 1925. Its warm climate made it an attractive place for vacations and retirement, once rail connections had been completed. Land values rose vertically in the early 1920s, enriching speculators. But two hurricanes devastated the Miami area in 1926, causing 400 deaths. Property price collapses left half-developed areas unfinished.

Minimal government regulation of the stock exchange, and the development of unsound financial practices, created unrealistic expectations among speculators in the late 1920s. The collapse of share prices on Wall Street in the fall of 1929 was traumatic, because it ruined many influential people and destroyed the savings of thousands more who had let themselves be deceived by false hopes.

The stock market prices also exceeded their real values. Investment trusts, buying on margin, and other speculative mechanisms enabled investors to spend more money than they possessed. Respectable national figures encouraged participation. The Wall Street crash of 1929 ended the fantasy. Only about one percent of the entire population had invested in the market, but it was the most influential one percent.

The years 1929–1933 witnessed a downward spiral of economic shrinkage, bankruptcies, factory closings, and rapidly worsening unemployment.

People riding a freight train during the Great Depression. As large numbers of workers during this period were unable to find work at home, some opted to travel around the country in search of better job prospects.

Its causes continue to be debated, but certainly, a principal factor was maldistribution of income throughout the population. Five percent of Americans possessed one-third of all personal income. Another cause was American overproduction. By 1890, the United States was producing more food (among other commodities) than it could consume. Short-sighted American tariff policy, which made it more difficult to export food and other products, made matters worse.

International financial instability also contributed to the Depression, especially the instability resulting from the Treaty of Versailles, which hindered German recovery. The Depression led to mass unemployment and underemployment. Individuals more often blamed themselves than the economic system.

Large numbers of migratory workers rode trains in search of work, and hobo communities became common. The downward spiral of the Depression perpetuated itself. Wage cuts and layoffs, the logical response of individual employers, shrank spending power and demand, which in turn, made recovery more difficult.

Now, President Hoover had to take the blame for the Great Depression.

Drought in the Great Plains states added the Dust Bowl to this catalogue of woe. Over-farming of the plains in the boom years of the 1910s had destroyed natural brakes on dust storms. And large numbers of bankrupt farmers, the Okies, sought an alternative way of life in California.

President Hoover, elected in 1928, became the scapegoat for these disasters. His own political and economic apprenticeship and an uninterrupted career of successes had provided no lessons for dealing with a national disaster of this magnitude. He was forced to take the blame. Until then, his life had been an uninterrupted line of successes:

- He was a prosperous mining engineer.

- He organized the evacuation of Americans from Europe at the beginning of the First World War.

- He organized famine relief in Belgium and, later, for postwar central Europe.

- As secretary of commerce under Presidents Harding and Coolidge, he contributed to a successful trade policy.

As president, Hoover spoke on behalf of the traditional American values of self-help and economic independence but was willing to intervene to restore economic confidence. He used military force against the Bonus Marchers, a group of World War I veterans who had been promised a bonus and asked for their money in advance. The spread of shantytowns, nicknamed "Hoovervilles," demonstrated his decline in popular esteem. His anti-Depression measures were too little and came too late to satisfy his critics.

He supported public works schemes, including the Boulder Dam and the Los Angeles Aqueduct, and was willing to incur federal government deficits, and he refused to support direct government-backed participation in industry. Ironically, Franklin Roosevelt criticized him for profligate spending during the campaign of 1932. ■

Suggested Reading

Martin L. Fausold, *The Presidency of Herbert Hoover*.

John Kenneth Galbraith, *The Great Crash*.

John Garraty, *The Great Depression*.

William Leuchtenberg, *The Perils of Prosperity, 1914–1932*.

Questions to Consider

1. In what ways did government actions create the conditions for the Wall Street crash and the Great Depression?

2. What were Herbert Hoover's strengths and weaknesses, and how did they serve him as president?

The New Deal
Lecture 66

> [Roosevelt's] efforts to prevent cutthroat competition among businesses, and his creation of federal agencies to oversee a wide variety of relief and regulatory tasks, marked a dramatic shift of power out of the states, and into the federal government.

President Franklin Roosevelt, elected in 1932, experimented boldly with political reforms in the first 100 days after his inauguration. His efforts to prevent cutthroat competition among businesses, and his creation of federal agencies to oversee a wide variety of relief and regulatory tasks, marked a dramatic shift of power out of the states and into the federal government. Many of his early innovations were nullified by the Supreme Court in 1935 and 1936, but they created a favorable impression on much of the nation, even though unemployment figures were slow to diminish. Roosevelt's New Deal began a shift of power from the states to the federal government but was unable to solve the basic dilemmas of the Depression.

Roosevelt had led a distinguished career in Democratic Party politics. A blueblood, related to President Theodore Roosevelt, he had enjoyed a privileged childhood. He rose to the post of assistant secretary of the Navy under Woodrow Wilson and was the Democrats' vice presidential candidate in 1920. He overcame polio to become governor of New York. He was better able to unite the disparate parts of the Democratic Party than Al Smith.

Nothing in Roosevelt's past augured the steps he took in beginning the New Deal. He was willing to experiment with unfamiliar methods and was more flexible than Hoover. The first 100 days of his administration, renamed as the New Deal, was one of the most creative periods in all of American political history. New agencies and programs included the National Recovery Act (NRA), the Civilian Conservation Corps (CCC), and the Tennessee Valley Authority (TVA). Roosevelt "sold" his policies by artful use of radio "fireside chats."

Innovation continued well into his first administration, with immense and lasting consequences. Creation of Social Security transformed old age in America. A dependable government pension made old age far more livable. The National Labor Relations Act (NLRA) strengthened American trade unions. NLRA protection set off a wave of union organizing and membership increases, despite Depression-era unemployment. The first sit-down strikes by striking auto workers in 1937 at Flint, Michigan, prevented the use of strike-breakers. The Supreme Court ruled in 1935 that several New Deal policies were unconstitutional. The National Recovery Administration and the Agricultural Adjustment Administration were overturned in cases in 1935 and 1936.

> **The first 100 days of what [Roosevelt] called the New Deal was one of the most creative periods in all of American political history.**

Among Roosevelt's more imaginative adversaries were Father Charles Coughlin, a Detroit priest whose skillful use of radio for political propaganda was equal to Roosevelt's own, and Huey Long the populist governor of Louisiana, a demagogue whose plans to oust the president were cut short by assassination. Roosevelt tried to safeguard his political innovations by enlarging the Supreme Court with pro-New Deal justices. Widespread resistance to the plan showed that, for all his popularity, he had overstepped his mandate.

Roosevelt's policies generated critics, some of them highly innovative, who threatened his bid for reelection in 1936. Father Coughlin began as a New Deal supporter but turned against FDR. Huey Long planned a challenge to FDR in 1936. Long's "Share Our Wealth" plan offered $5,000 per year to every family. And Francis Townsend, a California doctor, proposed to aid the elderly and jump-start the economy. Roosevelt overcame all rivals, including the Republican Alf Landon of Kansas, in the 1936 election, during which he won every state except Maine and Vermont.

Safely returned to the White House, Roosevelt rashly tried to reshape the Supreme Court. The number of justices is not specified in the Constitution but had been held at nine for a century by the time of the New Deal. FDR's plan to enlarge the court with Democratic appointees and to encourage old judges' retirement failed. Democratic Party critics assailed this partisan break with tradition. One judge, Owen Roberts, began to vote for, rather than against, New Deal legislation, prompting the quip: "A switch in time saves nine!"

The New Deal restored confidence in the nation but did little to alleviate unemployment, which remained high throughout the 1930s, until rearmament began at the decade's end. Memoirs recall the era's monotony and harshness. Sustained unemployment was particularly harmful to men's self-esteem. Poverty forced people to do without many of the labor-saving devices that had been available to those who could buy them for decades. ■

Suggested Reading

Alan Brinkley, *Voices of Protest: Huey Long, Father Coughlin, and the Great Depression*.

Paul Conkin, *The New Deal*.

Sidney Fine, *Sit Down: The General Motors Strike of 1936–1937*.

Arthur Schlesinger, Jr., *The Age of Roosevelt* (3 vols.).

Questions to Consider

1. Why did Roosevelt achieve such popularity, even though he was unable to solve the Great Depression?

2. How did the lives of trade unionists and old people change during the 1930s?

World War II—The Road to Pearl Harbor
Lecture 67

American popular opinion, aroused and inflamed and outraged by Pearl Harbor, meant that the very last thing the Americans would have done after that was to agree to withdraw their forces from the Pacific.

The New Deal alone never solved the Great Depression. Only the onset of a second global war in 1939, and the immense economic demands it made on America, could do that. Hitler's rise to power in Germany, facilitated by the faults of the Versailles treaty and the feebleness of the League of Nations, caused growing alarm in America. Lacking an American presence, the league proved powerless against aggressors in the 1930s. It was unable to prevent the Japanese invasion of China, and it was unable to prevent the Italian conquest of Ethiopia.

The United States did nothing to prevent Hitler's rise to power in Germany, where Germans nurtured an acute sense of grievance over the Versailles treaty. Hitler won the elections of 1933 and quickly cemented his position in power. Hitler's astonishingly successful attacks on his European neighbors in 1939 and 1940 and his vicious anti-Jewish policies caused many Americans to seek intervention on behalf of Britain.

By the summer of 1940, Britain was Hitler's only significant undefeated rival. American journalists' news of London in the blitz and of Churchill's resonant speeches swung more American opinion in favor of intervention. Roosevelt sent goods convoys and old destroyers to Britain on the lend-lease plan. American warships, such as the Reuben James (sunk in October 1941 by a German submarine), helped guard convoys to Britain when America was still nominally neutral.

Roosevelt was cautious. He was reelected to an unprecedented third term in November 1940 and began to give covert aid to Britain in the Atlantic antisubmarine war. He committed America to full-scale war, however, only after the Japanese attack on Pearl Harbor, Hawaii, in December 1941. America's military forces, small and unprepared for war, began to expand rapidly, but the prospect of victory appeared infinitely remote in early 1942. Meanwhile, anti-Japanese panic on the West Coast led to the mass internment of Japanese American citizens in relocation camps, one of the nation's worst civil rights violations.

Roosevelt defeated Wendell Willkie in November 1940. Willkie, a former Democrat, had been dismayed by the TVA and the rise of federal intervention in everyday life. His campaign, funded by private power companies, was nicknamed "the charge of the electric light brigade." Roosevelt denied that America might go to war. Hitler attacked Russia in the summer of 1941. In the long run, it ensured his defeat.

General MacArthur, U.S. commander in the Philippines in World War II.

The Japanese attack on Pearl Harbor, Hawaii, on December 7, 1941, finally brought America directly into the war. The Japanese government miscalculated American resolve to fight. They believed democracy had eroded the martial virtues. hey anticipated American withdrawal from the Pacific theater. Pearl Harbor was a severe setback but not ultimately decisive. American aircraft carriers and submarines, which were to prove decisive in the Pacific, survived. Claims that FDR knew the attack was coming are implausible. The attack silenced isolationists. Two days later, Hitler, Japan's ally, declared war on America.

Pearl Harbor news led to an invasion scare in California and prompted the policy of interning Japanese Americans. Accused of being actual or latent traitors, they were forced to sell or give away their property. Most were shipped to inland internment camps. Japanese American men were nevertheless expected to serve, but in the European theater.

Rearmament ended the Depression, while America hurried to enlarge its armed forces. In 1939, the American army was ranked about 20th in size in the world, but it began to grow rapidly with draftees and volunteers. The army discovered that many Depression-era Americans were unfit for service for want of regular medical care. It encountered a defeat in 1941 and 1942. American aircraft were destroyed on the ground in the Philippines. The Bataan garrison, besieged and without hope of relief, surrendered to a brutal captivity. General MacArthur, ordered to return to America, promised the men he had to leave behind in the Philippines that he would return. ■

> **The Japanese have totally misread America's resolve, which became steely hard after Pearl Harbor.**

Suggested Reading

John Keegan, *The Second World War.*

David O'Brien and Stephen Fugita, *The Japanese-American Experience.*

Gordon Prange, *At Dawn We Slept: The Untold Story of Pearl Harbor.*

Donald Watt, *How War Came: The Immediate Origins of the Second World War.*

Questions to Consider

1. Why did FDR delay America's participation in World War II for so long?

2. Why did America face short-term disadvantages and long-term advantages in its conflict with Germany and Japan?

World War II—The European Theater
Lecture 68

> Hitler himself was very struck by the incongruity of the alliance that he faced, a republic, America, an imperial monarchy, the British Empire, and a Marxist dictatorship, the Soviet Union, a very weird combination of allies against him.

Roosevelt and Churchill, believing Hitler to be the greater of their two enemies, agreed on a "Europe first" policy. Stalin urged them to split Germany's forces by launching an early second front in Western Europe as early as the summer of 1942. Churchill, content to see the two great totalitarians tearing each another to pieces, counseled delay. American forces fought in North Africa and Italy while the Army Air Force joined the Royal Air Force in massive bomber raids against German industry.

Transatlantic convoys braved submarine attacks to concentrate supplies to England, which supplied the D-Day invasion of France in June 1944. A year of hard campaigning led to the defeat of Germany, a junction with Soviet forces in central Europe, and discovery of the Holocaust's full horror. America itself was transformed in these years into a high-wage, high-employment economy, with women taking on many jobs previously reserved for men.

Soviet leader Stalin was eager to see them invade western Europe, to relieve some of the pressure on his own forces. From the summer of 1941 to the summer of 1944, the Russians faced almost the full weight of German power. America sent lend-lease aid to Russia on Arctic convoys. Churchill reminded FDR that Stalin had recently been Hitler's ally and should not be trusted too implicitly.

German fortification of the Atlantic coast made an invasion difficult. An Allied raid on Dieppe in 1942 was a bloody failure. America and Britain concentrated on air attacks against Germany. The air war was expensive in terms of men and materiel. Postwar surveys showed it to have been relatively ineffective and to have boosted the enemy's determination to resist. Occasionally, firestorm raids would be murderously destructive.

Keeping Atlantic shipping lanes open also demanded massive resources. Allied success in Europe depended on America's ability to ship goods to Britain en masse, against determined submariners. Allied code-breakers helped swing the war in their favor. American and German soldiers first clashed in North Africa. The reconquest of North Africa was followed by an Anglo-American invasion of Sicily and Italy.

Production of aircraft, landing craft, tanks, trucks, jeeps, and all other munitions, grew astronomically during the war years, making the success of the invasions possible.

The second front in Europe began on D-Day (June 6, 1944), and the European war finished 11 months later. Eisenhower's invasion force surprised the Germans by attacking Normandy, not the Calais area. Paratroopers behind enemy lines destroyed bridges to hamstring German reinforcements. Bombing and naval bombardment preceded the landing craft. Landings were nevertheless fiercely opposed, especially at Omaha Beach. The Allies built a powerful beachhead, then broke out into France. The American advance was checked in the Ardennes that winter (the Battle of the Bulge) but resumed in the spring and led to the invasion and conquest of western Germany.

Soviet armies rolled into Germany from the east while the "Big Three" leaders met at Yalta to decide the disposition of the postwar world. Stalin was determined not to relinquish his grip on the eastern European nations he had reclaimed from Hitler. He was embittered against Churchill and FDR for what he regarded as the tardiness of the second front. Hitler committed suicide in his bunker on April 30, 1945, and his successor, Admiral Doenitz, surrendered unconditionally a week later.

The war energized America, annihilated unemployment, and stimulated prodigious feats of technology and productivity. Large numbers of women worked at previously all-male tasks. A government campaign named the typical female factory worker "Rosie the Riveter." Government and most employers regarded the women as strictly temporary employees. Marriage rates and the birth rate rose sharply—the baby boom began in 1943.

Henry Kaiser developed and mass-produced Liberty Ships. He cut production time on a ship from 355 days in 1941 to 14 days in 1943. Production of aircraft, landing craft, tanks, trucks, jeeps, and other munitions grew astronomically during the war years.

The war bore witness to a significant redistribution of income. High wages made a return of the depression after the war less likely. Access to basic health care meant that, even including war casualties, American life expectancy increased during World War II.

Hollywood made patriotic and propaganda films to keep civilian morale high. Ronald Reagan and other stars worked on propaganda projects. ■

Suggested Reading

John Morton Blum, *V Was for Victory: Politics and American Culture during World War II*.

Max Hastings, *Overlord*.

John Keegan, *The Second World War*.

Studs Terkel, *The Good War*.

Questions to Consider

1. At what point did victory for Hitler become impossible?

2. What were the principal sources of tension between the Allies?

World War II—The Pacific Theater
Lecture 69

Early in 1943, American code-breakers worked out that a flight of aircraft was going to be carrying Admiral Yamamoto, the man who'd planned the Pearl Harbor raid. They were able to intercept his planes and shoot them down, a great morale booster for the Americans and a corresponding morale crusher for Japan itself.

America's aircraft carriers had survived Pearl Harbor and became the crucial weapon of the Pacific war. The battle of Midway was the first in history in which the rival fleets never even came over each other's horizon, being fought instead by carrier-based aircraft. American seaborne forces seized a succession of Pacific islands from which aircraft could bomb the Japanese mainland but found progress slow and enemy resistance tenacious.

Aircraft carriers and island air bases were central to American Pacific war strategy. The Doolittle raid was designed as a symbolic response to Pearl Harbor. Bombers flew from the carrier Hornet at maximum range on April 18, 1942, to bomb Tokyo. The raid demonstrated the Japanese emperor's vulnerability and horrified his generals.

The battles of Coral Sea and Midway in the spring of 1942 showed that the Americans could meet the Japanese on equal terms. Yorktown, damaged at Coral Sea, was repaired in 2 days instead of 90, as its captain had expected. At Midway, the two fleets never came over each other's horizon. Good luck enabled American dive-bombers to sink four enemy aircraft carriers in the space of five minutes. Seaborne aviators were acutely vulnerable.

American forces concentrated on seizing Japanese-held islands on which air bases for attacks on Japan and its shipping lanes could be built. American air power and submarines made it increasingly difficult for Japan to resupply its dispersed island holdings. Desperate land and sea battles gave America an eventual victory at Guadalcanal in the Solomon Islands and in subsequent island campaigns. The largest naval battle in history was fought at Leyte

Gulf, Philippines, in October 1944. American anti-Japanese propaganda created a harsh racial stereotype of the enemy.

As the war approached Japan itself in 1944 and 1945, Japan's resistance became even more ferocious, even though by then, its defeat was inevitable. The American campaign against Iwo Jima suffered heavy casualties, nearly 7,000 killed and 13,000 wounded.

> **Apart from everything else, the Americans' technological efficiency and technological superiority meant that they were able to keep their fleet running very effectively and repair it quickly.**

The Okinawa campaign was worse, taking 12,000 American lives, with 50,000 more wounded. Kamikaze (suicide) aircraft wrought destruction among American invasion forces. Japan prepared a civil defense army, some of whose members were expected to fight with nothing more than bows and arrows or sticks. From November 1944, American bombing planes, supported by long-range fighters, made round-the-clock raids on Japanese industry and cities.

The length and ferocity of the war, and the anticipation of worse things to come in an invasion of Japan itself, were the context in which the American atom bomb was perfected and used. Enrico Fermi's experiment at the University of Chicago in 1942 had shown that nuclear fission was possible and that it had a potential military application.

The Manhattan Project enjoyed secrecy and a high government priority. General Leslie Groves organized the project, which was conducted at Hanford, Washington; Oak Ridge, Tennessee; and Los Alamos, New Mexico. J. Robert Oppenheimer led the team of physicists at Los Alamos. The first bomb, tested in the New Mexico desert on July 16, 1945, proved spectacularly successful.

President Truman, elevated to office just before the end of the war in Europe, had to decide whether atomic bombs should be used against Japan. He had not been a member of Roosevelt's inner circle and had no foreign policy experience. He shared his advisors' belief that a conventional invasion of Japan would be costly in lives and might take years. He doubted the viability of arranging a demonstration.

Truman elected to use the bomb. The first, dropped from the B-29 Enola Gay, destroyed Hiroshima on August 6, 1945. The explosion killed 70,000 people outright. The second, dropped three days later, destroyed Nagasaki. Japan surrendered on August 14, with no conditions except the preservation of their emperor. American soldiers who would have participated in the invasion of Japan, and most civilians, were delighted.

General MacArthur accepted the formal Japanese surrender on September 2. At the time, he was on board the USS *Missouri*. ■

Suggested Reading

Richard Rhodes, *The Making of the Atomic Bomb*.

E. B. Sledge, *With the Old Breed at Peleliu and Okinawa*.

Ronald Spector, *Eagle against the Sun*.

John Toland, *The Rising Sun: The Decline and Fall of the Japanese Empire*.

Questions to Consider

1. What challenges did the American military have to overcome in its war against Japan?

2. What factors made the debate over use of the atomic bomb difficult?

The Cold War
Lecture 70

> Truman made the momentous decision *not* to revert to the customary American policy of isolationism, but, rather, to take up the burden of world leadership that Britain had relinquished.

World War II did not end with a general peace treaty. The principal victors, America and the Soviet Union, disagreeing over the future of eastern Europe and ideologically hostile to each other, fell out. Britain, severely weakened by the war, signaled to President Truman that it could no longer maintain a worldwide imperial policy. He made the momentous decision not to revert to the customary American policy of isolationism but, rather, to take up the burden Britain had relinquished. A temporary dividing line drawn through Europe became permanent—Churchill described it as the "Iron Curtain."

Soviet possession of nuclear weapons by 1949 created a geopolitical stalemate. Neither side could afford to upset the balance of terror. Nuclear weapons were much cheaper to maintain than conventional armies and were, thus, attractive foundations for American defense policy. Nevertheless, their proliferation over the ensuing decades to a point of mutual assured destruction caused anxiety and an intense moral debate about their legitimacy inside the United States.

The victors of the Second World War could not agree about the disposition of the postwar world. Presidents Roosevelt and Truman believed that European countries liberated from Germany should hold free elections. The "Big Three" leaders met at Teheran (November 1943), Yalta (February 1945), and Potsdam (July 1945) to discuss war policy and the postwar situation. Tensions and mistrust among them were already evident before the fighting finished.

Stalin was determined to create a pro-Soviet zone in eastern Europe. His armies were in place, enabling him to enforce his will. In the decades after

World War II, the "Iron Curtain became both an economic and a political dividing line.

Britain's uncertain future presented America with new international responsibilities. Winston Churchill was voted out of office during the Potsdam meeting, to be replaced by Labour Prime Minister Clement Attlee. War exhaustion prevented Britain from maintaining its world-spanning imperial role.

President Truman decided to maintain an American presence in Europe rather than withdraw into isolationism. America took over from the British in backing the anti-Communist regimes of Greece and Turkey in 1947. An influential American diplomat, George Kennan, conceived the policy of containment to prevent the worldwide spread of Communism. The Marshall Plan (1947) dedicated American resources to the economic revitalization of western Europe.

Soviet possession of nuclear weapons by 1949 created a geopolitical stalemate. Neither side could afford to upset the balance of terror.

NATO, formed in 1949, converted Germany from enemy to ally. Its creation followed an American victory in the Berlin airlift (1948–1949). NATO politics, as in the Suez crisis of 1956, added complex moral dilemmas to American foreign policymaking.

Nuclear weapons development continued and became a decisive factor in the postwar geopolitical situation. The first Soviet atom bomb was exploded in 1949; America tested its first hydrogen bomb in 1952. Rapid escalation in the explosive power of the bombs was matched by escalation in the development of delivery systems. Nuclear weapons were attractive because of their comparative cheapness. Their attractions to American taxpayers were offset by their excessive power.

Nuclear weapons underlay America's deterrence policy throughout the Cold War. Nuclear war-gaming created complex logical puzzles about what might happen and how targeting should be planned. New concepts included mutual assured destruction (MAD) and overkill. Appreciation of fallout dangers led to the Atmospheric Test Ban Treaty of 1963.

Influential Americans opposed dependence on nuclear weapons. The first antinuclear movement culminated in the early 1960s. A second campaign challenged the policy in the early 1980s.

The potential for nuclear-armed confrontation with the Soviet Union underlay every element of American foreign policy between World War II and 1990. Subsidiary wars in Korea and Vietnam, along with political struggles over ex-colonial Africa, all revolved around it. ■

Suggested Reading

Michael Mandelbaum, *The Nuclear Question: The United States and Nuclear Weapons*.

David McCullough, *Truman*.

Wilson Miscamble, *George Kennan and the Making of American Foreign Policy*.

Daniel Yergin, *Shattered Peace: The Origins of the Cold War and the National Security State*.

Questions to Consider

1. Did nuclear weapons make the Cold War more or less dangerous?

2. What were the effects of the Cold War on Europe and America's relations with it?

The Korean War and McCarthyism
Lecture 71

The American decision to resist the Communist North Korean invasion of South Korea in 1950 intensified anti-Communist fears inside America, and it gave a demagogue, Senator Joseph McCarthy, the opportunity to exploit public fears, some of which were irrational.

Rapid changes in the world situation during the late 1940s contributed to fears that Communist espionage had undermined American security. The Soviet Union's completion of its own atomic bomb in 1949, sooner than the Americans had expected, was attributable partly to spies. Two among them, Julius and Ethel Rosenberg, were sentenced to death and executed in 1953.

Mao's Chinese revolution in 1949 and the defeat of Chiang Kai Shek, America's client, intensified fears about internal loyalty. Rival Chinese armies under Chiang and Mao had postponed their enmity to fight the Japanese invasion during the 1930s and 1940s. American postwar aid to Chiang could not promote mass Chinese loyalty to his cause. He retreated to Taiwan and defended it with the help of the U.S. Navy. Anti-Communist Republicans in Congress denounced Truman for the "loss of China."

The Truman administration instituted background checks on federal employees in 1947, searching for Communist infiltrators. The Alger Hiss case indicated the presence of Communists in important government positions. American Communism had enjoyed a brief period of support during the Great Depression. Loyalty investigations by federal and state governments, and within industries, often compelled former Communists to redeem themselves by identifying former associates: "naming names."

The Korean War intensified domestic fears of Communism. Containment policy was put to the test when Kim Il-Sung, North Korea's Communist dictator, invaded South Korea in June 1950. Korea had been conquered by Japan and partitioned at the 38th parallel by America and the Soviet Union at the war's end. A speech by Secretary of State Dean Acheson appeared to exclude Korea from the nations under American protection.

President Truman decided almost at once to support Syngman Rhee, anti-Communist dictator of South Korea. A Soviet boycott of the United Nations Security Council (because of its refusal to seat a Chinese Communist member) enabled Truman to get unanimous Security Council support of U.N. action against North Korean aggression. General Douglas MacArthur took command of the American invasion. The Inchon landings, in September of 1950, were a brilliant strategic success. MacArthur expelled the invaders and went over to the offensive by invading North Korea.

His success prompted Mao to commit Chinese forces to the war. Their counterattack in November 1950 forced American troops into retreat. MacArthur advocated direct attacks on China, in pursuit of total victory. General Omar Bradley and the Joint Chiefs of Staff disagreed, fearing Russian entry into the war and nuclear escalation.

> **The Korean War bore witness to a technically brilliant campaign by General Douglas MacArthur following his invasion of Inchon.**

MacArthur's public challenge to Truman's orders prompted the president to dismiss him as commander. General Matthew Ridgway assumed command and stabilized the military situation. Congressional Republicans lionized MacArthur in their campaign against the Truman government. Truce negotiations began in July 1951, but fighting continued. The war continued until early 1953 when a new president, Eisenhower, arranged a truce that held for the next half century. Thirty-three thousand Americans—and two million Koreans—died.

Anti-Communist fears and the Korean War provided the conditions in which Senator Joseph R. McCarthy (R., Wisconsin) was able to make reckless allegations of disloyalty in high places. A former judge and non-combat war veteran, McCarthy needed a high-profile issue to ensure reelection. He had falsely claimed to be a decorated ex-aviator when he first ran for the Senate in 1946.

In a February 1950 speech, he claimed that Truman had failed to dismiss hundreds of "known Communists" in the State Department. His theatrical displays at the Senate Subcommittee on Investigations kept his adversaries on the defensive. Press and popular enthusiasm for his charges discouraged other Republicans from restraining or contradicting him. His defenders argued that he was right on the big question: that America must think of itself as being at war against Communism.

However, he overstepped the bounds of credibility by attacking the U.S. Army. The Army-McCarthy hearings (1954) were televised, enabling large numbers of citizens to witness his overbearing tactics firsthand. The Senate passed a motion of censure against him in 1954. ■

Suggested Reading

Richard Fried, *Nightmare in Red: The McCarthy Period in Perspective.*

Max Hastings, *The Korean War.*

Allen Weinstein, *Perjury: The Hiss-Chambers Case.*

Stephen J. Whitfield, *The Culture of the Cold War.*

Questions to Consider

1. Why were Americans' fears of Communism so intense in the late 1940s and early 1950s?

2. How did America's role in the Korean War differ from its role in the Second World War?

The Affluent Society
Lecture 72

America sprawled in the 1950s and became, incomparably, the wealthiest society in the entire history of the world. Anxiety about the Cold War peril was offset by domestic luxury, and a sense of almost boundless technologically enhanced possibilities for the future.

World War II had witnessed a dramatic redistribution of income throughout society. Generous veterans' benefits for the millions who had served in the war contributed to a transformation of everyday life in America. The GI Bill enabled veterans to gain low-cost education and mortgages. Congress unanimously passed the act in 1944. It dramatically raised the number of Americans graduating from college every year, from 160,000 graduates in the 1930s to half a million per year in 1950.

Levittown and other mass-produced suburbs contributed to suburban sprawl. William Levitt, the Henry Kaiser of prefabricated housing, built 17,500 houses at Levittown, Long Island, in 1947. Sunbelt cities, such as San Diego, Los Angeles, and Miami, were urban areas of low population density, built around their highway systems and made feasible by air conditioning.

Baby-boom children of the late 1940s and 1950s enjoyed more luxurious circumstances than any previous American generation. America's population rose from 140 million in 1945 to 200 million in 1967. Childhood and adolescence became distinct categories for marketing, entertainment, and psychologists. Disneyland (1955) is a prime example of such child-centered marketing. The rise of Las Vegas speaks to the amount of surplus money generated by the postwar American economy.

Citizens' mobility also increased. Possession of automobiles became almost universal. Building the interstate highway system stimulated the 1950s economy. Mass air travel began to displace the railroads.

High employment and high wages enabled most home-owning families to rely on single earners. The military-industrial complex contributed to economic buoyancy. The rapid spread of consumer credit facilitated this luxurious life.

Anxiety accompanied the new affluence. The shadow of nuclear war tempered national optimism. Children practiced civil defense drills against nuclear attack. Journalists and ministers debated the ethics of defending one's personal nuclear fallout shelters against negligent neighbors.

Intellectuals worried about a tendency to excessive conformity. Influential books, such as David Reisman's *The Lonely Crowd* (1950), argued that American individualism was in decline. Other social critics feared that advertising now obscured Americans' view of reality. American prisoners of war in Korea proved vulnerable to brainwashing.

Parents worried about their children's future in a complex world. One concern was the incidence of juvenile delinquency, depicted in such films as *Rebel Without a Cause* (1955) and *The Wild One* (1953). American public education did not seem equal to the era's technical and political challenges.

Of course, the shadow of nuclear war, which seemed very, very close in the late 1940s and early 1950s, tempered the national optimism.

American culture nevertheless enjoyed greater worldwide prestige than ever before. American literature no longer deferred to European masters. Norman Mailer, Saul Bellow, Ralph Ellison, Arthur Miller, and others were authors of the first rank. Meanwhile, New York became the capital of the art world. Abstract Expressionism, then Pop Art, were American-led movements in painting. Jackson Pollack, Andy Warhol, and Roy Lichtenstein made formidable reputations. And American corporations also dominated the world: among them Coca-Cola, Kodak, GM, Ford, Levi's, Exxon, I.T.T. In addition, American universities enjoyed a golden age of expansion, funding, and respect in the 1945–1965 era.

Galbraith's *The Affluent Society* (1957) gave a name to the era and pointed out many of its strengths and weaknesses. ■

Suggested Reading

John Kenneth Galbraith, *The Affluent Society*.

David Halberstam, *The Fifties*.

David Reisman et al., *The Lonely Crowd*.

Richard Pells, *The Liberal Mind in a Conservative Age*.

Questions to Consider

1. Why did an apparently successful situation create such a vigorous intellectual backlash?

2. What were the sources of sustained postwar prosperity?

The Civil Rights Movement
Lecture 73

The Supreme Court's decision in the *Brown* case, 1954, and then the Montgomery bus boycott of 1955 to 1956, inaugurated the legal and activist phases of the Civil Rights movement. By 1965, a combination of lobbying, direct action, and shifts in public sympathy had eventuated in the complete legal abolition of racial segregation.

The Supreme Court's decision in *Brown v. Board of Education* (1954) was the culmination of a long period of legal struggle for desegregation. After World War II, the federal government abandoned racial segregation. A government committee report, *To Secure These Rights* (1947), condemned American racial policy. Truman abolished racial discrimination in the military and in federal hiring in July 1948.

The Democratic Party divided over civil rights in 1948. Truman's victory showed that a pro-civil rights stance was not necessarily politically dangerous. Jackie Robinson's desegregation of major-league baseball in 1947 was symbolically important.

The *Brown* case (1954) delighted civil rights advocates and horrified segregationists. The Warren Court used sociological and psychological evidence to show that separate education for a racial minority was inherently unequal. The Court's 1955 order for "all deliberate speed" in desegregation was ambiguous.

Civil rights activism accelerated in the late 1950s and early 1960s. Perhaps most significant were the events surrounding the Montgomery bus boycott led by Martin Luther King, Jr., in 1955 and 1956. Rosa Parks agreed to test the local segregation laws and was arrested. NAACP women arranged a protest meeting, calling for the boycott and appointing King to lead it. Regular church meetings maintained community solidarity during the ensuing year-long boycott, which succeeded.

Martin Luther King, Jr. (1929–1968). For his leadership in the nonviolent civil rights movement in the United States, King was awarded the Nobel Peace Prize in 1964. He was assassinated in 1968.

Civil rights groups mounted campaigns in which confrontation and, hence, press coverage seemed likely. Sit-ins at lunch counters, beginning in Greensboro, North Carolina, and "freedom rides" on interstate buses provoked white aggression.

As with Mohandas Gandhi, nonviolence was an effective weapon against antagonists who had a conscience. Atlanta politicians realized the importance of desegregating nonviolently to preserve their city's public image. However, the Kennedy government dragged its feet for fear of losing votes in the "Solid South."

The Birmingham campaign of 1963 provoked Bull Connor to violent reaction, as King had expected. His "Letter from Birmingham Jail" argued the nationwide importance of seemingly local events. The Birmingham bombings prompted more vigorous federal support for the movement. Bomb attacks on churches killed four girls during their Sunday-school classes in 1963. In August, King made his "I Have a Dream" speech, and getting the Nobel Peace Prize in 1964 made him a world-famous figure.

Malcolm X and Elijah Muhammad offered an alternative model of black citizenship. The Nation of Islam offered a mirror image of white racism, relying as it did on a creation story that included "white devils." It rehabilitated drug addicts and criminals, offering them pride and dignity. Malcolm X became the most influential advocate of black separatism and criticized King's version of integration. His militancy made King seem, by comparison, a mild and mainstream reform advocate.

Legally sanctioned segregation disappeared quickly, but efforts to destroy de facto segregation proved far more difficult. "Massive resistance" collapsed quickly. Prince Edward County, Virginia, was unusual in closing its public schools (1958) rather than desegregating them. The policy of token integration was taken by most southern school districts.

By the end of the millennium, the end of the century, affirmative action programs themselves were in retreat in most parts of America.

The Civil Rights and Voting Rights Acts of 1964 and 1965 abolished racial categories. "Freedom Summer" in 1964 witnessed black and white students registering black voters in Mississippi. But destructive race riots in the "long, hot summers" of the 1960s soured the good feeling that had been generated by the Civil Rights movement. Political rights, though vital, had not reduced immense disparities of wealth.

Affirmative action programs reintroduced racial categories in 1965, but now with an integrationist rather than a segregationist intent. Opposition to busing and affirmative action spread in the American north. Militant white parents and students attacked school buses in Boston. "White flight" accelerated suburban growth and racial re-segregation. *Griggs v. Duke Power* (1971) upheld affirmative action, but the *Bakke* case (1978) began its dissolution. ■

Suggested Reading

David Garrow, *Bearing the Cross: Martin Luther King, Jr. and the Southern Christian Leadership Conference*.

Alex Haley, *The Autobiography of Malcolm X*.

Martin Luther King, Jr., *Stride toward Freedom*.

J. Harvie Wilkinson, *From Brown to Bakke: The Supreme Court and School Integration, 1954–1978*.

Questions to Consider

1. Why was the Civil Rights movement able to overcome segregation relatively quickly after 1954?

2. What problems persisted in the African American community after the movement's victory, and how effectively were they resolved?

The New Frontier and the Great Society
Lecture 74

Youthful, handsome President Kennedy brought charisma to the White House in 1961. His election ... contributed to a decline in inter-religious tensions in America. Kennedy's escalation of the Cold War ... was offset by a new concern for legislating on behalf of the poor and minorities.

Kennedy's family history and personal attributes made him an attractive candidate and president. His father, Joseph Kennedy, was wealthy and ambitious for himself and his sons. He profited from the liquor business during and after Prohibition. He was American ambassador to Britain at the start of World War II. He schemed to attain the presidency for his oldest son Joseph, Jr., but the young man was killed in a plane crash. John, the younger son, became the focus of his ambitions.

John Kennedy had a distinguished war record and made rapid progress through the Democratic ranks. His adventures on P.T. 109, the boat he captained during the war, became the basis of a book and film. He was elected to the House of Representatives in 1946. He became the junior Massachusetts senator in 1952. His wife, Jacqueline Bouvier (married, 1953), was elegant, beautiful, and politically accomplished.

His presidential campaign in 1960 led to one of the narrowest victories in

John F. Kennedy (1917–1963), 35th president of the United States from 1961 to 1963.

American history. Adlai Stephenson, having lost twice to Eisenhower, was an unconvincing candidate. Kennedy managed to allay fears that his Catholicism made him unsuitable for the presidency. The two candidates, Kennedy and Nixon, debated on TV, Kennedy being the more photogenic. Nixon accepted the razor-thin electoral verdict against him, despite widespread rumors of election fraud in Chicago.

> [The inner-city riots] very, very severely undercut the good feeling that had been generated by the Civil Rights movement.

The Kennedy administration believed in a more aggressive pursuit of the Cold War than had Eisenhower. Kennedy argued for "flexible response" and "brushfire wars" around the periphery of the Cold War. He supported vigorous anti-Communist action in Vietnam. He reacted to the Cuban Revolution first by supporting, then by abandoning, the Bay of Pigs counter-invasion (1961).

Kennedy attempted to regain the initiative in the Cuban missile crisis of 1962. The U.S. Navy created a "quarantine" line in October 1962 that Soviet ships, carrying missiles to Cuba, must not cross. The prospect of war prompted Soviet Premier Krushchev to back down.

In domestic politics, Kennedy took limited initiatives on behalf of women, minorities, and the poor. Progress was inhibited by his slender electoral victory and the power of conservative southern white Democrats in Congress. He became progressively more sympathetic to the Civil Rights movement as segregationist violence intensified.

Lyndon B. Johnson (1908–1973), 36th president of the United States (from 1963 to 1969).

He was assassinated in November 1963. Mystery surrounds the incident. The Warren Commission report only intensified speculation about the assassination. Lyndon Johnson was sworn in as president on Air Force One. Kennedy's good looks, charismatic personality, and "Camelot" mystique have turned him retrospectively into a larger-than-life figure.

The Johnson administration continued, and escalated, the work Kennedy had begun. Johnson, from humble Texan origins, was already a Washington veteran when Kennedy arrived. Relations between the two men, former rivals in the 1960s primaries, were never close. Johnson felt overshadowed by the Kennedy mystique and was scorned by the Kennedy loyalists. He was genuinely committed to abolishing racial segregation. He ushered the Civil Rights, Voting Rights, and Immigration Reform Acts through Congress in 1964 and 1965.

Johnson won reelection in 1964 against conservative Republican Barry Goldwater, an Arizona senator. Goldwater offered "a choice, not an echo." He was a tactless, outspoken campaigner and lost severely. Goldwater's allegation that Johnson was insufficiently resolute in opposing Communism contributed to the escalation of the Vietnam War.

Johnson's War on Poverty program argued for "maximum feasible participation" by the poor themselves. The Economic Opportunity Bill created numerous organizations to combat poverty and helplessness. Overcoming longstanding opposition from the American Medical Association, Congress created Medicare and Medicaid. Inner-city race riots, beginning in Los Angeles, severely undercut the program's political popularity. ∎

Suggested Reading

Robert Dallek, *Flawed Giant: Lyndon Johnson and His Times, 1961–1973*.

Doris Kearns Goodwin, *Lyndon Johnson and the American Dream*.

Arthur Schlesinger, Jr., *A Thousand Days: John F. Kennedy in the White House*.

Garry Wills, *The Kennedy Imprisonment*.

Questions to Consider

1. Why is President Kennedy remembered so fondly by most Americans?
2. How did President Johnson advance the cause of American liberalism?

The Rise of Mass Media
Lecture 75

Twentieth-century America was almost universally literate, at least at some level. Thousands of newspapers throughout the century, including numerous foreign language papers that helped immigrants to adapt to the New World, were complemented by radio stations from the 1920s, and by television stations from the late 1940s.

Public schooling assured the rapid assimilation of new immigrants. Early 20th-century America also had a massive foreign-language press. Newspapers could embody the character of late 19th- and early 20th-century cities that were too big for face-to-face relations.

Joseph Pulitzer and William Randolph Hearst were the most skillful promoters of mass-circulation newspapers. They understood the value of big headlines, illustrations, low prices, and high-quality writing. They promoted sales by embarking on campaigns and "crusades."

Magazine editors developed the muckraking style. Ida Tarbell exposed the Standard Oil scandal for *McClure's* in 1904. Lincoln Steffens's *The Shame of the Cities* (1904) enjoyed mass circulation in journal and book form. Later muckrakers, such as Jessica Mitford (*The American Way of Death*, 1963), followed in their footsteps.

Radio broadcasting extended communication possibilities. Radio technology was developed out of telegraphy. By 1900, ship-to-shore Morse code messages were possible. Invention of the "audion tube" in 1906 made voice and music broadcasting possible. Amateurs and enthusiasts tinkered with radio until 1917, when the U.S. Navy took control of it, for fear of its espionage possibilities.

Regular civilian broadcasting began in the 1920s. Evangelical preachers, such as Amy Semple McPherson, quickly appreciated its possibilities. Radio was commercial and private in America; public and by license in Britain.

Ownership of radios in America grew from nearly nothing in 1919 to 12 million in 1930.

President Franklin Roosevelt realized the immense potential of broadcasting to give him direct access to voters. Radio ownership was close to universal by the Depression era. "Fireside chats" enabled FDR to explain his policies in person. His powerful rivals, such as Father Charles Coughlin, a master of negative campaigning, also enjoyed radio access.

Radio, like the movie industry, created widely loved fictional characters, along with news personalities:

- Freeman Gosden and Charles Correll created "Amos 'n Andy" in 1928.

- The Lone Ranger made his debut on a Detroit radio station in 1933.

- Edward Murrow became a highly respected news broadcaster, reporting from England during the German blitz.

Orson Welles created a brief national panic with his "War of the Worlds" broadcast in 1938.

Television intensified the effects established by radio. Television was technologically viable by the late 1930s, but World War II postponed its mass development. TV grew meteorically in the late 1940s and early 1950s. By 1960, it was almost universally available in America. It revived the careers of some fading Hollywood stars, such as Ronald Reagan. Its spectacles, such as *Twenty-One,* garnered massive audiences.

Television, too, began to play a crucial role in political life. Senator Estes Kefauver became famous for his televised hearings on organized crime in 1951, and Senator Joseph McCarthy was discredited by the televised Army-McCarthy hearings in 1954. The Kennedy-Nixon debate (1960) gave an advantage to the more physically attractive man. And Joe Maginnis's *The Selling of the President* (1969) is the classic account of how the candidate was "packaged" for electoral success by gifted and cynical TV professionals.

Television enabled citizens to follow dramatic and controversial events that were physically remote. It played an important role in turning American public opinion against the Vietnam War. And it followed the first human landings on the moon in 1969.

Religious groups made use of television, as of radio. Fulton Sheen, a Catholic priest, was the first major religious TV star in the 1950s. Television was also central to the ministries of Jerry Falwell and Jim and Tammy Bakker.

I think it's also worthwhile bearing in mind that we ... have, by far, the most access to competing sources of information and interpretation of that information.

Computers revolutionized personal communications and information access in the last decades of the 20th century. Phenomenal developments in transistor technology and miniaturization made computers possible. Transistors, invented in 1947, replaced cumbersome vacuum tubes. Jack Kilby invented the silicon-based integrated circuit in 1958, eliminating the problem of overheating.

Miniaturization, improvements in user-friendliness, and a gradual decline in cost brought computers to the business world in the 1960s and 1970s. The first video games, including PacMan, also appeared in the late 1970s. Intensification of these trends inaugurated a boom in personal computer ownership in the 1980s. IBM launched the first PC in 1981. The spread of the Internet and e-mail in the 1990s gave ordinary citizens almost instant access to one another around the world. ■

Suggested Reading

R. W. Burns, *Television: An International History of the Formative Years*.

Susan Douglas, *Listening In: Radio and the American Imagination*.

Joe McGinniss, *The Selling of the President, 1968*.

John Naughton, *A Brief History of the Future: From Radio Days to Internet Years in a Lifetime*.

Questions to Consider

1. Are there social costs, as well as benefits, to having extremely high levels of access to information?

2. How did the development of broadcasting change American politics?

The Vietnam War
Lecture 76

Vietnam was a French colony in the early 20th century. Japan invaded in 1942 but was ousted by the victorious allies in 1945. Ho Chi Minh, the Vietnamese nationalist leader, issued a Declaration of Independence based on the American model. To his dismay, the French Empire returned, aided by America as a quid pro quo for French participation in the defense of West Germany and NATO.

American defense planners became involved in Vietnam as part of the containment policy and because they were determined to "avoid another Munich." The events of the late 1930s suggested that the enemy should be fought earlier rather than later and that to delay would simply increase the enemy's power. Most Americans did not know where Vietnam was in the 1950s, and few could speak its language.

America became involved in the French colonial war in return for French cooperation in NATO in the late 1940s and early 1950s. Dien Bien Phu (1954) showed Ho's military skill and the decline of French imperial power. American support of South Vietnam enabled it to avoid elections after the Geneva Treaty.

A steady escalation of American civil and military aid in the late 1950s and early 1960s shored up Diem's regime. For young Americans, including Dr. Tom Dooley, who helped relocate Catholic Vietnamese from north to south, anti-Communism in Southeast Asia was an idealistic cause.

Presidents Kennedy and Johnson enlarged the American presence in Vietnam. Among Kennedy's difficulties was the deep unpopularity of the Diem regime. A Catholic minority ruled corruptly and heavy handedly. Kennedy finally permitted the assassination of Diem in 1963. South Vietnam never found a stable or popular alternative to Diem, which forced America to collaborate with a succession of corrupt and unpopular military dictators.

Johnson aimed to show that he was as stern an anti-Communist as Goldwater. The Gulf of Tonkin incident in 1964 provided the justification for direct military intervention in force. By 1968, more than half a million Americans were fighting in Vietnam.

The American expectation of success was reasonable. The American military had perfected long-range amphibious and jungle warfare techniques in World War II and Korea. Plus, the North Vietnamese army and the Viet Cong guerrillas in the south were poorly armed.

Enemy control of the countryside, especially at night, prevented the American and South Vietnamese forces from gaining ground. The terrain and the enemy's fighting style proved unsuitable to American tanks and high-tech weapons. Reliance on helicopters gave the Americans mobility and temporary local advantage, and they inflicted much heavier casualties than they suffered.

Uncertainty about the enemy's identity contributed to American commission of atrocities, such as the My Lai massacre. Declining morale among American troops also led to more than 700 "fragging" incidents. Drug addiction among the troops also became widespread.

Domestic opposition to the war increased after 1966. Growing numbers of young men resisted the draft or deserted. Student deferments brought thousands more into colleges, leaving the poor and minorities to take on a disproportionate share of the fighting. Sympathetic faculty at some schools aided draft resistance.

Demonstrations against the war attracted massive crowds. Martin Luther King Jr., Dr. Spock, Norman Mailer, and other celebrities became vocal opponents of the war. Antiwar intellectuals, such as Susan Sontag, began to visit Hanoi, the enemy capital, and to eulogize the North Vietnamese. Hatred of the war prompted Lyndon Johnson to abandon his plans for reelection in 1968. The Tet offensive sealed his fate.

The election campaign of 1968 witnessed scenes of massive disruption over the war issue. Democratic candidates split over whether to support the war policy—their Chicago convention was chaotic. Richard Nixon, the veteran Republican candidate, campaigned on behalf of the "silent majority" in making his comeback. The Paris peace talks made slow progress because Ho used them for political advantage and because Nixon wanted to achieve "peace with honor." Nixon's decision to attack North Vietnamese sanctuaries in Cambodia in 1970 set off another wave of protests.

The outcome of the Vietnam War influenced America in profound ways.

The outcome of the war influenced America in profound ways. American disengagement was complete by 1973. American POWs returned home. The Watergate crisis and the unpopularity of the war prevented an American return to Vietnam when intense fighting resumed. Saigon fell to North Vietnamese forces in 1975.

Repression and persecution in postwar Vietnam prompted some Americans to rethink their wartime attitudes. Neoconservatives, such as Michael Novak and Norman Podhoretz, argued that the American role had been justified after all, not least on human rights grounds. Government, constrained by the Vietnam syndrome, became cautious about subsequent interventions. The army restricted media access to operations. And politicians sought potential exit strategies before becoming engaged. Keeping American casualties low became a higher priority than ever. ■

Suggested Reading

Herr, *Dispatches*.

Karnow, *Vietnam: A History*.

Podhoretz, *Why We Were in Vietnam*.

Sheehan, *A Bright Shining Lie: John Paul Vann and America in Vietnam*.

Questions to Consider

1. Why did American intervention in Vietnam seem justifiable in the early 1960s?

2. How did the Vietnam War transform the character of American politics in the 1960s and 1970s?

The Women's Movement
Lecture 77

Postwar America idealized families in which father worked outside the home and mother didn't. Betty Friedan's book, *The Feminine Mystique*, published in 1963, showed that many middle-class women were bored by being confined to housework and mothering. Friedan's organization, the National Organization for Women (NOW), campaigned successfully for the abolition of gender discrimination in employment.

American women of the 1950s and 1960s were among the most privileged in world history, but many felt that their lives were being wasted. Their material circumstances were more luxurious than those of earlier generations. The massive middle class had access to better foods and more labor-saving devices than any earlier generation.

Those with college degrees felt their education was underused. Betty Friedan's *The Feminine Mystique* (1963) argued their case and identified "the problem that has no name." And employed women were vulnerable to discrimination in the workplace and pay differentials by gender.

President Kennedy appointed a Commission on the Status of Women in 1961, with Eleanor Roosevelt as its first head. Its 1963 report detailed discrimination against women in jobs, payment, and the law.

The women's movement began as a moderate lobbying effort, but radical women's liberation upstaged it in the late 1960s. Friedan's National Organization for Women (NOW, founded in 1966) campaigned for the abolition of gender discrimination in employment. Legislation in 1963 and 1964 included clauses preventing gender discrimination and stipulating equal pay for equal work. The 1960s and after saw a sharp rise in the number of women in previously all-male, high-profile jobs. Access to high-quality childcare became, and remained, a vital issue among feminists.

Women in the Civil Rights, student, and antiwar movements became critical of the sexism they encountered among their male comrades. They sought to oppose sexism and women's self-delusion by conducting "consciousness-raising" workshops. They denounced such conventional forms of female display as beauty contests. They compared themselves to other minority groups, especially African Americans.

A minority of radical feminists viewed the world as a perpetual conflict between men and women. Susan Brownmiller's *Against Our Will* (1975) was a notorious literary example of this outlook. There was also the question as to where lesbianism should be placed in the movement, which created tension among feminists in the 1970s.

The sexual revolution and its effects contributed to tension about questions of men's and women's roles. The Kinsey Reports on male (1948) and female (1953) sexuality found high levels of premarital and extramarital sex and of homosexuality. *Playboy* (1953) and other literature promoted a hedonistic philosophy of sex. And in 1962, Helen Gurley Brown published *Sex and the Single Girl*.

The dramatic improvement of contraceptives with the birth-control pill in the early 1960s made it possible to reliably separate sex from procreation. Concern about the "population explosion" also made contraception seem benign. Many American Catholics were indignant when, in 1968, their church affirmed its ban on contraceptives.

Taboos on cohabitation and childbearing outside of marriage declined sharply. Abortion gained legal protection in 1973 with the Supreme Court's decision in *Roe v. Wade*. And the gay liberation movement began in 1969, making analogous claims to those of the feminists and the Civil Rights movement.

Ronald Reagan with Sandra Day O'Connor, the first woman to become a U.S. Supreme Court Justice.

These rapid changes in social mores and gender roles led to an antifeminist backlash and some unanticipated consequences. Phyllis Schlafly led the campaign against the ERA. Passed through Congress easily in 1972, the amendment seemed sure to become part of the Constitution. Schlafly's "StopERA" opposed it for its perceived assault on traditional gender distinctions.

> **By the close of the 20th century, it was necessary for both partners to be working in order for the continued rise in standards of living to be maintained … .**

Religious groups campaigned against abortion. Some leaders offered powerful analogies from slavery and the Holocaust era. Operation Rescue in the 1980s tried to apply the techniques of the Civil Rights movement to the anti-abortion cause.

Women's participation in the workforce became more widespread than ever and eventually more necessary, too. Family incomes continued to rise into the 1990s but only by having both spouses in the workforce. ∎

Suggested Reading

Ehrenreich, *Re-Making Love: The Feminization of Sex*.

D'Emilio and Freedman, *Intimate Matters: A History of Sexuality in America*.

Friedan, *The Feminine Mystique*.

Steinem, *Outrageous Acts and Everyday Rebellions*.

Questions to Consider

1. What issues in American life led to the sudden emergence of feminism in the 1960s?

2. Why did American women divide over the benefits and drawbacks of the Equal Rights Amendment?

Nixon and Watergate
Lecture 78

Nixon's unnecessary decision to eavesdrop electronically on the McGovern campaign in the Watergate complex during the summer of 1972 led to the arrest of his agents, the "plumbers." Nixon won easily that fall but was ruined by an escalating series of revelations over the next two years.

Nixon's early career marked him as a talented and able politician. He, like John F. Kennedy, entered Congress in 1946. He was a graduate of Whittier College and Duke Law School, and he had served in the Pacific during World War II. His support for Whittaker Chambers in the Alger Hiss case brought him early prominence as an anti-Communist. He campaigned against Helen Gahagan Douglas in 1950 for a California seat in the U.S. Senate. Allegations that she was "soft on Communism" again proved effective.

Then, as Eisenhower's running mate in 1952, Nixon survived another challenge to his candidacy, when although he hadn't taken any illegal campaign contributions, he and his children had accepted a cocker spaniel dog. Nixon delivered the "Checkers" speech, an early masterpiece of TV political rhetoric, which generated a lot of support for his candidacy and enabled him to stay on the ticket when his candidacy and his political future had appeared to be jeopardized.

But during his eight years as president, Eisenhower restricted Nixon's actual political role. Then, even though he had been vice president for eight years, Nixon lost in one of the narrowest elections of the century to John F. Kennedy. In 1962, attempting to repair his political fortunes, Nixon ran for the job of governor of California, hoping that he could then restore his fortunes, but he lost again.

But all was not lost. Nixon took advantage of the social upheavals of the 1960s to strengthen the Republican Party and his own role in it. He realized that white southerners—who fiercely opposed policies like affirmative action—were now willing to vote Republican. He appealed for their support, calling them the "silent majority," that is, people who weren't out demonstrating in the streets.

Nixon's primary challenger was George Wallace, who shared one of Nixon's principal issues—law and order. Nixon's use of the media was disciplined now, but he was up against Wallace, who had a great genius for inflammatory rhetoric. Nonetheless, Nixon capably distinguished himself from Wallace and went on to win the presidency with 31 million votes to Wallace's 10 million.

As president, Nixon undertook important foreign policy initiatives. Perhaps most important of all, he opened diplomatic negotiations with China in 1972. Then he negotiated the SALT I Treaty with the Soviet Union in the same year. By 1973, he extricated America from Vietnam and abolished the draft—mission accomplished, yes—but he took too long. By then, the Kent State massacre had already occurred, which meant that he remained as hated a figure by the American political left as Johnson had been. Not to mention that Nixon wasn't able to preserve South Vietnam's permanent viability.

> **The combination of the Vietnam War and then the Watergate scandal created a sour mood of suspicion and betrayal inside the United States.**

Domestically, Nixon accepted most of the legacy of Johnson's Great Society, partly because he had to. Both houses of Congress were in Democratic hands in his first administration. School desegregation went forward faster now than it had in either of the Democratic administrations preceding it.

One colorful figure from the era was Nixon's vice president, Spiro Agnew, who publicized the administration's dislike of radicals and the media. Agnew was the Republicans' leading fundraiser in Nixon's first administration, and he had some wonderful speechmakers who came up with phrases like describing the press as "an effete corps of impudent snobs."

Then there was the Watergate break-in—totally unnecessary—and it ruined Nixon. The "plumbers" bugged the Democratic Party's headquarters in the Watergate complex (July 1972) and were caught. *Washington Post* journalists Robert Woodward and Carl Bernstein pursued the story tenaciously. They cultivated sources who enabled them to trace links back to the Oval Office.

Nixon won reelection easily in the fall of 1972. His opponent, George McGovern, represented the Democratic left, which had a passionate following, but only among a minority of voters.

After the reinauguration, Nixon was in a very awkward position. He had to give the appearance of prosecuting the Watergate investigation vigorously while he was actually involved in covering it up. A series of National hearings of a U.S. Senate committee drew massive TV audiences in the summer of 1973.

Bit by bit, investigators started finding, with the help of journalists like Woodward and Bernstein, evidence that Nixon and his aides had been involved in burglary, bribery, spying on the sex lives of their political opponents, blackmail, destruction of evidence, perjury, and even pledges of executive pardons to perpetrators who kept quiet. Investigators were also astonished to discover that Nixon had tape-recorded all of his Oval Office conversations. Nixon tried to claim "executive privilege" but was eventually forced to turn over the tapes, which incriminated him.

In the summer of 1974, the House of Representatives prepared to indict Nixon for "high crimes and misdemeanors." It denied his appeal for renewed military efforts in Vietnam. Nixon resigned rather than face trial in Congress. Vice President Gerald Ford took over until the next presidential election in 1976. ■

Suggested Reading

Kutler, *The Wars of Watergate: The Last Crisis of Richard Nixon.*

Nixon, *RN: The Memoirs of Richard Nixon.*

Wills, *Nixon Agonistes.*

Woodward and Bernstein, *All the President's Men.*

Questions to Consider

1. How did the social turmoil of the 1960s help Nixon in his rise to power?

2. What does Watergate tell us about the nature of the American political system in the mid- and late 20th century?

Environmentalism
Lecture 79

Theodore Roosevelt, as president, had established a national policy toward forests, parks, and national land use. Modern environmentalism began with Rachel Carson's book *Silent Spring*, published in 1962, a surprise bestseller that criticized the indiscriminate use of pesticides. By 1968, widespread concerns over pollution, chemicals in the atmosphere, and world overpopulation had gelled into what was at first called the "ecology movement."

Rachel Carson's bestseller *Silent Spring* was sharp in condemning the seemingly miraculous pesticide, DDT, in the effective killing of mosquitoes and lice. She pointed out that after a few years, new generations of the insects developed resistance to DDT. Her skillful rhetoric also made a strong case about the threat of the chemical entering the food chain and poisoning animals and humans.

This new public awareness sparked the publishing of several other books on the subject of the environment. For example, Ralph Nader's *Unsafe at Any Speed* (1965) inaugurated consumer advocacy and a new willingness among citizens to criticize corporations. And Paul Ehrlich's *The Population Bomb* (1968) argued that catastrophic famines due to overpopulation were inevitable and imminent. Meanwhile, the Sierra Club and other environmental groups campaigned to prevent the building of a dam in the Grand Canyon.

The first Earth Day, April 22, 1970, popularized the environmental cause. Activists invented symbolic and theatrical ways of drawing citizens' attention to environmental issues. The decade's tradition of protests and skepticism about government claims aided the environmental cause.

Congressional legislation after 1960 gave greater protection to the environment than ever before. Acts to improve air and water quality reduced ambient pollution levels. The National Environmental Policy Act (1969–1970) created the Environmental Protection Agency, which mandated environmental impact statements before new construction. Legislation enhanced the status of national parks, national forests, wilderness areas, and wild and scenic rivers. And the Endangered Species Act (1973) helped preserve threatened animals and their habitats.

Energy crises in the 1970s tested the nation's dedication to environmental protection. The oil crises of 1973 prompted Congress to vote in favor of a trans-Alaska pipeline. The pipeline was a technical triumph, but the transfer point, Port Valdez, was the scene of a severe oil spill in 1989.

Nuclear power stations seemed superior to coal-fired and hydroelectric stations in the 1950s but did not fulfill their advocates' hopes. The federal government encouraged utility companies to invest in nuclear power generation. Problems with thermal pollution, disposal of spent nuclear fuel rods, and poor construction practices led to widespread public doubts about the industry in the 1970s. The Three-Mile Island accident (1979) energized the antinuclear movement and effectively ended the technology's political viability.

After about 1975, concern for—and attention to—the jeopardized environment has been a central issue in American political life.

By the early 1980s, support for the environment was bipartisan, and it remained a central issue on the national agenda for both parties through the millennium. President Reagan's first secretary of the interior, James Watt, scorned environmental concerns, while membership in the environmental lobbies boomed. After two years, Watt and his EPA head, Ann Gorsuch, were both forced to resign. Reagan tried to recover by reappointing the original EPA administrator, William Ruckelshaus, to repair the damage.

In the late 1980s and early 1990s, both parties' candidates claimed the environment as a priority. George Bush Sr. declared in 1988 that he would be "the environmental president" and criticized his opponent Michael Dukakis for the pollution of Boston harbor. In 1992, democrat Al Gore published *Earth in the Balance* and brought his environmental concerns to the Clinton White House. ∎

Suggested Reading

Carson, *Silent Spring*.

Leopold, *A Sand-County Almanac*.

Opie, *Nature's Nation: An Environmental History of the United States*.

Reisner, *Rivers of Empire: The American West and Its Disappearing Water*.

Questions to Consider

1. Why did the environment become an important political issue only after World War II?

2. What were the strengths and weaknesses of the American response to environmental protection?

Religion in Twentieth-Century America
Lecture 80

By the early 20th century, America was the most ethnically and religiously diverse nation in the world. In the 20th century, it showed a continuing capacity to assimilate new ethnic types and new religions from all over the world. The First Amendment ensured separation of church and state.

Separation of church and state, along with freedom of religion, enabled many denominations and faiths to coexist in the United States. America's long tradition of religious revivals, already two centuries old, found its latest embodiment in the Billy Graham sensation of the late 1940s.

After World War I, the nation came to terms with its multireligious character. Protestants were still numerically dominant. They split between liberal and evangelical groups. The Scopes "Monkey Trial" (1925) exposed this fracture. Liberal Protestants tried to adapt to the most recent intellectual trends; fundamentalists to resist them.

Catholics, almost a third of the population, assimilated ethnically diverse peoples and lobbied for full American inclusion. Catholics asserted their place with great architectural monuments. Catholic machines dominated the political life of many cities. And the Legion of Decency influenced Hollywood productions.

Jews, about three percent of the population, debated the merits of assimilation. Reform Jews emphasized the ethical side of their tradition. Orthodox Jews tried to resist assimilation. Conservative Judaism, an American invention of the late 19th century, steered a middle course.

Mutual tolerance increased during the second half of the 20th century. The Holocaust and the creation of Israel contributed to the end of American anti-Semitism. Already mild by European standards, it became an impermissible breach of national standards after 1950. Will Herberg, in *Protestant,*

Catholic, Jew (1955), treated Judaism as one of the three main forms of American identity.

John F. Kennedy's electoral success and the Second Vatican Council contributed to the end of American anti-Catholicism. Paul Blanshard was the last of the "highbrow" anti-Catholics. Organizations to prevent the election of John F. Kennedy failed and had no successors. An American Jesuit, John Courtney Murray, advised the Vatican Council on its religious liberty document.

A series of Supreme Court decisions clarified the separation between church and state. School prayer and Bible-reading decisions (1962 and 1963) excluded all sectarianism from public schools. And the *Pierce v. Society of Sisters* case (1925) had upheld the constitutionality of religious and private education.

> **It remains true that America is unusual for its religious vitality and for its religious diversity, much more so than the other Western industrial nations.**

The 1960s social movements gave rise to new religions and new versions of old ones. Hippie Christians created the Jesus movement. Ted Wise's "Living Room" was an evangelical Christian sanctuary for hippies of the Haight-Ashbury district. Arthur Blessitt served the same function in Los Angeles. However, Jim Jones's "People's Temple" demonstrated that new religious movements could be unstable.

Women began to question their traditional religious roles. Liberal churches began to ordain women to the ministry, but Catholics and Orthodox Jews refused to change. Feminist theologians reinterpreted familiar biblical stories.

Americans who were disenchanted by the Judeo-Christian tradition turned to Asian spiritual alternatives. The Beatles' journey to the Maharishi Mahesh Yogi and their practice of transcendental meditation influenced young Americans. And Zen meditation attracted men and women who hoped to adapt it to their secular lives rather than become monks.

New immigrant generations further diversified America's religious landscape. Immigration reform laws in 1965 abolished discrimination based on national origin, enabling people from everywhere in the world to enter America.

American Islam was composed partly of African American converts and partly of immigrants. Malcolm X and, later, Louis Farrakhan helped popularize Islam among African Americans. Immigrants from India, Pakistan, Iran, Yemen, and other Middle Eastern nations brought a more traditional Islam to America. Political tensions after 1980 subjected some American Muslims to discrimination and assault.

American Hindus found their way of life changing, too, even as they tried to preserve it. Like earlier groups, their children's assimilation was difficult to forestall. ∎

Suggested Reading

Allitt, *Major Problems in American Religious History*.

Morris, *American Catholic: The Saints and Sinners Who Built America's Most Powerful Church*.

Noll, *The Old Religion in a New World: The History of North American Christianity*.

Smith, *Islam in America*.

Questions to Consider

1. Why was America so successful at incorporating new religious groups?

2. How did social movements affect religious life after 1960?

Carter and the Reagan Revolution
Lecture 81

Jimmy Carter, a born-again Christian with an unblemished moral reputation, benefited from Watergate to win the 1976 presidential race in a campaign that featured campaigning against Washington. He was unlucky, however, and confronted an ugly combination of economic stagnation and inflation, which was nicknamed stagflation.

The media had a great time exploiting the unusual circumstances of President Jimmy Carter's early life. Carter's religious views surprised journalists and policy professionals. Many evangelical ministers were very angered by the interview that Carter gave *Playboy* magazine. And his eccentric family provided plentiful material for colorful media stories. They had almost a Flannery O'Connor flavor, of a strange, gothic group living in the old, rustic South.

Carter was sincere in wanting to establish a foreign policy based on Christian principles, so far as that was possible. That's why he withdrew American support for the shah of Iran and for the Nicaraguan dictator Somoza. He also tried to promote lasting peace in the Middle East. The Camp David Accord between Israel and Egypt (1978) was his most important contribution to world stability. Carter also presided over the American relinquishment of the Panama Canal.

But the Carter administration ended in a foreign-policy crisis. Iranian revolutionaries seized 71 American diplomats and embassy staff members in November 1979 and held 52 of them as hostages for 444 days. Carter hoped to be able to preside over an extension of world peace, but instead, world tension seemed to be ratcheting up rather than down.

To rub salt in the wound, Iran, although clearly it intended eventually to release the hostages, waited until the very day of Ronald Reagan's inauguration. Once Reagan had actually taken the oath of office, then the hostages were released. It was clearly a calculated insult to Carter, not to release them into his care.

Meanwhile, Carter's economic policies were hamstrung by an awkward combination of slow growth and inflation (stagflation). The 1979 oil crisis intensified inflation. This caused great hardship for American auto makers, in particular Chrysler, which went bankrupt and had to be bailed out by a federal loan. With all this on his watch, Carter faced a bruising challenge in the Democratic Party for the 1980 nomination.

Ronald Reagan's victory over Carter in 1980 indicated a shift in the Republican Party and the new energy of the Religious Right. The Moral Majority, led by Jerry Falwell, brought the concerns of evangelical Christians into the political arena for the first time since the 1920s. They objected to the "permissive society," the sexual revolution, feminism, and a perceived breakdown of the family. They aimed to restore religion to a central place in public life.

Reagan's earlier fame, based on his radio, Hollywood, and television careers, gave Republican conservatives a handsome, relaxed, media-savvy

Iran waited until the day of Ronald Reagan's inauguration to release its American hostages.

representative. Reagan, like Eisenhower, deliberately gave the impression of being less politically capable than he in fact was. Surviving an assassination attempt soon after his inauguration enhanced his popularity.

His persona, as much as his policies, helped to ensure Reagan's reelection in 1984, especially when the Democrats pursued controversial policies and candidates. The Democrats' choice of a female vice-presidential candidate backfired. Jesse Jackson's role in the Democratic Party also contributed to the party's disarray.

Reagan abandoned the bipartisan consensus of recent decades in both domestic and foreign policy. He espoused the supply-side revolution in economic policy. Tax cuts, providing entrepreneurial incentives, would increase economic growth and enhance revenue.

Once Reagan had actually taken the oath of office, then the hostages were released. It was clearly a calculated insult to Carter.

The libertarian side of Republicanism gained more than the profamily and evangelical side, whose policy plans presupposed more government intervention and surveillance. Reagan, despite his rhetoric, did little to legislate against abortion or for school prayers. He also found it difficult to follow through on his promise to diminish the reach of the federal government.

Reagan's militant Cold War posture strained relations with the Soviet Union and contributed to bitter conflict in Latin America. Reagan supported the antiregime Contras in Nicaragua's civil war and the pro-United States regime in El Salvador. The "Star Wars" program prepared to militarize even beyond the Earth's atmosphere. Concessions in the START (Strategic Arms Reduction Treaty) talks augured the Soviet Union's internal crisis.

His "Teflon" image enabled Reagan to weather even the embarrassing Iran-Contra scandal of his second term. A press sensation followed with congressional hearings featuring Colonel Oliver North, who justified his unconstitutional activities by claiming the necessity of national security, claiming, "Yes, it's true that sometimes we have to conduct policies that may not live up to our highest ideals, but we do it in the name of forestalling something much worse."

President Reagan was clearly involved in these affairs but claimed not to have understood that arms were being traded for hostages. There was talk then of the impeachment of the president, but congressmen were very reluctant to do it, because they knew that Reagan remained very, very popular personally as president, even though clearly some of his policies had overstepped the bounds of legality. ■

Suggested Reading

Bourne, *Jimmy Carter: A Comprehensive Biography from Plains to Post-Presidency*.

Carroll, *It Seemed Like Nothing Happened: America in the 1970s*.

Johnson, *Sleepwalking through History: America in the Reagan Years*.

Wills, *Reagan's America: Innocents at Home*.

Questions to Consider

1. Why did evangelical Christian voters abandon Jimmy Carter even though he was more like them in most respects than was Ronald Reagan?

2. How did Cold War and Middle Eastern crises affect Presidents Carter and Reagan, and in what ways did their responses differ?

The New World Order
Lecture 82

The pressure of the arms race in the 1980s and military failure in Afghanistan combined to bring the great postwar Soviet Empire to and end that year. Joyful students demolished the Berlin Wall. Two years later, the Soviet Union itself went through a peaceful transition to democracy and survived an attempted countercoup.

The fall of the Soviet Union left the United States as the world's one great superpower, able to preside over the creation of numerous new nations with more or less democratic and America-inspired political systems. The sudden end of the Soviet Empire took the United States by surprise. The Soviet Union's participation in an unwinnable war in Afghanistan intensified hatred for the regime, especially among the non-Russian nationalities. And Mikhail Gorbachev's policies of Perestroika and Glasnost were too little, too late. After Russia's collapse, President George Bush Sr., announced that America would continue to monitor what he described as the "New World Order."

The Iron Curtain collapsed in 1989. Its most famous section, the Berlin Wall, had been a symbol of the Cold War confrontation since 1961. President Bush welcomed the birth of democracy in Russia, its former Soviet neighbors, and Eastern Europe. Meanwhile, China's regime crushed prodemocracy demonstrations in Beijing's Tiananmen Square in 1989.

The long nuclear standoff of the era had not ended in nuclear war; deterrence had worked. But the Gulf War tested the world's new geopolitical alignment in 1990 and 1991. Saddam Hussein's Iraq invaded its oil-rich neighbor Kuwait in August 1990. The United Nations, with strong American leadership, imposed trade sanctions on Iraq. When the sanctions yielded no result, the United Nations began air raids on January 15, 1991. When Hussein still refused to evacuate Kuwait, a ground force invasion of Kuwait, and of Iraq itself, followed on February 24, 1991. Very rapidly, the Iraqi invaders of Kuwait were repelled, and the war ended with total victory for the United Nations forces, not surprisingly, because the overwhelming preponderance of force was on their side. America's "smart bombs" and overwhelming technological superiority kept American casualties low and ensured rapid victory. American media were also kept far from the fighting, and the army controlled access to the news.

President Bush made the momentous decision not to pursue and overthrow Saddam Hussein. Had he done so, clearly he and his forces would very rapidly have been able to occupy Baghdad, the Iraqi capital, and overthrow the dictator, but then what?

> **The United States remained the one unquestioned superpower, and everything the Americans did mattered. It mattered if the Americans did act, and it mattered if they decided not to.**

Foreign policy dilemmas in the 1990s arose in southeastern Europe, east Africa, and in the form of terrorism from internal and external sources. Post-Communist Yugoslavia broke up into warring, and sometimes genocidal, ethnic fragments. NATO, the United Nations, and the United States attempted to stop the bloodshed without becoming overcommitted in the region. Intertribal genocide in Rwanda drew no effective American response.

Anti-American terrorism created an undercurrent of anxiety through the 1990s and into the new millennium. From the 1960s onward, political groups hijacked aircraft for purposes of political leverage and publicity. A car bomb attack on the World Trade Center in February 1993 killed 6 people and injured another 1,000. Even more vexing, enemies were harder to identify because they no longer always correlated directly with nation-states. Sometimes they were covert organizations and, in the case of Timothy McVeigh, organizations of American citizens themselves.

Still, the general picture was nevertheless a bright one. The United States remained the one unquestioned superpower, and everything the Americans did mattered. It mattered if the Americans did act, and it mattered if they decided not to. America had profound impact on the rest of the world. Something that not all Americans realized was that America itself had an immense cultural radiance around the world. Millions of people wanted to get into America. ■

Suggested Reading

Grosscup, *The Newest Explosions of Terrorism.*

Hutchings, *American Diplomacy at the End of the Cold War.*

Serrano, *One of Ours: Timothy McVeigh and the Oklahoma City Bombing.*

Trainor and Gordon, *The Generals' War.*

Questions to Consider

1. Why did the Soviet Empire collapse between 1989 and 1991?

2. What issues made the conduct of post–Cold War foreign policy difficult for Bush Sr. and Clinton?

Clinton's America and the Millennium
Lecture 83

> [President Bill Clinton] surrendered much of the Democratic Party's liberal heritage and presented himself as a vigorous probusiness president. His eight-year administration witnessed an incredible period of economic growth in America but also a continued growth in the gap between the richest and the poorest Americans.

President Clinton was, like every president in so many ways, an intriguing and controversial figure. He was a man with great skills on one hand but ruinous weaknesses on the other. Highly educated (a Rhodes scholar) and hard working, he had risen rapidly in politics. But two controversies overshadowed him: He avoided the draft in Vietnam, which to some undermined his credibility in dealing with military affairs, and there were well-substantiated rumors that he was a philanderer.

He became, however, a surprise Democratic favorite in 1992. The expectation was that George Bush Sr., was going to win reelection, because he'd just won a the Gulf War, and there's almost no surer way of ensuring your popularity. But America very rapidly went into an economic recession, so that the aura that had surrounded George Bush for his victory in the Gulf War began to dissipate in the ugly economic realities of 1992.

Clinton's initiatives on healthcare generated intense Republican resistance. Hillary Clinton's role in the healthcare plan was the most important political work ever undertaken by a First Lady, but her efforts were not the most tactful. It wasn't long before she faced the opposition of the American Medical Association, the doctors' union, the insurance companies, the pharmaceutical companies, and the Republican Party. That's too many adversaries to face. She should have done more to conciliate them if this plan was going to take place.

Like Hilary, Newt Gingrich didn't understand that usually you've got to get to your objective through a very circuitous route by building up alliances. He had a plan called the "Contract with America" to balance the federal budget, a plan that was blocked by the incredible tenacity of people who were going to lose their jobs if it really did shrink.

The most dramatic manifestation of this plan was that, in the face of Democratic reluctance to cooperate with the idea, they closed the federal government down altogether, briefly in December 1995 and again in January 1996, hoping to be able to make the case that it was Democratic intransigence and the president's stubbornness that led to the situation. This confrontational closure backfired against the Republicans, and Clinton was reelected in November 1996.

Clinton's second administration was hamstrung by the Lewinsky affair. Lewinsky, by talking to her friends about her affair with the president, contributed to press leaks. Clinton's lies about the affair led to his impeachment in December 1988. Democratic support in Congress and some Republican crossover votes enabled Clinton to win acquittal despite evidence of his improper conduct. The Republicans won back the White House, but only after a controversial count of Florida votes, when George W. Bush ran against Al Gore, Clinton's vice president.

Sustained economic boom times through the 1990s did nothing to narrow the gap between America's richest and poorest citizens. High technology created a new generation of entrepreneurial wizards, who gained almost the same social prestige of that afforded to the brilliant entrepreneurs of the 1860s and 1870s—people like Rockefeller and Carnegie. The failure of the Great Society's War on Poverty led to a drastic overhaul of Welfare and Aid to Families with Dependent Children in 1996.

The nation was riven by bitter debates over affirmative action, political correctness, and "culture wars." Powerful lobbies supported affirmative action, but the Supreme Court and voter initiatives began to restrict it in the 1990s. University campuses debated whether free speech was an absolute right. Also, American crime and imprisonment rates remained far higher than in most industrially developed nations, and its dependence on the death penalty made it unpopular among human rights groups.

The al Qaeda attack on the World Trade Center on September 11, 2001, emphasized the world's continuing instability. The well-planned attack took advantage of America's open society, porous immigration system, and high technology. The attackers' willingness to sacrifice their own lives made the event difficult to foresee or prevent. Conspiracy theories about 9/11 are implausible.

President George W. Bush and his cabinet drew the conclusion that America must take a more proactive approach to foreign policy. They attacked Afghanistan to oust the Taliban regime, which supported al Qaeda. Their military success there stood in striking contrast to the agonizing 10-year campaign that had contributed to bringing down the Soviet Union. The political aftermath of this victory was, however, ambiguous.

The painful and divisive events of 2001–2003 demonstrated that although America had overwhelming military power ... it could not enjoy domestic consensus about its proper role in the world.

In the opening months of 2003, Bush also decided to attack Iraq, claiming that it was preparing weapons of mass destruction. In justification of the attack was Iraq's consistent failure to cooperate with 10 years of U.N. resolutions and Saddam Hussein's human rights abuses. Against it was the danger of being sucked into a Vietnam-like quagmire, of arousing even more passionate anti-Americanism in the Arab world, and of being unable to create a stable political alternative to Hussein's despotism.

The war began in March 2003 and was another overwhelming American military success, annihilating the enemy in four weeks with scarcely 100 U.S. casualties. As in Afghanistan, the political aftermath was far less decisive.

The painful and devisive events of 2001–2003 demonstrated that although America had overwhelming military power at its disposal, it could not look forward to presiding over a harmonious world and could not enjoy domestic consensus about its proper role in the world. ■

Suggested Reading

Drew, *Showdown: The Struggle between the Gingrich Congress and the Clinton White House.*

Gitlin, *The Twilight of Common Dreams: Why America Is Wracked by Culture Wars.*

Klein, *The Natural: The Misunderstood Presidency of Bill Clinton.*

Langewiesche, *American Ground: Unbuilding the World Trade Center.*

Questions to Consider

1. What domestic problems continued to mar post–Cold War America?

2. What were the strengths and weaknesses of President Clinton?

Reflections
Lecture 84

It's easy to assume that history is something that happened once and for all in the past. Actually, it's continuous, and we live with history's burdens, as well as its benefits.

The 84 lectures of this course have shown that the immense vitality and diversity of American life have been underlain by certain recurrent themes. First, America's development has differed from that of most of the rest of the world in religiosity, in national confidence and sense of destiny, and in the nation's incredible good fortune.

Second, and closely related, America has enjoyed unprecedented wealth, an abundance of raw materials, plenty of entrepreneurial and inventive talent, and a gradual widening of the population that could share in the benefits of prosperity. By the millennium, it set standards for the rest of the world to follow and was a decisive leader of the whole world's economy.

Third, its political and social systems ensured that citizens enjoyed a wide range of freedoms, that its class system was fluid, and that democracy was as much a reality as an aspiration.

Fourth, it was more successful than any other nation in bringing immigrants from every corner of the world and assimilating them into the American system. Compared to its high ideals, America always fell short. Compared to the other nations of the world, however, America was far more impressive for its successes than for its failings.

American historians' use of the idea of American exceptionalism is justified. Americans never lost the sense of being a chosen people. This sense contributed to some of the initial settlers' motivation in the 17th century. It shaped the idea of manifest destiny in the 19th century.

A combination of cultural and environmental circumstances enabled America to become the richest nation in the history of the world. It was lucky in its access to great natural resources. For three centuries, it was able to develop fertile land and plentiful timber supplies. Iron ore and coal deposits fueled America's Industrial Revolution. Crude oil, vital to the later stages of industrial development, was also abundant. Even the secondary minerals (gold, copper, mercury, uranium) were plentiful in America.

The capitalist system encouraged the rapid exploitation of these resources. Individual incentives to entrepreneurs proved more effective than alternative economic systems. Capitalism sometimes led to reckless or delusional activity. It also ensured massive inequality of incomes.

Wealth, freedom, democracy, and the capacity to include newcomers have all contributed to America's exceptional character.

Meanwhile, America's political institutions nurtured and protected vital freedoms. The Constitution, written under difficult conditions, proved itself effective for the next two centuries. Political stability and political freedom combined to nurture prosperity. Democracy, steadily widened since the 1780s, has made the political system responsive to citizens' interests. Most white males gained the vote before 1860. Women participated in electoral politics after 1919. Full participation by African Americans was delayed until the Civil Rights movement of the 1950s and 1960s.

The Bill of Rights and the Supreme Court prevented democracy from degenerating into demagogy. And new generations learned to take the principles of democracy and equality very seriously.

America has welcomed and assimilated more varied immigrant groups than any other nation. European, African, and Asian immigrants, voluntary and coerced, all adapted to a single language, polity, and culture. "Multiculturalism" has demonstrated great internal variation and richness. British institutions largely decided the shape of the melting pot, but its savor came from the languages, foods, and cultures of those it combined.

America's educational achievements have matched its assimilative power. It has a distinguished literary and artistic tradition. Since the mid-20th century, it has led the world in scientific research. In America, the endowment of education sanitizes ill-gotten fortunes. ■

Suggested Reading

Hofstadter, *The American Political Tradition and the Men Who Made It.*

Lerner, *America as a Civilization.*

Lukacs, *Outgrowing Democracy: A History of America in the Twentieth Century.*

Phillips, *The Cousins' Wars: Religion, Politics, and the Triumph of Anglo-America.*

Questions to Consider

1. Why has American history been so different from that of the other industrial democracies?

2. Should historians pass moral judgments on their subject, or should they simply explain what happened and why?.

Timeline (Lectures 49–84)

1869	Completion of the first transcontinental railroad.
1869	Completion of the Suez Canal.
1873	Invention of barbed wire (which made fencing of the Great Plains possible).
1876	Battle of the Little Bighorn; death of General Custer.
1876	Invention of the telephone by Alexander Graham Bell.
1877	Great Railroad Strike.
1879	Invention of the light bulb by Edison.
1880	Election of President James Garfield (Rep.).
1881	Assassination of President Garfield by a disappointed job-seeker, Guiteau; Vice President Chester Arthur becomes president.
1884	Election of President Grover Cleveland (Dem.).
1886	Founding of the American Federation of Labor.
1886	Haymarket (Chicago) anarchist bombing.
1888	Election of President Benjamin Harrison (Rep.).
1889	Jane Addams founds Hull House.
1890	U.S. Census announces the closing of the frontier.

Timeline (Lectures 49–84)

1892	Election of President Grover Cleveland (Dem.).
1892	Homestead Strike, Pennsylvania.
1894	Pullman Strike, Illinois.
1896	Supreme Court decision in *Plessy v. Ferguson* upholds racial segregation laws.
1896	Election of President William McKinley (R.) over William Jennings Bryan (D. and Populist).
1898	U.S. war against Spain in Cuba and the Philippines; Theodore Roosevelt victorious on San Juan Hill.
1900	Reelection of President McKinley, with Theodore Roosevelt as vice president.
1901	Assassination of President McKinley by anarchist Czolgosz. Vice President Roosevelt becomes president.
1903	Wright Brothers' first flight.
1904	Reelection of President Theodore Roosevelt.
1906	San Francisco earthquake.
1906	Publication of Upton Sinclair's *The Jungle*.
1908	Election of President William Howard Taft (R.).
1908	Henry Ford builds the prototype Model T.
1912	Election of President Woodrow Wilson (D.) over Taft and Roosevelt (Progressive).

1914	Completion (by American companies) and opening of the Panama Canal.
1914	World War I begins in Europe.
1915	German submarine sinks the *Lusitania*; Wilson protests to Germany and W. J. Bryan resigns as secretary of state.
1916	Wilson reelected under the slogan "He kept us out of war."
1917	German declaration of unrestricted submarine warfare prompts American entry into the war.
1917	Russian Revolution; Bolsheviks, led by Vladimir Lenin, seize power.
1918	American forces on the Western Front contribute to Allied victory in World War I.
1919	President Wilson at the Treaty of Versailles is unable to prevent a vengeful, anti-German settlement. U.S. Senate refuses to participate in League of Nations.
1919	Constitutional Amendments give votes to women and prohibit alcohol.
1920	Election of President Warren G. Harding (R.).
1921	Commercial radio broadcasting begins.
1921 (and 1924)	Congress passes restrictive legislation against immigration.
1923	President Harding dies in office. Vice President Calvin Coolidge becomes president.

1924	Reelection of President Coolidge.
1925	Scopes "Monkey Trial" upholds Tennessee law against teaching evolution in schools.
1925	Supreme Court decision in *Pierce v. Society of Sisters* upholds constitutional right to private education.
1927	Charles Lindbergh makes first solo transatlantic flight in the *Spirit of St. Louis*.
1928	Election of President Herbert Hoover (R.) over Al Smith (D.), America's first Catholic presidential candidate.
1929	Wall Street Crash.
1932	Election of President Franklin Roosevelt (D.) over Hoover.
1933	First 100 days of the New Deal creates powerful new federal agencies.
1933	Adolf Hitler elected to German leadership.
1935	Legislation establishes Social Security.
1935	Supreme Court decision in *Schechter v. United States* overturns crucial New Deal legislation.
1936	President Roosevelt reelected over Alf Landon (R.).
1937	Failure of Roosevelt's "court-packing" plan.
1939	Hitler's Germany invades Poland: World War II begins.

1940	President Roosevelt reelected over Wendell Willkie (R.).
1941 (summer)	Hitler's invasion of the Soviet Union.
1941 (December)	Japanese attack on Pearl Harbor brings United States into the war against Germany and Japan.
1942	Battle of Midway, first significant American military success of World War II.
1943	American forces participate in Allied invasion of Sicily and Italy.
1944	Allied invasion of France (D-Day), led by General Dwight Eisenhower.
1944 (November)	Reelection of President Roosevelt over Thomas Dewey (R.).
1945 (April)	Death of President Roosevelt. Vice President Harry Truman becomes president.
1945 (May)	Unconditional German surrender ends war in Europe.
1945 (August)	Atomic bombs at Hiroshima and Nagasaki end war in Asia.
1946	Allied deadlock over the future of Eastern Europe begins Cold War.
1948	Reelection of President Truman over Dewey (R.), Henry Wallace (Progressive), and Strom Thurmond (Dixiecrat).
1950	Korean War begins.
1950	Senator Joseph McCarthy's accusations intensify American anti-Communism.

1952	President Dwight Eisenhower (R.) elected over Adlai Stevenson (D.).
1953	Truce ends fighting in Korea.
1954	Supreme Court's decision in *Brown v. Board of Education of Topeka, Kansas* condemns racial segregation in education.
1955	Martin Luther King, Jr., leads Montgomery bus boycott against segregated city transportation.
1956	Reelection of President Eisenhower over Stevenson.
1957	Soviet launch of *Sputnik* inaugurates the "space race."
1960	Election of President John F. Kennedy (D.), America's first Catholic president, over Richard Nixon (R.).
1962	Cuban missile crisis.
1963	Assassination of President Kennedy by Lee Harvey Oswald. Vice President Lyndon Johnson becomes president.
1964	Gulf of Tonkin incident escalates American role in Vietnam.
1964	Reelection of President Johnson over Barry Goldwater (R.).
1964 and 1965	Legislation on civil rights, voting rights, and immigration abolishes all forms of government-sponsored racial discrimination.
1967	Hippie "summer of love" in San Francisco Haight-Ashbury district.

1968	Tet offensive further undermines American credibility in Vietnam.
1968	Assassinations of Martin Luther King Jr., and Robert Kennedy; urban rioting.
1968	Election of President Richard Nixon (R.) over Hubert Humphrey (D.).
1969	Neil Armstrong and Buzz Aldrin, the first men on the moon.
1969	Congress passes National Environmental Policy Act.
1970	Cambodian campaign and Kent State shootings intensify Vietnam controversy.
1972	President Nixon visits China and opens diplomatic contacts.
1972	Reelection of President Nixon over George McGovern (D.).
1973	American military withdrawal from Vietnam completed.
1974	President Nixon forced to resign over Watergate scandal. Vice President Gerald Ford becomes president.
1976	Election of President Jimmy Carter (D.) over Ford.
1977	Opening of trans-Alaska pipeline.
1978	President Carter brokers Camp David Peace Accords between Israel and Egypt.
1979	Accident at Three Mile Island nuclear power station.

1979	American embassy staff in Teheran, Iran, imprisoned by revolutionary students.
1979	Soviet invasion of Afghanistan sours 1970s Cold War *detente*.
1980	Election of President Ronald Reagan (R.) over Carter.
1981	Reagan military escalation intensifies Cold War.
1984	President Reagan reelected over Walter Mondale (D.), whose running mate, Geraldine Ferraro, was the first major-party female candidate in U.S. history.
1986	Soviet Premier Gorbachev attempts radical internal reforms, *glasnost* and *perestroika*.
1987	Congressional investigation of the Iran-Contra scandal.
1988	Election of President George Bush, Sr., over Michael Dukakis (D.).
1989	Soviet Union abandons its Eastern European satellites. Berlin Wall demolished.
1990	Iraq invades Kuwait and creates an emergency for the "New World Order."
1991	U.N. forces led by the United States eject Iraqi forces from Kuwait in the Gulf War.
1991	Soviet Union collapses. Democracy established in Russia.
1992	Election of President Bill Clinton (D.) over George Bush, Sr.

1995	Attack on federal building in Oklahoma City.
1996	Reelection of President Clinton over Bob Dole (R.)
2000	Election of President George W. Bush, Jr., (R.) over Al Gore (D.) by narrowest possible margin.
2001	Al Qaeda attack on World Trade Center and Pentagon.
2001–2002	U.N. forces led by the United States fight in Afghanistan.
2003	U.S. and coalition forces fight in Iraq.

Glossary (Lectures 49–84)

affirmative action: Government policies designed after the civil rights laws of 1965 to achieve actual racial integration by setting aside places in schools and workplaces for racial minorities and women.

agrarianism: The belief that farmers are the most important element in the nation and that government policy should be more attentive to their interests than those of any other element.

anarchism: The belief that government and capitalism are always oppressive and should be abolished. Some American anarchists in the 1880–1920 era, notably Alexander Berkman and Emma Goldman, believed that violence in pursuit of these ends was justifiable.

anti-Communism: The belief that Communism poses a mortal threat to America and that legal measures at home and military measures abroad are necessary to thwart it. Anti-Communism was the central informing idea of American policy from 1946–1990.

Black Power: Advocacy of black political assertion and rejection of Martin Luther King's pacifist and integrationist ideals by a second generation of civil rights activists after about 1965. Malcolm X was its most well-known advocate.

Bull Moose: Nickname for Theodore Roosevelt's Progressive Party in the election of 1912.

busing: Moving public school children from one district to another to achieve actual racial integration in education (the policy prevailed between the 1970s and 1990s but had been abandoned by 2000).

conservative: A politician, intellectual, or citizen who believes in conserving society's main institutions and principles. American conservatism has always been paradoxical because the nation's commercial dynamism has made it change more rapidly than virtually all others in the world. American conservatives in the 20th century supported capitalism and opposed liberalism and Communism.

containment: The theoretical basis of America's Cold War-era defense policy; deterring and preventing Soviet aggression wherever it appeared, diplomatically if possible but with the threat of nuclear strikes if necessary.

ecumenism: The belief—widespread in 20th-century America—that different religious groups can coexist and that they should cooperate.

Evil Empire: President Reagan's name for the Soviet Union and its satellites in the early 1980s. Advocates of peaceful coexistence criticized such provocative language.

feminism: The belief that society ought not to make invidious distinctions between men and women and ought not to deny education, work, or other opportunities to women because of their gender. Early 20th-century feminism was dedicated chiefly to women's suffrage; late-20th–century feminism, to jobs and educational equality.

free silver: The belief, common among farmers in the late 19th century, that silver, as well as gold, should be the basis of American currency, a policy that would have been inflationary and would have tended to increase farm incomes. Free silver was the central economic issue of the 1896 election.

fundamentalism: The religion of conservative American Protestants who opposed the intellectual developments in science and comparative religion of the late 19th and early 20th centuries. Fundamentalists continued to assert the inerrancy (perfect accuracy) of all the Bible, which led them to reject evolutionary theory and ecumenism.

Germany First: American policy in World War II, based on the recognition that Germany, the greater military and industrial threat, should be attacked and defeated before Japan.

imperialism: The policy, common among Western European powers in the late 19th century, of conquering African and Asian nations. Influential turn-of-the-century politicians in America, including Theodore Roosevelt, favored a comparable policy after the Spanish-American War, and the idea influenced America's role in the Philippines, Cuba, and Latin America.

integrationist: A black or white advocate of racial integration.

interchangeability: Manufacture of identical parts, first fully achieved in the bicycle industry, which was essential to mass production.

isolationism: The belief that American 20th-century foreign policy should carry on the 19th-century tradition of disengagement from European affairs. Americans who opposed participation in World War II between 1939 and Pearl Harbor (1941), including aviation hero Charles Lindbergh and ex-president Herbert Hoover, were labeled isolationists.

liberal: In the 19th century, a politician, intellectual, or citizen who believed in human equality, free institutions, and a free-market economy, while opposing inherited privilege and hierarchy. The word's American meaning shifted in the 1930s to signify a supporter of the New Deal and a stronger government role in combating poverty and social vulnerability.

libertarian: Advocate of an extreme form of 19th-century "classical" liberalism, taking the view that the entire economy should be privatized and that government's role should be minimal.

massive resistance: The declared policy of white southern congressmen and senators after the *Brown* case (1954), who threatened absolute non-cooperation with the federal government and judiciary in their policy of racial integration.

massive retaliation: The Eisenhower-era defense policy, which economized on conventional forces by relying on the threat of nuclear retaliation against Soviet aggression.

New Freedom and New Nationalism: The economic policy proposals of Woodrow Wilson and Theodore Roosevelt, respectively, in the 1912 election campaign. Wilson's New Freedom sought to restore free competition in each industry by breaking up monopolies and oligopolies. Roosevelt's New Nationalism accepted the existence of economic giants but advocated their close regulation by government.

overkill: The ability of the world's nuclear weapons stockpiles to kill the world's entire population more than once; a situation already in existence by the mid-1960s.

political correctness: The social orthodoxy of late-20th–century America. The term meant to favor feminism, affirmative action, gay rights, and abortion rights and to condemn humor that satirized any social, ethnic, or racial group, especially if it was disadvantaged. Influential, especially on college campuses; opponents saw it as antithetical to freedom of thought, expression, and speech.

Populist: A supporter of the People's Party in the 1890s, advocating agrarian and free silver policies. More generally, populism is support for "the people" against "the experts" or "the intellectuals." Politicians with a populist image included Huey Long, Joe McCarthy, and George Wallace.

progressive: An early 20th-century advocate of political and social reforms, emphasizing democratic accountability, efficiency, and the application of rationality and expertise to all problems. By 1912, nearly all politicians claimed to be Progressives.

spin: Techniques for manipulating and interpreting the news so that, whatever its content, it can be made to reflect favorably on one's own group. "Spin-doctors" became a central feature of political life in the late 20th century.

temperance: Originally the word meant moderation in drinking, but it had come to mean complete abstinence from alcohol by the late 19th century. National temperance was the objective of the Women's Christian Temperance Union and other lobbies for a prohibition amendment to the Constitution.

trust: Early 20th-century name for a monopoly or a price-fixing agreement between the biggest companies in an industry. Antitrust legislation from 1890 was designed to prevent trusts from forming or to prosecute those that did form, if they acted in restraint of competition and free trade.

Biographical Notes (Lectures 49–84)

Jane Addams (1860–1935). Progressive reformer and founder of Hull House social settlement. Addams suffered from psychosomatic illnesses in her youth and sought an outlet in philanthropic, socially useful work. Reluctant to marry and live the parasitic life of an upper-middle-class woman, she was impressed by the British settlement house movement, which brought privileged young men and women into the slums of London. She bought Hull House in the midst of a poor, working-class Chicago district in 1889 and turned it into a shelter, day-care center, and educational resource, living and working there for the rest of her life. Hull House helped generations of immigrants from southern and eastern Europe to adapt to American city life, and it lobbied the city government on their behalf, attempting to rid it of corrupt machine politicians. It also served as a high-pressure training school for middle-class women in the temperance, suffrage, and social work movements, with many of its alumnae becoming nationally important figures in their own right. Addams helped incipient trade unions in the area and created a Labor Museum, as well. She respected and tried to preserve the folkways, languages, and cultures of immigrant groups, and she was among the founders of the American Civil Liberties Union. She became a nationally famous peace advocate during World War I and won the Nobel Peace Prize in 1931.

Louis Brandeis (1856–1941). First Jewish member of the Supreme Court. Born to Czech immigrant parents in Louisville, Kentucky, Brandeis excelled as a student, graduating at the head of his Harvard Law School class at age 21. He created a successful practice in Boston and became interested in public interest questions, as well as profitable cases. His "Brandeis Brief," first tried in *Muller v. Oregon* (1908), used not only legal information but also sociological and medical evidence in support of a law restricting women to an eight-hour work day. A friend of trade unions and women's rights and a tenacious courtroom critic of monopoly businesses, he became an economic policy advisor to Woodrow Wilson. Wilson appointed him to the Supreme Court in 1916, where he served with distinction until his retirement in 1939. He opposed the repressive Espionage Act during World War I and maintained a distinguished record on civil liberties through the 1920s. He was, however, one of the justices who enraged President Franklin Roosevelt by concluding that such New Deal initiatives as the National Recovery Administration exceeded the limits of the Constitution.

Andrew Carnegie (1835–1919). Poor Scottish immigrant who became a steel manufacturer and philanthropist. Son of a poor handloom weaver, Carnegie came to America at age 13 and became a cotton factory worker, then a railroad messenger boy. Self-educated and an avid reader, he soon learned how to seize business opportunities and invest his savings, making small amounts increase dramatically. By the end of the Civil War, he was a senior railroad employee but left to start his own company in the metal bridge business. As the American railroad network continued to spread nationwide, Carnegie's steel factories in the Pittsburgh area provided the raw iron and steel, eventually making him one of the richest men in America. The bitter Homestead Strike of 1892 took place at his factories; he was doggedly opposed to trade unions. He sold out at the end of the century to J. P. Morgan, who used Carnegie's factories as the basis of the U.S. Steel Corporation. Carnegie wrote in *The Gospel of Wealth* (1889) that rich men should use their wealth for the public good, and he gave away more than $350 million in his lifetime. The most famous of his charities was the building of public libraries in Britain and America, giving access to books to the thousands of working people for whom they were otherwise out of reach.

Hillary Clinton (b. 1947). The first First Lady to piggyback on her husband's political career and create one of her own. Raised in Park Ridge, Illinois, Hillary Rodham became an outstanding student at Wellesley College (Massachusetts) and Yale Law School in the late 1960s. She served on the staff of the Watergate-era Judiciary Committee in Congress; then, after President Nixon's resignation, she went to Arkansas to marry Bill Clinton, whom she had met in law school. He became governor of the state in 1978, and she became a practicing lawyer, law school professor, and the state's First Lady, involving herself in educational and children's affairs. Clinton's election to the presidency in 1992 brought her into the national spotlight where, more than any previous First Lady, she sought a substantive policy-making role. She chaired a task force on national health care reform but was unable to bring to fruition her plans for an American national health service. During her husband's second administration, she had to endure the humiliating evidence of his infidelity with White House intern Monica Lewinsky. She stuck by him during his own impeachment crisis, but they separated when his term in office ended, by which time she had been elected New York's junior senator in the election of 2000.

Thomas Edison (1847–1931). America's most prolific inventor, who eventually held more than a thousand patents. The Ohio-born son of a carpenter, Edison became a railroad messenger at age 12, learned how to operate the telegraph, and began inventing devices to improve the quality and speed of telegraphy. After six years on the railroads, traveling the Midwest and Canada, Edison became an independent inventor, moving in 1876 to Menlo Park, New Jersey, where he spent the next 10 years, working systematically on new inventions. He moved again to a bigger lab in West Orange, New Jersey, in 1886, where he employed a staff of 60 assistants. Among his most important inventions were the incandescent electric light bulb, the phonograph (earliest device for recording music), and several elements of moving photography, including the world's first "talkie" in 1913. Recognizing the transforming possibilities of electricity, he established a generating company for Manhattan in 1882, with the backing of several major financiers who had learned to trust, and invest heavily in, his innovations. He also improved telephones, batteries, and duplication machines, becoming, in his later years, a living legend of inventiveness and ingenuity.

Dwight Eisenhower (1890–1969). Victorious World War II general and 34th president. A career army officer from Abilene, Kansas, Eisenhower graduated from West Point in 1916 but did not see action in World War I. He was an outstanding staff officer, however, and drew the favorable attention of Douglas MacArthur and other senior officers. He worked with MacArthur in the Philippines in the 1930s but was recalled to America after Pearl Harbor. Eisenhower led the American invasion of North Africa in 1942 and was supreme Allied Commander for the D-Day invasion of Normandy in 1944, showing great political skill, as well as logistical and strategic brilliance. His success made him one of the great heroes of the war and an attractive candidate to both political parties in the early Cold War years. With no prior political record, he could have accepted either bid but chose the Republicans and ran successfully in the election of 1952 against Adlai Stevenson. As president, Eisenhower cultivated the impression of being less intelligent than he really was, delegated effectively to a powerful staff, and found time for almost daily golf. He presided over many of the tensest years of the Cold War but had a realistic sense, from his military years, of what the nation could and could not do in the face of a nuclear-armed enemy. He helped create a truce in Korea and resisted the temptation to escalate in Vietnam, meanwhile presiding over boom conditions at home. Reelected in 1956 despite a serious heart attack, he acted cautiously to aid the Civil Rights movement and, on his retirement from office after the 1960 election, warned Americans about the potential hazards of an over-mighty "military-industrial complex."

Henry Ford (1863–1947). First manufacturer of cheap, mass-produced cars. Ford, the son of Irish immigrant parents in Michigan, was among the earliest Americans to study internal combustion engines and automobiles. He built his own first car in 1896, founded his company in 1903, and introduced the immortal Model T in 1908. He continued to build the same model between then and 1927, switching to the moving assembly line method in 1913, first, at Highland Park and, later, at an even larger factory in River Rouge, Michigan. To ensure workers' loyalty despite the job's boredom, he paid them $5 per day, far higher than industrial wages elsewhere. When General Motors and Chrysler began to challenge his dominance of the business, he shut down for five months in 1927, retooling to produce the Model A. Dictatorial and intolerant, he spied on workers who attempted to unionize in the 1930s and never really relinquished power to his son Edsel, who was nominal chief from 1919. Among his many interests and obsessions were industrial history (he founded a museum and named it after Edison, whom he had known as a teenager) and an exaggerated fear of Jewish power.

Betty Friedan (b. 1921). Author of *The Feminine Mystique* and founder of the National Organization of Women (NOW). Betty Goldstein (her maiden name) was an enthusiastic leftist during the 1930s and 1940s but, after college at Smith, she attempted to settle down with her new husband to suburban middle-class life. Finding it stifling and discovering that many of her former college friends felt the same way, she published *The Feminine Mystique* in 1963. Vigorous and scathing, it denounced the values and assumptions that directed American women into motherhood and home building. It became an immense bestseller. Friedan cofounded NOW in 1966 to lobby against gender discrimination in legislation, pay, and work; under her powerful guidance, it became an effective lobby. Her stormy, violent marriage ended in 1969, and she feuded with other central figures in the new feminism, notably Bella Abzug and Gloria Steinem. Her later work included campaigning for the Equal Rights Amendment, contradicting some radical feminists' claim that lesbianism was superior to heterosexuality, and advocacy (in *The Fountain of Age* [1993]) on behalf of elderly people.

Bill Gates (b. 1955). High-tech business wizard, head of Microsoft, and multi-billionaire. Gates, son of a Seattle attorney and a schoolteacher, became a computer enthusiast in his early teens and was already building innovative software systems as a Harvard freshman in the early 1970s. He dropped out of Harvard as a junior and founded Microsoft in 1975, building software that shrewdly anticipated the coming of personal computers. Constant dedication to company growth and to innovative research and development enabled him to dominate the field by the late 1980s and to pioneer the Internet boom. In the 1990s, government regulators who regarded him as a monopolist prosecuted Gates for violation of the antitrust statutes. He generated popular good will, however, with philanthropy on a massive scale, donating $800 million to education, libraries, public health, and the arts, establishing a foundation that at once became one of the world's most munificent. His book on his experiences and the computer industry, *The Road Ahead* (1995), became a bestseller and, by 2000, he was almost certainly the richest man in the world.

Emma Goldman (1869–1940). Russian immigrant who advocated anarchism, feminism, and free love. Born and raised in Russia, Goldman migrated to America as a teenager and worked in clothing-trade sweatshops in Rochester and New York. After the 1886 Haymarket bombing, she joined the anarchists and made passionate public speeches urging the overthrow of capitalism. She was deeply attached to Alexander Berkmann, another anarchist immigrant, and supported his decision to attempt the assassination of Henry Clay Frick for his anti-union tactics at Homestead during the bitter steelworkers' strike of 1892. She even tried to raise money to buy him a gun and train fare by becoming a prostitute, but her first potential customer told her that she was unsuited to the business. Berkmann wounded but did not kill Frick and went to prison for 14 years. Goldman became an advocate of birth control for working-class women, made speeches on behalf of the idea, and was also imprisoned for it, because it violated the Comstock Acts against public indecency. When America joined the First World War in 1917, she and Berkmann spoke against American involvement in a capitalist war. Arrested again, they were deported and spent the years from 1917 to 1921 in Russia, where they witnessed (and were disillusioned by) the early years of the Russian Revolution. As anarchists, they were opposed to all forms of government and soon found that Lenin and Trotsky's Bolsheviks favored a strong and repressive state. Goldman spent her later years partly in Britain, partly touring and speaking—she even went to Spain at the outbreak of its civil war in 1936 to speak on behalf of the anarchist forces there.

Samuel Gompers (1850–1924). Immigrant cigar maker and trade unionist who became the president of the American Federation of Labor. Born in London to Dutch parents, he emigrated to America at the age of 13. Gompers worked in the cigar-making trade, which flourished in thousands of New York sweatshops. Becoming a trade unionist, he represented the Cigar Makers' Union at early efforts to create an association of trade unions and, in 1886, played a leading role in founding the American Federation of Labor, remaining its president from then until his death except for one "sabbatical" year, 1895. A pragmatic, down-to-earth workingman, he avoided radical politics and concentrated on his member unions' efforts to bargain for better pay, shorter hours, and safe, sanitary working conditions. His leadership skills enabled the AFL to gain a membership of over a million by 1890 and to continue its growth through the early 20th century. He concentrated on skilled workers who could not easily be replaced by strikebreakers and, therefore, had greater bargaining leverage against their employers. Admired on both sides of the negotiating table, Gompers often gave testimony in Congress, joined civic groups, and became a member of President Wilson's Council of National Defense during World War I. He attended the Versailles Peace Treaty negotiations as a member of the Commission on International Labor Legislation.

Billy Graham (b. 1918). Evangelical revival preacher. Raised on a farm in North Carolina, Billy Graham attended a series of Bible colleges and earned a reputation for magnetic preaching. With Youth for Christ International, he spoke at youth rallies in the later days of World War II and gained national recognition among evangelicals for his preaching gifts. Henry Luce's decision to publicize his Los Angeles revival in 1949 made him famous beyond the evangelical subculture and, throughout the rest of the century, he remained one of the most famous men in America. Unlike many fundamentalist contemporaries, he preached love, compassion, and understanding more than fire and brimstone. He deplored divisions among the Protestant churches and tried to diminish them rather than insist on theological purity. President Truman thought him a charlatan, but every subsequent occupant of the White House cultivated Graham—he was a particular favorite of Presidents Eisenhower and Nixon. When other evangelical preachers, such as Jim Bakker and Jimmy Swaggart, were damaged by sex and money scandals, Graham remained unblemished. The end of the Cold War enabled him to take his revival meetings even to Russia.

Herbert Hoover (1874–1964). Thirty-first president whose heroic reputation was destroyed by his inability to halt the Great Depression. Hoover, born in Iowa but raised by relatives in Oregon, graduated from Stanford in 1891 as a mining engineer. He spent most of his 20s and 30s in China, Australia, and other parts of the developing world, becoming rich and widely respected as an engineer. He was in Europe when World War I began and supervised the evacuation of Americans from France. During the war, he worked to bring famine relief to Belgians caught between the lines, and when the war ended, he organized emergency food supplies to the starving people of Germany, central Europe, and Russia. Highly regarded as a philanthropist, businessman, and statesman, he occupied senior cabinet positions under Presidents Harding and Coolidge, becoming the Republican Party's presidential candidate in 1928. He won easily over America's first major-party Catholic candidate, Al Smith, but soon after his inauguration, was confronted by the Wall Street Crash and the slide into economic depression. Hoover believed strongly in the traditional American virtues of self-discipline and self-help and was reluctant to get the federal government involved in poverty relief. The scale of the Depression, however, made his remedial alternatives seem ineffective to the point of insensitivity, and he was swept out of office in the election of 1932, disliked and discredited. Poor shantytown dwellers nicknamed their hovels "Hoovervilles." He became an outspoken critic of the New Deal's statist policies in the 1930s and was an isolationist in the early years of World War II but returned to favor in the late 1940s and early 1950s as chair of a commission to rationalize the government's executive departments.

Martin Luther King, Jr. (1929–1968). Leader of the nonviolent phase of the Civil Rights movement, and a Nobel Peace Prize winner. King, son and grandson of Atlanta ministers, was educated at Morehouse College near his home, then at Crozer Theological Seminary (Pennsylvania) and Boston University. Accepting a call to the ministry at Dexter Road Baptist Church in segregated Montgomery, Alabama, he arrived in 1954 and, a year later, became leader of the Montgomery bus boycott. Its success, and his eloquence as spokesman for the movement, catapulted him to national fame. Skilled in the manipulation of the media, he knew how to provoke racist law-enforcement officials into attacking his peaceful demonstrations and was willing to suffer assault and imprisonment to gain the moral high ground. In 1963, Bull Connor, public safety chief of Birmingham, Alabama, met King's marchers with fire hoses and attack dogs. King was arrested but won an immense public relations victory there, not least through publication of his "Letter from a Birmingham Jail." Later that year, his "I have a dream" speech in Washington marked a climax of his career, and he received worldwide recognition with the Nobel Prize the following year. Urban riots after 1964 and challenges to nonviolence from Black Power advocates troubled King's later years, and he began to devote energy to the anti-Vietnam War movement, as well as to civil rights. He was assassinated by James Earl Ray in Memphis, where he had gone on behalf of striking black garbage workers, in 1968.

Sinclair Lewis (1885–1951). Satirical novelist and America's first Nobel Prize winner for literature. Lewis was born in Sauk Center, Minnesota, to a doctor's family. Fascinated by books from the beginning of his life, he graduated from Yale in 1908 and went to work in the New York publishing business, devoting every spare moment to writing of his own. His first book appeared in 1912, but his first great success came with *Main Street* (1920). From then on, he had a mass audience throughout his life and won all the major literary prizes open to him, including the Pulitzer (1926) and Nobel (1930) Prizes. Among his most famous works are *Babbitt* (1922), about a midwestern businessman's shallow self-confidence, consumerism, and inability to think outside the crowd, and *Arrowsmith* (1925), on the heroic asceticism of a true scientist. His works from the 1920s paint a vivid picture of an America becoming urban and prosperous but often backward-looking and foolish.

Walter Lippmann (1889–1974). Influential liberal journalist and commentator. A Harvard graduate in the Progressive era, Lippmann worked first for the muckraker Lincoln Steffens. His first book, *A Preface to Politics* (1913), won him an editorial job at *The New Republic*. He wrote extensively on the problems of democracy in an age of specialists and expertise and was among the century's most effective critics of utopianism. Woodrow Wilson asked his advice on the peace treaty that ended World War I and brought him to Versailles as an advisor. Born to a Reform Jewish family, Lippmann nevertheless contributed to a Harvard policy of restricting Jewish admissions in the 1920s. By the New Deal era, he was the most influential columnist and commentator in the nation. Presidents were careful not to cross him if they could avoid it, and he knew all of them, from Franklin Roosevelt onward. His book *The Public Philosophy* (1955) endorsed natural law theories of politics and showed that the Cold War had made him more conservative. Nevertheless, he became an outspoken critic of President Johnson's escalation of the Vietnam War in the 1960s.

John D. Rockefeller (1839–1937). Oil business entrepreneur who became the richest man in America. Born on a farm in upstate New York, Rockefeller moved as a teenager to Cleveland and became an oil refiner during the early days of the Pennsylvania oil rush. Shrewd, sober, and a Baptist Sunday-school teacher, but also with a flair for good investments and profitable entrepreneurial risks, he rapidly increased his share of the refining business until, in 1870, his company, Standard Oil, was the largest in the trade. Oil in those pre-automobile days was used as lamp fuel, and Rockefeller specialized in creating high-quality lamp kerosene, which was sold nationwide in distinctive red cans. After passage of the Sherman Anti-Trust Act of 1890, Standard was prosecuted and broken up by order of the Ohio courts because it had monopolized the business. It moved to New Jersey and, through Rockefeller's ingenious management, was rapidly reassembled, though it succumbed to another prosecution in 1911. Rockefeller himself, retiring from the everyday running of the business in 1896, turned his attention to philanthropy, giving tens of millions of dollars to educational, church, and missionary charities. Among his biggest bequests was $35 million to the University of Chicago, founded with his encouragement and supervision in 1890. His name was a byword for financial power; he was widely hated for his hard business approach, but he contributed as much as anyone to the creation of the 20th century style of big business.

Theodore Roosevelt (1858–1919). Twenty-sixth president. Born to a rich New York family in 1858, Roosevelt regretted that he was too young to fight in the Civil War. Overcoming childhood illnesses and physical weakness, he learned to box and challenged himself in arduous outdoor activities, becoming an advocate of the "strenuous life." Roosevelt graduated from Harvard and began a career in New York state politics, where he defied the corrupt Tammany Hall Democratic regime on behalf of honest Republican principles. The death of his wife and his mother on the same day in 1884 led to a nervous breakdown. Roosevelt recovered by spending several months hunting on his ranch in the Dakota Badlands, about which he wrote two excellent books. Remarried in 1886 and continuing a rapid political ascent, he became Assistant Secretary of the Navy in the McKinley administration after the election of 1896. He gave up this post when America went to war against Spain in 1898, creating the famous "Rough Riders," a troop of cavalry made up of friends from Harvard and cowboy friends from the West. Becoming a hero for seizing San Juan Hill, he returned in glory to America and won the governorship of New York later that year. McKinley selected him as his running mate in the election of 1900, and Roosevelt became president a few months after the inauguration, when McKinley was assassinated by an anarchist. As president (the youngest in the nation's history to that point), he prosecuted abusive monopolies and took a more active and interventionist role in the economy than his predecessors. Popular and widely admired, he was reelected in 1904 but left the White House after the 1908 election. Even an African safari was insufficient to keep his attention after that, and in 1912, he tried to regain the Republican nomination from his successor, William Howard Taft. Thwarted, he ran for president as a Progressive "Bull Moose" candidate, split the Republican vote, and enabled the Democrat Woodrow Wilson to prevail instead.

Booker T. Washington (1856–1915). Black educator and the most influential African American in the early 20th century. Washington was born in slavery to a Virginia family and was six years old at the time of Lincoln's Emancipation Proclamation. Eager for education, he worked his way through Hampton Institute and admired the philanthropic whites, led by Hampton's

General Samuel Armstrong, who attempted to improve the lives of freedmen in the Reconstruction South. In 1881, he became principal of the Tuskegee Institute, a college dedicated to basic literacy and preparation for the practical careers that most African Americans could expect. He raised money for the school through successful speaking tours, mainly among such northern industrialists as John D. Rockefeller and Andrew Carnegie. Washington did not welcome the racial segregation system of the post-Reconstruction era, but in a famous speech at the Cotton States Exposition, Atlanta, in 1895, he argued that blacks could accommodate to it while earning whites' respect and trust. His autobiography, *Up from Slavery* (1901), was hailed at the time and contributed to President Theodore Roosevelt's much-criticized decision to invite him to dine at the White House. W. E. B. DuBois and other black leaders of less accommodationist views deplored what looked to them like Washington's acceptance of second-class status.

Malcolm X (1925–1965). Black Muslim missionary and Black Power advocate. Malcolm Little grew up in the predominantly white community of Lansing, Michigan, but witnessed racist violence when the family home was burned down and when his father was murdered. Moving to Boston as a teenager, he became a petty criminal. Arrested and imprisoned for burglary, his life was transformed when he joined the Nation of Islam (NOI) in 1946. Its members preached black pride and dignity; they believed that whites were genetically engineered mutants and devils. Released in 1952, Malcolm (who took the name "X" to stand for his family's African name, which had been stolen by slavery), became the NOI's leading spokesman. His mesmerizing stage presence, eloquence, and apparent fearlessness inspired a generation of black activists. Scornful of Martin Luther King's advocacy of integration through Christian nonviolence, he argued for racial separatism and violence when necessary in self-defense. In the early 1960s, however, he made the Hajj pilgrimage to Mecca, which prompted a reorientation of his beliefs to a more orthodox form of Islam. He parted on bad terms from NOI, whose leader, Elijah Muhammad, resented his success. Soon after a series of meetings with the writer Alex Haley that formed the basis of his book *The Autobiography of Malcolm X*, Malcolm X was assassinated by three members of the NOI.

Bibliography (Lectures 49–84)

General Works

Beard, Charles, and Mary Beard. *The Rise of American Civilization*. New York: Macmillan, 1930. Outdated big history of the whole thing, but still very much worth reading because it emphasizes issues, especially economics, that contemporary historians tend to scant.

Boorstin, Daniel. *The Americans: The Democratic Experience*. New York: Viking, 1974. The grand old man of American history at the height of his powers. He can make you interested in things you thought you didn't care about.

Brown, Dee. *The American West*. New York: Simon and Schuster, 1994. Folksy history of the Old West: cowboys, Indians, soldiers, miners, and lots of great photographs.

Hofstadter, Richard. *The American Political Tradition and the Men Who Made It*. New York: Knopf, 1948. Old but good; a classic study of the nation's most important politicians from the nation's best professional historian of the 20th century.

Johnson, Paul. *A History of the American People*. New York: Harper Perennial, 1997. A quirky, irritable British Catholic with fiercely conservative views tells the whole story, sometimes enchantingly, sometimes infuriatingly. He's also the author of *Modern Times*, a history of the world since World War I (same remarks apply).

Perry, Lewis. *Intellectual Life in America: A History*. New York: Franklin Watts, 1984. Useful overview of the main themes in American history of ideas, with a glance at all the big thinkers.

Phillips, Kevin. *The Cousins' Wars: Religion, Politics, and the Triumph of Anglo-America*. New York: Basic, 1999. Well-told story of the strong and enduring links between America and the "mother country."

Tindall, George, and David Shi. *America: A Narrative History*. 4th ed. New York: Norton, 1996. Currently the most reliable single-volume history of the nation.

Specialized Works

Note: Some of the following books may be out of print. Internet sites such as www.abebooks.com and www.amazon.com may be helpful in locating copies.

Abrams, Ray. *Preachers Present Arms*. New York: Round Table Press, 1933.

Addams, Jane. *Twenty Years at Hull House*. New York: Signet Classic, 1981 (originally published, 1910). Autobiography of the philanthropic founder of a Chicago settlement house and her battles on behalf of impoverished immigrants.

Ahlstrom, Sydney. *Religious History of the American People*. 2 vols. New Haven: Yale University Press, 1972. An even better source than my Teaching Company course on *American Religious History*!

Allen, Frederick Lewis. *Only Yesterday*. New York: Harper Perennial, 1964. On-the-spot journalist's gossipy history of the 1920s. His *Since Yesterday* did the same kind of job for the 1930s.

Allitt, Patrick. *Major Problems in American Religious History*. Boston: Houghton Mifflin, 2000. Meet the characters who made sure it would be one nation under God.

Ambrose, Stephen. *Nothing Like It in the World: The Men Who Built the Transcontinental Railroad*. New York: Simon and Schuster, 2000.

Anderson, Jervis. *This Was Harlem: A Cultural Portrait*. New York: Farrar, Straus and Giroux, 1982.

Antin, Mary. *The Promised Land*. Boston: Houghton Mifflin, 1912. Life of a Russian Jewish immigrant to New York and her enthusiasm for the new country.

Athearn, Robert. *Union Pacific Country*. Chicago: Rand McNally, 1971.

Baum, Frank. *The Wizard of Oz*. Indianapolis: Bobbs Merrill, 1900.

Bell, Daniel. *The End of Ideology*. Glencoe, IL: Free Press, 1960. No sociologist ever wrote more luminous prose. A great book on the history of ideas in the mid-20th century.

Benfield, Ben Barker. *Horrors of the Half-Known Life*. New York: Harper and Row, 1976. How 19th-century doctors, particularly pioneer gynecologists, thought about sex differences. Not for the queasy or delicate reader.

Blum, John Morton. *V Was for Victory: Politics and American Culture during World War II*. New York: Harcourt Brace Jovanovich, 1976.

Bourne, Peter G. *Jimmy Carter: A Comprehensive Biography from Plains to Post-Presidency*. New York: Scribner, 1997.

Brinkley, Alan. *Voices of Protest: Huey Long, Father Coughlin, and the Great Depression*. New York: Knopf, 1982.

Burns, R. W. *Television: An International History of the Formative Years*. London: Institution of Electrical Engineers, 1998.

Cahan, Abraham. *The Rise of David Levinsky*. New York: Harper Colophon, 1966 (originally published, 1917). Superb novel about the ambiguities of the immigrant experience in the early 20th century—a mix of commercial success and spiritual decline.

Carnegie, Andrew. *Autobiography*. New York: Houghton Mifflin, 1920.

Carroll, Peter. *It Seemed Like Nothing Happened: America in the 1970s*. New York: Holt, Rinehart and Winston, 1982.

Carson, Rachel. *Silent Spring*. Boston: Houghton Mifflin, 1962.

Cather, Willa. *My Antonia*. Boston: Houghton Mifflin, 1918.

Clark, Norman H. *Deliver Us from Evil: An Interpretation of American Prohibition*. New York: Norton, 1976.

Conkin, Paul. *The New Deal*. Arlington Heights, IL: Harlan Davidson, 1975.

Cooper, John Milton. *The Warrior and the Priest*. Cambridge, MA: Belknap of Harvard University Press, 1983. Double biography of the two great Progressive presidents, Theodore Roosevelt and Woodrow Wilson.

Cox, Harvey. *Religion in the Secular City*. New York: Simon and Schuster/ Touchstone, 1984. Harvey Cox is the most likable liberal Protestant in America and the author whose dozen books on the subject, from 1960 to the present, are approachable and entertaining.

Cronon, William. *Nature's Metropolis: Chicago and the Great West*. New York: Norton, 1991. I think this is the single best U.S. history book of the 1990s. It explains how Chicago grew by transforming the western environment into money.

Crosby, Alfred. *America's Forgotten Pandemic: The Influenza of 1918*. Westport, CT: Greenwood Press, 1976.

Dallek, Robert. *Flawed Giant: Lyndon Johnson and His Times, 1961–1973*. New York: Oxford University Press, 1998.

Daniel, Pete. *Standing at the Crossroads: Southern Life in the Twentieth Century*. New York: Hill and Wang, 1986. Excellent introduction to the whole subject, including the true story of an elephant-lynching in Tennessee.

Douglas, Ann. *The Feminization of American Culture*. New York: Avon, 1977. A modern classic about women's indirect but powerful influence over 19th-century society.

Douglas, Susan. *Listening In: Radio and the American Imagination*. New York: Times Books, 1999.

Drew, Elizabeth. *Showdown: The Struggle between the Gingrich Congress and the Clinton White House*. New York: Simon and Schuster, 1996.

DuBois, Ellen. *Feminism and Suffrage*. Ithaca, NY: Cornell University Press, 1978.

DuBois, W. E. B. *The Souls of Black Folk*. New York: Signet Classics, 1969 (originally published, 1903). Harvard's first black history Ph.D. on the history and condition of African Americans at the turn of the century.

Ehrenreich, Barbara. *Re-Making Love: The Feminization of Sex*. Garden City, NY: Anchor Doubleday, 1986.

Fausold, Martin L. *The Presidency of Herbert Hoover*. Lawrence, KS: University Press of Kansas, 1985.

Ferrell, Robert H. *Woodrow Wilson and World War I, 1917–1921*. New York: Harper and Row, 1985.

Fine, Sidney. *Sit Down: The General Motors Strike of 1936–1937*. Ann Arbor, MI: University of Michigan Press, 1969.

Fink, Leon. *Workingmen's Democracy: The Knights of Labor and American Politics*. Urbana, IL: University of Illinois Press, 1983.

Fisher, James T. *Dr. America: The Lives of Thomas A. Dooley*. Amherst: University of Massachusetts Press, 1997. Amazing saga of the pious gay doctor who made the war in Vietnam seem like an idealistic crusade.

Fitzgerald, F. Scott. *The Great Gatsby*. New York: Grosset and Dunlap, 1925.

Fried, Richard. *Nightmare in Red: The McCarthy Period in Perspective*. New York: Oxford University Press, 1990.

Friedan, Betty. *The Feminine Mystique*. New York: Norton, 1963.

Friedman, Estelle, and John D'Emilio. *Intimate Matters: A History of Sexuality in America*. New York: Harper and Row, 1988.

Galbraith, John Kenneth. *The Affluent Society*. Boston: Houghton Mifflin, 1958. The best description and analysis of America's widespread prosperity in the 1950s and the problems it created.

———. *The Great Crash*. Boston: Houghton Mifflin, 1972. The great liberal economist explains 1929 with keen insight and brilliant deadpan humor.

Garland, Hamlin. *Main Traveled Roads*. New York: Harper, 1899.

Garraty, John. *The Great Depression*. New York: Harcourt, Brace Jovanovich, 1986.

Garrow, David. *Bearing the Cross: Martin Luther King, Jr., and the Southern Christian Leadership Conference*. New York: William Morrow, 1986. Pulitzer-prize winner on the Civil Rights movement's central figure.

Gitlin, Todd. *The Twilight of Common Dreams: Why America Is Wracked by Culture Wars*. New York: Henry Holt, 1995.

Glazer, Nathan. *American Judaism*, 2nd ed., rev. Chicago: University of Chicago Press, 1972.

Goodwin, Doris Kearns. *Lyndon Johnson and the American Dream*. New York: Harper and Row, 1976.

Goodwyn, Lawrence. *The Populist Moment*. New York: Oxford University Press, 1978.

Gordon, Sarah. *Passage to Union: How the Railroads Transformed American Life, 1829–1929*. Chicago: Ivan Dee, 1996.

Gourley, Catherine. *Wheels of Time: A Biography of Henry Ford*. New York: Millbrook Press, 1999.

Grosscup, Philip. *The Newest Explosions of Terrorism*. Far Hills, NJ: New Horizon, 2002.

Gutman, Herbert. *Work Culture and Society in Industrializing America*. New York: Vintage, 1977. Vivid history of workingmen's experiences adapting to factories and industrial life.

Halberstam, David. *The Fifties*. New York: Villard, 1993.

Haley, Alex. *Autobiography of Malcolm X*. New York: Grove Press, 1964. Electrifying story of the convict-turned-Muslim missionary and Black Power advocate.

Hastings, Max. *The Korean War*. New York: Simon and Schuster, 1987.

———. *Overlord*. London: M. Joseph, 1984.

Herr, Michael. *Dispatches*. New York: Avon, 1977. Combat reporter's tales of Vietnam fighting give the authentic sense of fear, horror, and futility.

Hofstadter, Richard. *The Age of Reform*, sections I–III. New York: Knopf, 1955.

Hounshell, David. *From the American System to Mass Production*. Baltimore: Johns Hopkins University Press, 1984. Irresistibly fascinating account of how things actually got made and how hard it was to make identical parts for successful mass production.

Hutchings, Robert. *American Diplomacy at the End of the Cold War*. Baltimore: Johns Hopkins University Press, 1997.

Johnson, Haynes. *Sleepwalking through History: America in the Reagan Years*. New York: Norton, 1991.

Jones, Maldwyn. *Destination America*. New York: Holt, Rinehart and Winston, 1976.

Josephson, Matthew. *The Robber-Barons*. New York: Harcourt Brace, 1934.

Kanigel, Robert. *The One Best Way: Frederick Winslow Taylor and the Enigma of Efficiency*. New York: Viking, 1997.

Karnow, Stanley. *Vietnam: A History*. New York: Viking, 1983.

Keegan, John. *The Second World War*. New York: Viking Penguin, 1990.

Kennedy, David M. *Over Here: The First World War and American Society*. New York: Oxford University Press, 1980.

Keynes, John Maynard. *The Economic Consequences of the Peace*. New York: Harcourt, Brace, and Howe, 1920.

King, Martin Luther, Jr. *Stride toward Freedom*. New York: Harper, 1958.

Klein, Joe. *The Natural: The Misunderstood Presidency of Bill Clinton*. New York: Doubleday, 2002.

Kline, Benjamin. *First along the River: A Brief History of the U.S. Environmental Movement*. San Francisco: Acada Books, 1997. Short, tight, and accessible history of where environmental ideas began, why they caught on, and what the nation did to put them into practice.

Kutler, Stanley. *The Wars of Watergate: The Last Crisis of Richard Nixon*. New York: Knopf/Random House, 1990.

Langewiesche, William. *American Ground: Unbuilding the World Trade Center*. New York: North Point Press, 2002.

Leopold, Aldo. *A Sand-County Almanac*. New York: Oxford University Press, 1949.

Lerner, Max. *America as a Civilization*. New York: Simon and Schuster, 1957.

Leuchtenberg, William. *The Perils of Prosperity, 1914–1932*. Chicago: University of Chicago Press, 1958.

Levin, Norman Gordon. *Woodrow Wilson and World Politics: America's Response to War and Revolution*. New York: Oxford University Press, 1968.

Lewis, Sinclair. *Babbitt*. New York: Signet Classic, 1991 (originally published, 1922). America's first Nobel laureate in literature pictures a midwestern businessman's life in the early 1920s.

Limerick, Patricia. *The Legacy of Conquest: The Unbroken Past of the American West*. New York: Norton, 1987. What was wild about the West? Mainly the economic uncertainties, seen here through Limerick's shrewd and unsentimental eyes.

Livesay, Harold. *Samuel Gompers and Organized Labor in America*. Boston: Little Brown, 1978.

Lukacs, John. *Outgrowing Democracy: A History of America in the Twentieth Century*. Garden City, NY: Doubleday, 1984.

Lynd, Robert, and Helen Lynd. *Middletown: A Study in Modern American Culture*. New York: Harcourt Brace, 1929. The great sociological classic about small-town life (Muncie, Indiana) in the 1920s. Still full of vitality and amazingly perceptive.

Mandelbaum, Michael. *The Nuclear Question: The United States and Nuclear Weapons*. New York: Cambridge University Press, 1979.

Marsden, George. *Fundamentalism and American Culture*. New York: Oxford University Press, 1980. Fundamentalists *are* intellectuals, Marsden shows; it's just that they have directed their intelligence down different paths than their antagonists.

May, Elaine Tyler. *Homeward Bound: American Families in the Cold War Era*. New York: Basic, 1988. Dad goes to work, Mom stays home, and the anxious kids help to build a fallout shelter in the backyard.

May, Henry. *Protestant Churches and Industrial America*. New York: Harper and Brothers, 1949. How do Jesus's rural parables play out in industrial cities? The social gospel movement tried to make the switch.

McCullough, David. *Truman*. New York: Simon and Schuster, 1992.

McDougall, Walter. *The Heavens and the Earth: A Political History of the Space Age*. New York: Basic, 1985. Pulitzer Prize winner about the hard political and military calculation that lay behind the astronauts' derring-do.

McGinniss, Joe. *The Selling of the President, 1968*. New York: Trident, 1969.

McGreevy, John. *Parish Boundaries: The Catholic Encounter with Race in the Twentieth Century Urban North*. Chicago: University of Chicago Press, 1996. Horrified churchgoers discover, in 1965, that their priests *favor* racial integration. Superb book despite the dry title.

McMurtry, Larry. *Crazy Horse*. New York: Lipper/Viking, 1999.

Melosi, Martin. *Thomas A. Edison and the Modernization of America*. New York: Harper Collins, 1990.

Miller, Nathan. *Theodore Roosevelt: A Life*. New York: Morrow, 1992.

Miscamble, Wilson. *George Kennan and the Making of American Foreign Policy*. Princeton, NJ: Princeton University Press, 1992.

Moody, Anne. *Coming of Age in Mississippi*. New York: Doubleday, 1968. I-was-there memoir about Freedom Summer, the sit-ins, freedom rides, and gradual disillusionment of a nonviolent black student activist.

Morris, Charles. *American Catholic: The Saints and Sinners Who Built America's Most Powerful Church*. New York: Random House/Times Books, 1997.

Naughton, John. *A Brief History of the Future: From Radio Days to Internet Years in a Lifetime*. Woodstock, NY: Overlook, 2000.

Niehardt, John, ed., *Black Elk Speaks*. Lincoln: University of Nebraska Press/Bison, 2000 (originally published, 1930). Old Sioux medicine man who fought at the Little Bighorn as a teenager recounts his life to a sympathetic anthropologist 50 years later.

Nixon, Richard. *RN: The Memoirs of Richard Nixon*. New York: Grosset and Dunlap, 1978.

Noll, Mark. *History of Christianity in the United States and Canada*. Grand Rapids, MI: Eerdman's, 1992.

———. *The Old Religion in a New World: The History of North American Christianity*. Grand Rapids, MI: Eerdman's, 2002.

O'Brien, David, and Stephen Fugita. *The Japanese-American Experience*. Bloomington, IN: Indiana University Press, 1991.

Olsen, Otto. *Reconstruction and Redemption in the South*. Baton Rouge, LA: Louisiana State University Press, 1980.

Opie, John. *Nature's Nation: An Environmental History of the United States*. Fort Worth, TX: Harcourt Brace College Publishers, 1998.

Overland, Orm. *Immigrant Minds, American Identities: Making the United States Home, 1870–1930*. Urbana, IL: University of Illinois Press, 2000.

Parkman, Francis. *The Oregon Trail*. New York: Oxford University Press/World's Classics, 1996 (originally published, 1849). Wonderful firsthand account of life with the Sioux Indians on the Great Plains 30 years before Custer.

Pells, Richard. *The Liberal Mind in a Conservative Age*. New York: Harper and Row, 1985.

———. *Radical Visions and American Dreams: Cultural and Social Thought in the Depression Years*. Middletown, CT: Wesleyan University Press, 1973. Americans' sensible and nutty ideas from the 1930s about how to solve the Great Depression.

Perrett, Geoffrey. *Days of Sadness, Years of Triumph: The American People, 1939–1945*. Madison, WI: University of Wisconsin Press, 1985. What happened inside America while the entire world was at war? Watch *Rosie the Riveter*, then read this book!

Phelps, Elizabeth Stuart. *The Gates Ajar*. Boston: Fields, Osgood, 1868.

Podhoretz, Norman. *Why We Were in Vietnam*. New York: Simon and Schuster, 1982.

Prange, Gordon. *At Dawn We Slept: The Untold Story of Pearl Harbor*. New York: McGraw Hill, 1981.

Ramsay, David. *Lusitania: Saga and Myth*. New York: Norton, 2002.

Reisner, Marc. *Rivers of Empire: The American West and Its Disappearing Water*. New York: Viking, 1986.

Rhodes, Richard. *The Making of the Atomic Bomb*. New York: Simon and Schuster, 1986.

Riesman, David, Nathan Glazer, and Reuel Denney. *The Lonely Crowd: A Study of the Changing American Character*. New Haven, CT: Yale University Press, 1950. Classic study of American character types and how they changed with industrialization and modernization. Still full of shrewd and relevant ideas.

Riis, Jacob. *How the Other Half Lives*. New York: Scribner's, 1890. Danish immigrant and pioneer slum photographer gives graphic testimony in words and pictures about the horrors of late-19th–century life in New York tenements.

Rolvaag, Ole. *Giants in the Earth*. New York: Harper, 1927.

Roosevelt, Theodore. *The Rough Riders*. New York: Scribner's, 1899. Blow-by-blow description of the Cuban campaign (1898) from the hero of the Spanish-American War who went from San Juan Hill to the White House. No understatements here.

Rosengarten, Theodore. *All God's Dangers: The Life of Nate Shaw*. New York: Knopf, 1975. A moving firsthand account of an Alabama sharecropper's life under segregation in the early 20th century.

Salvatore, Nick. *Eugene V. Debs: Citizen and Socialist*. Urbana: University of Illinois Press, 1982. Biography of the trade union leader who became a five-time Socialist candidate for president of the United States.

Schlesinger, Arthur, Jr. *The Age of Roosevelt*. 3 vols. Boston: Houghton Mifflin, 1957–1960. Pro-FDR classic on the early New Deal. Massive, but very readable, especially if you're a Democrat.

———. *A Thousand Days: John F. Kennedy in the White House*. Boston: Houghton Mifflin, 1965.

Serrano, Richard. *One of Ours: Timothy McVeigh and the Oklahoma City Bombing*. New York: Norton, 1998.

Sheehan, Neil. *A Bright Shining Lie: John Paul Vann and America in Vietnam*. New York: Random House, 1988.

Sheldon, Charles. *In His Steps*. Elgin, IL: David Cook Publishing, 1900.

Sinclair, Upton. *The Jungle*. New York: Bantam Classic, 1981 (originally published, 1906). One of the great American novels, it revealed the disgusting truth about the Chicago meat-packing yards and led to federal laws regulating the food industry.

Slatta, Richard. *Cowboys of the Americas*. New Haven: Yale University Press, 1990. Excellent on U.S. cowboys, especially because it compares them with their Mexican, Argentinean, and Brazilian counterparts.

Sledge, E. B. *With the Old Breed at Peleliu and Okinawa*. Novato, CA: Presidio Press, 1981.

Smith, Jane I. *Islam in America*. New York: Columbia University Press, 1999.

Sowell, Thomas. *Ethnic America*. New York: Basic, 1981.

Spector, Ronald. *Eagle against the Sun*. New York: Free Press, 1985.

Starr, Kevin. *Inventing the Dream: California through the Progressive Era*. New York: Oxford University Press, 1985. What happened on the West Coast after the gold rush but before the postwar L.A. sprawl? Find out and be entertained here.

Steffens, Lincoln. *The Shame of the Cities*. New York: Hill and Wang, 1957 (originally published, 1904). Evils of corrupt city government, circa 1900, exposed in this muckraking classic.

Stegner, Wallace. *Beyond the Hundredth Meridian: John Wesley Powell and the Opening of the American West*. New York: Penguin, 1992 (originally published, 1954). Biography of the man who first boated down the Grand Canyon and later became head of the U.S. Geological Survey.

Steinem, Gloria. *Outrageous Acts and Everyday Rebellions*. New York: Holt, Rinehart, and Winston, 1983.

Stilgoe, John R. *Metropolitan Corridor: Railroads and the American Scene*. New Haven, CT: Yale University Press, 1983. How railroads transformed the landscape and our ideas about it. One of my personal favorites (but in fairness I should caution that most Emory students think it's a great bore).

Stover, John F. *American Railroads*. 2nd ed. Chicago: University of Chicago Press, 1997. Brisk, no-nonsense explanation of how trains linked up and speeded up the nation and of what happened to them after the automobile and aircraft revolution.

Stowell, David. *Streets, Railroads, and the Great Strike of 1877*. Chicago: University of Chicago Press, 1999.

Stratton, Joanna. *Pioneer Women: Voices from the Kansas Frontier*. New York: Simon and Schuster, 1981. Desperate struggles of Kansas farm women in the 1870s and 1880s, mainly told in their own words. You'll never sentimentalize pioneers again.

Tanenhaus, Sam. *Whittaker Chambers: A Biography*. New York: Random House, 1997. Sympathetic account of the passionate Communist spy turned anti-Communist informer and his McCarthy-era confrontation with Alger Hiss.

Terkel, Studs. *The Good War*. New York: Pantheon, 1984.

Thomas, Brook, ed. *Plessy v. Ferguson*. Boston: Bedford, 1997. A collection of documents, including the Supreme Court's decision upholding racial segregation in 1896, and arguments for and against the decision, then and later.

Toland, John. *The Rising Sun: The Decline and Fall of the Japanese Empire*. New York: Random House, 1970.

Trainor, Bernard, and Michael Gordon. *The Generals' War*. Boston: Little Brown, 1995.

Wallace, Lew. *Ben Hur*. New York: Harper, 1880.

Warner, Sam Bass. *Streetcar Suburbs*. Cambridge, MA: Harvard University Press, 1962.

Washington, Booker T. *Up from Slavery*. New York: Dover, 1995 (originally published, 1901). Autobiography of the famous black educator and college president who was born a slave.

Watt, Donald. *How War Came: The Immediate Origins of the Second World War*. London: Heinemann, 1989.

Weinstein, Allen. *Perjury: The Hiss-Chambers Case*. New York: Random House, 1978.

Whitfield, Stephen J. *The Culture of the Cold War*. Baltimore: Johns Hopkins University Press, 1991.

Wiebe, Robert. *The Search for Order: 1877–1920*. New York: Hill and Wang, 1967. Dense but durable explanation of how America's old "island-communities" got linked up to make the modern industrial nation. Take with black coffee.

Wilkinson, J. Harvie. *From Brown to Bakke: The Supreme Court and School Integration, 1954–1978*. New York: Oxford University Press, 1979.

Williams, John Hoyt. *A Great and Shining Road*. New York: Times Books, 1988. Superior account (in a crowded field) of how the first transcontinental railroad got built.

Wills, Garry. *The Kennedy Imprisonment*. Boston: Little Brown, 1982.

———. *Nixon Agonistes: The Crisis of the Self-Made Man*. Boston: Houghton Mifflin, 1970. One of the first biographies of Nixon but still one of the best (even though written pre-Watergate); full of piercing and painful insights.

———. *Reagan's America: Innocents at Home*. Garden City, NY: Doubleday, 1987. Another masterpiece; sharp, perceptive, wounding, and illuminating.

Woodward, C. Vann. *Origins of the New South, 1877–1913*. Baton Rouge, LA: Louisiana State University Press, 1915. Grizzled veteran of a thousand graduate seminars and still the best place to start in understanding the South after Reconstruction.

———. *The Strange Career of Jim Crow*. New York: Oxford University Press, 1955.

———. *Tom Watson: Agrarian Rebel*. New York: Oxford University Press, 1963.

Woodward, Robert, and Carl Bernstein. *All the President's Men*. New York: Simon and Schuster, 1974.

Worster, Donald. *Dust Bowl: The Southern Plains in the 1930s*. New York: Oxford University Press, 1979. How a mixture of human and natural forces caused the Dust Bowl and how obtuse people declined to learn obvious lessons from it.

Yergin, Daniel. *The Prize: The Epic Quest for Oil, Money, and Power*. New York: Simon and Schuster, 1991.

———. *Shattered Peace: The Origins of the Cold War and the National Security State*. Boston: Houghton Mifflin, 1977.

Ziff, Larzer. *The American 1890s: Life and Times of a Lost Generation*. New York: Viking, 1966. The American literary scene in which Mark Twain, Henry James, Edith Wharton, and William Dean Howells thrived.